Social Voices

Social Voices

The Cultural Politics of Singers around the Globe

Edited by
LEVI S. GIBBS

Publication of this book was supported by Dartmouth College.

© 2023 by the Board of Trustees
of the University of Illinois
All rights reserved
1 2 3 4 5 C P 5 4 3 2 1
♾ This book is printed on acid-free paper.

Library of Congress Cataloging-in-Publication Data
Names: Gibbs, Levi, 1980– editor.
Title: Social voices : the cultural politics of singers around the globe / edited by Levi S. Gibbs.
Description: Urbana : University of Illinois Press, 2023. | Includes bibliographical references and index.
Identifiers: LCCN 2022058885 (print) | LCCN 2022058886 (ebook) | ISBN 9780252045240 (hardcover) | ISBN 9780252087387 (paperback) | ISBN 9780252054761 (ebook)
Subjects: LCSH: Music—Social aspects. | Music—Political aspects. | Popular music—History and criticism. | Vocal music—History and criticism. | Singers—Social conditions.
Classification: LCC ML3916.S656 2023 (print) | LCC ML3916 (ebook) | DDC 306.4/842—dc23/eng/20221207
LC record available at https://lccn.loc.gov/2022058885
LC ebook record available at https://lccn.loc.gov/2022058886

Contents

Acknowledgments vii

Introduction: The Cultural Politics of Singers 1
Levi S. Gibbs

PART I. THE POLITICS OF AUTHENTICITY AND ICONICITY

Introduction 25
Jeff Todd Titon

1. Becoming a "Folk" Icon: Pete Seeger and Musical Activism 29
Anthony Seeger

2. An Ordinary Icon: Cassettes, Counternarratives, and Shaykh Imam 47
Andrew Simon

3. Idolatry and Iconoclasm in K-Pop Fandom 63
John Lie

PART II. RACE, GENDER, ETHNICITY, AND CLASS

Introduction 79
Eric Lott

4. All On They Mouth Like Liquor 83
Treva B. Lindsey

5. Compromise and Competition: The Musical Identities of Afro-Cuban Women Singers   98
Christina D. Abreu

6. Challenging the Divide Between Elite and Mass Cultures: Opera Icon Beverly Sills   115
Nancy Guy

PART III. MULTIPLICITIES OF REPRESENTATIONS

Introduction   135
Ruth Hellier

7. Artful Politics of the Voice: "Queen of Romani Music" Esma Redžepova   139
Carol Silverman

8. Teresa Teng: Embodying Asia's Cold Wars   161
Michael K. Bourdaghs

9. Women, Political Voice, and the South African Diaspora, 1959–2020   178
Carol A. Muller

PART IV. SINGERS AND SONGS AS INTERWEAVING NARRATIVES

Introduction   195
Kwame Dawes

10. The Vocal Narratives of Lata Mangeshkar: Gender, Politics, and Nation in India   201
Natalie Sarrazin

11. Ya Toyour: One Song in Two Voices   219
Katherine Meizel

Afterword: The Power of Song   237
Elijah Wald

Contributors   241

Index   249

Acknowledgments

This volume has been several years in the making, and there are many people to thank for their support in helping it come to fruition. The contributors presented and discussed earlier drafts of the chapters of *Social Voices*, along with the edited volume's key themes, at a two-day Dartmouth College conference—"The Power of Song: The Cultural Politics of Singers Around the Globe"—held on Zoom in December 2020. Elijah Wald delivered a wonderful public keynote address, and William Cheng gave an inspired keynote response, tying together the chapters and panels presented, and providing a unified overview of this future volume. Jeff Todd Titon, Eric Lott, Ruth Hellier, and Kwame Dawes graciously served as discussants for the four conference panels corresponding to the four sections of this book. I am grateful to all of the conference participants for their enthusiastic participation and flexibility during the difficult and rapidly evolving early stages of the COVID-19 pandemic, and for their hard work and patience as this volume has come together.

This project would not have been possible without the generous support of Dartmouth College's Dean of the Faculty's Dartmouth Conference Award from the Leslie Conference Gift Fund and a project grant from the Leslie Center for the Humanities, with additional support from Dartmouth's Asian Societies, Cultures, and Languages Program, Dean for International Studies and Interdisciplinary Programs, Department of Music, Middle Eastern Studies Program, Department of Spanish and Portuguese, and Office of the Vice Provost for Research. For their funding support and encouragement for this project, I am indebted to Dennis Washburn, Elizabeth Smith, Rebecca Biron, Allen Hockley, Matthew Delmont, Isabel Lozano-Renieblas, Tarek El-Ariss,

Kui Dong, and Dean Madden. For their assistance with the logistics of planning and running the conference, I want to thank Catherine Darragh, Mary Fletcher, Erin Bennett, Ann Fenton, Darshana Griggs, and Nyla Waddell. Roy Schmidt did a fantastic job designing and facilitating the conference website.

For their fruitful conversations, suggestions, and support during the planning and refining of this volume over the past six years, I am grateful to Alan Tansman, Helen Rees, William Cheng, Theodore Levin, Ruth Hellier, Eman Morsi, Yana Stainova, Farzaneh Hemmasi, Andrew Simon, Charlotte Bacon, Andrew F. Jones, Thomas A. DuBois, Walter Armbrust, Martin Stokes, Douglas Haynes, Pavitra Sundar, James Dorsey, Leigh H. Edwards, James Engelhardt, Lauren Gorfinkel, and Emily J. Lordi. Chapter 5 is a revised version of Christina D. Abreu's 2018 article "*Más que una reina*: Race, Gender, and the Musical Careers of Graciela, Celia, and La Lupe, 1950s–1970s" in *Journal of Social History* 52(2): 332–52, and used with the permission of Oxford University Press. Portions of chapter 6 are taken from Nancy Guy's 2015 book, *The Magic of Beverly Sills*, and used with the permission of the University of Illinois Press.

Overseeing the publication of this volume, we are extremely fortunate to have Laurie Matheson, Mariah Schaefer, Gary Smith, Angela Burton, Jennie Fisher, Jennifer Argo, Kevin Cunningham, Heather Gernenz, Kristina Stonehill, Denise Peeler, Michael Roux, Roberta Sparenberg, and Jim Proefrock at the University of Illinois Press. Thanks are also due to Amber Williams for her excellent copyediting, to Judy Davis for creating the index, and to the Press's three anonymous reviewers, whose helpful suggestions and comments inspired many improvements. Finally, I want to thank my wife, Aída, my daughter, Rose, and my son, Henry, for their patience, love, and support as this volume has come together.

Social Voices

Introduction

The Cultural Politics of Singers

LEVI S. GIBBS

This book is about professional singers from around the world who become topics for discussions regarding a range of cultural politics. It brings together an interdisciplinary group of scholars of anthropology, sociology, literature, music, ethnomusicology, and performance studies, who together explore how singers of different genres have come to represent regions, nations, groups of people, and historic moments while simultaneously becoming rich sites through which to consider questions of individual and collective identities.

People can experience the performances of professional singers in different ways. The singers' songs can express personal and collective feelings and ideas, molded by the circumstances in which one encounters them. Popular singers can "enable listeners to enter into community with other listeners" (Hellier 2013b, 31), with their songs acting as "spaces where [audiences] can publicly share deep experiences of selfhood and connection" (Powers 2017, xxviii). After a song emerges from deep within a singer's body, its powerful reverberations enter the bodies of other people and are frequently interpreted as expressions of emotions and ideas—either those of the person singing, those of the person listening (e.g., "this song really speaks to me"), or some notion of a collective body that may or may not include the singer, the listener, or both. One can experience a singer's song both inside oneself and as an external thing, the singer's voice "simultaneously social and at once deeply intimate and physiological" (Gray 2013, 196). Often, even without paying attention to a song's words, the texture or "grain" (Barthes 1977) of a singer's voice can tell us things about identity, power, vulnerability, and inequality, about love, desire, pain, disappointment, and consolation.

Part of this symbolic power is connected to the way a song's melody "can get into your head even before you know what the lyrics are about" (Seeger, this volume). Because we are able to experience a professional singer's song again and again, that repetition can breed familiarity and intimacy. In this volume, Anthony Seeger cites labor songwriter Joe Hill's idea that "a pamphlet, no matter how good, is read only once, but a song is learned by heart and repeated over and over" (Taylor 1990, 1, quoted in Seeger, this volume). Seeger also points to jazz writer Charles Edward Smith's observation that a singer's voice and lyrics are "fused . . . in the fire of singing so that words and music, are, for that moment of creation, inseparable" (Smith in P. Seeger 1993, 18, quoted in Seeger, this volume). Indeed, research has suggested that the more times we hear a song, the more the music and lyrics appear to be fused together and, more importantly, the more meaningful the lyrics seem to us when compared to "the same lyrics presented as spoken text" (Thompson and Russo 2004, 51).

In addition, the way one experiences a singer's song—how it "reads" you at this moment in your life—is interconnected with how it "reads" and has read everyone else who has experienced it. Whether you are hearing the song for the first or hundredth time, the context(s) in which you hear it or have heard it in the past add color—and baggage—to your experience. You may, for example, identify with or detest aspects of the singer's persona, and those emotional responses color how you hear the song. You may feel the song's rhythm in your body, perhaps as a backdrop to other activities. You might only catch its hook or chorus, or maybe you memorize the whole song so you can sing along. You might think about the singer, contemplating how their life story resonates with the song's lyrics and the world as you know it.

Because the experiences of singers' performances frequently involve issues of representation—how people see other people and perspectives—such performances can bring to mind all of the issues that underlie how we relate to one another, such as class, gender, sexual orientation, race, ethnicity, nationality, political persuasion, personality, attitude, and so on. For songs that people perceive to simultaneously speak for groups *and* individuals, what and whom a song, and by extension its singer, represent are topics for constant debate—there is a powerful ambiguity in a singer's voice as an expressive form. You may like a particular singer and feel that they speak to you or a group (or groups) with which you identify. On the other hand, another singer may strike you as disagreeable or a bad influence if you feel that the messages they convey promote problematic worldviews, behaviors, or ideologies. And your attitude may change over time. Singers' songs are public expressions—performed and experienced again and again—and professional singers become public figures through a series of live and mediated interactions with audiences. In the process, these singers become "conversation topic[s] ... around which publics gather, debate, and contest" (Fleetwood 2015, 9), or, in other words, sites where public values are negotiated. These discussions of values are ongoing; as consensuses ebb and flow and perspectives clash and dissipate, the singers' performances live on, along with the many meanings they come to represent.

Singers as Carousel Mirrors

Because singers' performances lie at the intersection of the personal and the social (Gray 2013, 196), professional singers make ideal sites for discussions of cultural politics. As focal points where individual and collective feelings and ways of thinking clash and interweave, such singers, when we examine them in greater detail, provide rich insights into complex social discussions and how those discussions evolve over time. Rather than conveying a single, fixed perspective, individual singers come to represent different things to different people—they are polysemic (cf. Fiske 2011; Edwards 2009). Their songs create worlds where multiple viewpoints are represented (cf. Kun 2005; Gibbs 2018), opening up "boundless social world[s] of difference and possibility" that allow listeners "to try out different versions" of themselves and their relations with other people and society at large (Kun 2005, 2). In a sense, a person's experience of such a song intersects with how that person is experiencing the world at that moment—their positionality in relation to other people. Different people may experience the same singer's performance in vastly different ways.

A useful metaphor for thinking about this phenomenon is to imagine the singer as a multipaneled mirror at the center of a carousel. As you stand looking at it, the mirror panel you see represents its meaning *for you at that moment*—determined in part by your own position and perspective, a mixture of your emotions, values, and sense of right and wrong. Your perspective and perceived image of the singer take on further depth when you consider the overlapping or contrasting perspectives of other people standing to your right or left, or on the opposite side of the carousel, who each see a different mirror panel and interpret the singer in other ways. When you try to have a conversation with those people about the singer, you will probably disagree. Some of the people may find the singer meaningless, in which case the singer has failed to strike a chord with them. Some people may love the singer; others hate them. Those who admire the singer may see the singer as giving voice to a group that needs to be heard; those who do not like the singer may see the singer as promoting social agendas with which they do not identify.

Rather than producing a singular meaning for everyone, the singer instead acts as a polysemic center around which, "through performance, multiple and conflicting categories of the social can be expressed simultaneously and left in conflict without resolution" (Santana 2020, 186).

The singers discussed in this volume thus become topics for multiple, sometimes parallel, sometimes overlapping conversations, often with critics and fans talking past one another. Each singer, like each of us, "contain[s] multitudes" (Cheng 2020b), presenting a combination of "virtues, threats, *and* dangers" (Wald 2020), and each "listener listens with their own multiple identities which are layered and complex" (Hellier, this volume). Yet, when we look at and listen to the singer-carousel from a particular perspective at a particular moment, we tend to see one thing; we assume that the singer sings a particular genre (cf. Wald 2012) and has a particular voice representing a particular point of view (cf. Meizel 2020 and this volume). When we focus on aspects of a singer that we see as virtues, we move toward elevating the singer as an icon. On the other hand, when we focus on aspects that we perceive to be dangers, we see the singer as a threat. If different people focus on different things in the same singer—hearing and seeing that singer in vastly different lights—it is almost as if they are responding to different singers. Given that, although we may feel offended when someone criticizes a singer with whom we identify or one of their songs that we like, let us instead try to dig deeper and understand where those other observers are coming from and what they are seeing in the singer. Then, we can begin to see how singers work as sites where different politics, perspectives, and approaches intersect.

Social Conversations

An example of such intersections can be seen in some of the reactions to the American pop singer Jennifer Lopez's performance of the song "This Land Is Your Land" at the 2021 inauguration of US President Joseph R. Biden. Lopez's performance and its broader meanings were interpreted in the media in different ways. For some, her presence in the gala proceeding, which also included country music singer Garth Brooks, pop singer Lady Gaga, and the newly introduced young poet laureate Amanda Gorman, represented a celebration of "Latinx inclusion and representation" in America (Azizi 2021b). In an article on Lopez's performance at the inauguration, one writer and scholar wrote,

> As symbolism goes, it could hardly have been stronger. During Donald Trump's four years in office, he outraged many in the Hispanic commu-

nity with his racist outbursts and inhumane immigration policies. In Joe Biden's very inauguration, he struck a far different note by inviting the Latina icon Jennifer Lopez to perform the American classics "This Land Is Your Land" and "America the Beautiful." J.Lo gave rousing renditions and bridged the two songs by loudly chanting part of the Pledge of Allegiance in Spanish: "One nation, under God, indivisible, with liberty and justice for all." (Azizi 2021a)

When seen in this light, Lopez's performance of "This Land Is Your Land" sought to rebut the outgoing Trump administration's racist rhetoric and exclusionary policies and reaffirm an inclusive vision of American identity—a sentiment further reinforced by the way protesters had sung that song "to passengers who'd been detained at JFK and Philadelphia International Airport" amid "the tense period of President Trump's proposed travel ban" (Blair 2019) and the fact that New York US Representative Alexandria Ocasio-Cortez had tweeted the song's lyrics in response to Donald Trump saying that a group of congressional women of color should "go back where they came from" (quoted in Kaufman 2019).

Other publications chose to focus on Lopez's decision to dress in "white, a color associated with the women's suffrage movement" (Gold 2021). Bianca Betancourt, the Culture Editor for HarpersBAZAAR.com, described Lopez's clothing as "an all-white, suffragette-inspired suit by Chanel that included a sweeping overcoat, sequined wide-leg trousers, and a ruffled high-neck blouse" (Betancourt 2021), while Joey Hadden, a lifestyle reporter at Insider Inc., speculated that Lopez's addition of pearls to her "patent JLo bling . . . likely honors Vice President Kamala Harris" (Hadden 2021), the first woman to hold the office of Vice President in the country's history. Underscoring that "Lopez's all white outfit was a nod to the suffragettes," writer Christian Allaire (2021) added, in *Vogue* magazine's online edition, that at the inauguration, "[Kamala] Harris and Hillary Clinton also wore purple, the other official color of the US women's suffrage movement . . . a decades-long fight for the right for women to vote." Such attempts to interpret Lopez's symbolism via comparisons with the clothing of others present were furthered by fashion and beauty writer Sophie Shaw, who also noted Lady Gaga's "chic suffragette white Inauguration Day coat and mask" worn upon her arrival at the White House before her performance that day (Shaw 2021). Highlighting the fact that both Gaga and Lopez had worn "suffragette white for the occasion" (although Gaga would shed the white coat for her actual performance), Shaw pointed to the way the pair's fashion choices echoed those of Kamala Harris, who "when accepting her Vice Presidential nomination . . . wore white as a nod to the suffragettes and female trailblazers in US politics who came before her" (ibid.).

Lopez's performance was also interpreted via her choice of song and its political history. For some, Lopez was echoing earlier performances where "This Land Is Your Land" had been seen as a progressive manifesto. The American folksinger Woody Guthrie (1912–1967) had originally composed the song in 1940 as "a Marxist response to [Irving Berlin's song] 'God Bless America,'" and "This Land Is Your Land" would go on to become what has been described as "an alternative national anthem" (Spitzer 2012). Two of its original verses critiqued the social inequalities caused by American capitalism but were not published at the time due the rising tide of anti-communist sentiment during the McCarthy era (ibid.), and by the 1960s, the song had come to be seen by many as "a progressive anthem of social revolution" (Kun 2005, 35; cf. Denning 1996). Although the song was later sung by the likes of conservative politicians, including Richard Nixon and Ronald Reagan, when the singers Bruce Springsteen and Pete Seeger performed it at the 2009 inauguration of President Barack Obama, Seeger insisted on singing the original anti-capitalist verses (Greene 2021). Following Jennifer Lopez's 2021 inauguration performance, which did not include the controversial verses, one article asked, "Did Jennifer Lopez really know what she was singing?" and then answered the question by suggesting that "Lopez was singing the lyrics of a devout socialist, some say even a communist, who would be turning in his grave to see his song rendered as a patriotic song of hope" (Grant 2021). As I was writing this introduction, the same song once again made headlines, described as a "'Communist' song" in a right-wing media article about a protest led by a group of progressive Democratic congresspeople who sang "This Land Is Your Land" as they urged President Biden to extend a moratorium on evictions that had been issued during the COVID-19 pandemic (Hubbard 2021).

Following Lopez's 2021 inauguration performance, other people found Lopez's choice of song insensitive to the history of erasure of Indigenous people from US territory (cf. Fonseca 2021). In an article critiquing Lopez's performance of the song, the journalist Sam Yellowhorse Kesler noted, "Native Americans will just as soon point out that the core of the song, that 'this land was made for you and me,' is a wholly colonialist message" (Kesler 2021). The Abenaki musician and writer Mali Obomsawin had previously suggested that the song's "lyrics as they are embraced today evoke Manifest Destiny and expansionism ('this land is made for you and me')," writing, "In the context of America, a nation-state built by settler colonialism, Woody Guthrie's protest anthem exemplifies the particular blind spot that Americans have in regard to Natives: American patriotism erases us, even if it comes in the form of a leftist protest song. Why? Because this land 'was' our land" (Obomsawin

2019). This sentiment, in turn, echoed controversies surrounding the song from the 1960s, when the Cree musician Buffy Sainte-Marie refused to sing it with Pete Seeger, later recalling, "I just cried through it. I thought, 'This used to be my land and you guys aren't even smart enough to be sensitive to this?'" (Kesler 2021). Seeger later often performed an additional verse that mentioned the stealing of Native Americans' land (ibid.). In the context of the Biden inauguration, decolonizing critics felt that Lopez's inclusion of the song in the festivities went against the new administration's promoted message of diversity and inclusion by poignantly excluding Indigenous people.

The conversations surrounding Lopez's performance highlight the social roles that singers play as focal points for discussions of cultural politics. On the one hand, the debates over the significance of Lopez's performance are tied to different views of Lopez as a singer—whether she is primarily a mainstream pop singer (who gaffed by ignoring the history of Indigenous people in this country), a female singer promoting women's political agency, or a powerful voice celebrating Latinx identity. On the other hand, the ways in which her performance was interpreted were also connected to the song's history—its composition, previous singers, and prior performances. Whether one sees Lopez as celebrating Latinx identity in the face of Trumpian racism or as a pop star promoting US hegemony and the erasure of Indigenous people, such perspectives point to the singular ways in which people view and interpret singers as enacting a particular type of social work—they look at the singer and see one side of the carousel mirror.

When singers like this perform songs that other singers have sung before them, they enter into and add to a stream of ongoing social conversations. The praise, critiques, and controversies surrounding singers of "This Land Is Your Land" show how different singers performing a song over time can produce "a tapestry of meanings" (Gibbs 2019, 111) where new stories and contexts can be continually woven in—an ongoing, available space where social conversations can be picked up again and again from different angles (cf. Nora 1989). We see this when a song that Bob Dylan composed and sang in the 1960s to protest the Vietnam War (1955–1975) found new relevance during the Iraq War in 2003 (Kennedy 2003). We also see it when a singer's biting critiques of the Egyptian government, clandestinely distributed on noncommercial cassette tapes in the 1970s, found new meaning on social media in the new millennium during the "Arab Spring" (Simon, this volume). And we see it when an American singer competing in *Arabs Got Talent* in Beirut in 2013 and a Syrian singer performing at a cross-cultural event in Ohio in 2016 both found expression in the same hybrid-style song, composed over eight decades earlier (Meizel, this volume). In each case, the later singers' performances of earlier songs conjure up fluid sites of memory, drawing audiences in with opportunities to process and socialize individual experiences in conversation with the experiences of others amid social change (cf. Grossberg 1992; DuBois 2006; Gibbs 2019).

Representation via song, however, is a double-edged sword. Because the act of "giving voice" through song is often tied to unequal power relations, a singer's performances can simultaneously unite *and* divide, bringing together groups large and small, ranging from nations (Gray 2013; Hemmasi 2020; Tansman 1996; Danielson 1997; Weidman 2021; Sarrazin, this volume) to civil rights movements (P. Seeger and Reiser 2009; Eyerman 2002) to summer camps (A. Seeger and K. Seeger 2006), while also strengthening hegemonies, mainstream media networks, and structural racism/misogyny. Elijah Wald (2020) notes how "the powers singers access and employ may overlap or even be the same as the powers they are fighting to dismantle," and such tensions are present in many of the chapters in this volume. In *Lions of the North: Sounds of the New Nordic Radical Nationalism*, Benjamin Teitelbaum (2017) highlights the dangers of bringing people together through song by showing how white nationalist singers' songs have provided a means to coalesce and seek to rationalize various forms of radical white nationalism, bringing audiences together as they tear societies apart (cf. Eyerman 2002). The tricky part is that any strength gained in giving voice to some can either be viewed as providing support and solidarity to those who lack it or as taking away from others' power. Raising certain voices can eclipse the voices of others, and decisions about *who* gets to represent and *what* they are seen as representing are implicitly tied to contrasting social values.

At the heart of this paradox is the way that each encounter with a singer's song can challenge our notions of fixity, essentialism, and stable identities. "Every time we listen to a song," writes Josh Kun in *Audiotopia: Music, Race, and America*, "a stranger enters the gates, an identity is menaced, an identity is questioned" (2005, 12). Popular music, like popular culture more generally, provides us with "a contact zone for defining one's self in relation to others" (Weintraub and Barendregt 2017, 21; cf. Lipsitz 1994). And significantly—as many of the singers discussed in this volume are women—Andrew N. Weintraub and Bart Barendregt have noted in *Vamping the Stage: Female Voices of Asian Modernities* how pioneering women singers have been "instrumental in the construction of new identities, through questioning and rejecting conventional forms of presentation," giving voice to "(counter) hegemonic positions in specific contexts" and thereby "contribut[ing] to new processes of social differentiation, of culture formation, and of history making" (2017, 15).

If singers' performances are a medium through which different points of view come into contact with one another, the meanings that people find in them are ever-changing and inherently dialogic. The same singers who may be praised by some can be denigrated by others who do not want the singers to express the things they do in the ways they do—the desires expressed in their songs do not resonate with those critics, who may want to keep the social hierarchy as it is or desire to shift society in a different direction, perhaps outlined by other, contrasting singers. Between praise and condemnation, every reaction to a singer represents an attempt to find and assert one's point of view, a desire to have others share that point of view, an appeal to frame collective identities in relation to one's own.

Chapter Overview

In this book, we look at some of the social conversations inspired by popular singers from around the world. Intended as a textbook for advanced undergraduates coming from different disciplines, the book's chapters provide examples of different disciplinary approaches you can use to look at singers you know or in whom you have an interest. Some chapters may talk about singers you have not heard of, while others may talk about singers you know, albeit in new ways.

Because singers come to embody a wide range of meanings, the scholars in this volume make use of a range of perspectives from sociology, literary studies, ethnomusicology, cultural studies, and so on to address the singers they study. In addition, the types of source material they use in their research vary, including everything from newspaper articles to films, personal interviews to online comments, music videos to Saturday Night Live sketches, YouTube clips to SoundCloud plays, and more. These approaches and sources represent only some of a plethora of possibilities; you may find discussions of a particular singer across a range of media, and the genres of discussion and the media you encounter—whether you look at clashing comments posted on a YouTube video or peer-reviewed journal articles and books—may determine, in part, the types and tenors of the conversations you end up writing about (cf. Briggs and Bauman 1992). As you read the chapters that follow, try to pay attention to the types of sources and approaches the authors are using and how those choices might inspire you on your own journey to explore your own singers of interest.

In addition, to help readers connect more closely with the volume's contributors and show how interests in singers can develop into professional pursuits, each introduction to the volume's four parts begins with an autobiographical interlude showing how its author came to research the particular topic and/or singer(s) at hand, how their academic interests developed and deepened, and how they have used approaches from different disciplines to examine and talk about singers. Jeff Todd Titon, for example, developed an interest in blues into an academic interest in issues of authenticity among singers, while Eric Lott's interest in the dynamics of race led him to explore ways in which singers negotiate race and gender. Ruth Hellier, in turn, worked as a creative artist, singer, actor, teacher, and researcher, which led to her interest in performance studies, feminist studies, and her research on the multiplicities of representations among singers. Kwame Dawes, as a writer, scholar, and artist searching for "a poetics and an aesthetic" of "sites of origin long denigrated and ignored by the colonial enterprise" (Dawes, this volume), turned to reggae singers for inspiration, later leading him to write about the lyrical genius of Bob Marley, highlighting the interplay of singers' lived experiences and their songs (Dawes 2007). Each of these autobiographical interludes shows ways in which personal interests can evolve into academic research on singers, at the same time highlighting why the four section themes matter—what is at stake. In addition, for those readers who would like to explore more of the songs, genres, and milieus of the singers discussed throughout the volume, there are multimedia playlists at the end of the chapters that can be explored at one's leisure through online searches.

As you read the following chapters, you will notice that each writer focuses on a particular aspect or set of aspects with regard to the singer(s) they discuss. It is important to keep in mind that these are a subset of potential approaches that one can take in observing the career of each singer, and that the perspective with which one approaches a singer is intertwined with the resulting view of that singer. As highlighted by the carousel mirror metaphor discussed earlier, there is a tendency to essentialize—to place the singer within a particular paradigm or between two paradigms. Although one cannot avoid how the light cast by a writer's perspective influences the resulting image of the singer, it is important to remember that singers are complex, multisided figures. With that in mind, we encourage you to question how a chapter portrays a particular singer—through questioning those representations, we can better understand how singers reflect back different images to different people who approach the singers from different points of view. This act of comparing alternative representations can show us how a singer's position at the intersection of contrasting perspectives makes them powerful topics for conversations about different social values.

By engaging with the approaches used in the following four parts of this volume—each of which contains a short introduction followed by several chapters—you will come away with a new set of ways of thinking about the singers you encounter in the Cloud, movies, television, and the news. You will come to see biopics, scandals involving singers, and glowing obituaries of iconic singers not as isolated cases, but instead as forming part of a larger pattern through which society processes divergent opinions and social change.

The Politics of Authenticity and Iconicity

In part one of the volume, the authors ask the following questions: As singers grow in fame and become symbolic icons, how do different claims to authenticity and authority come into play? And, how do different media pathways, including records, cassettes, social media, television, and so on, connect singers to different audiences and position the singers in relation to competing singers over the course of their careers?

A singer's fans and naysayers each see and judge the singer through the lens of particular values. Professional singers come to embody different claims to authenticity—tied to particular values—as they become icons. As different values come to be venerated, that changes *who* the idols are. To put it another way, when people choose to idolize a singer, it says a great deal about the values they view as important and the narratives they believe in. As Jeff Todd Titon notes, "Authenticity involves a process in which an interpretive community validates a story" (Titon 2012, 230). As particular singers and stories are raised up, it is often at the expense of other singers and stories. For example, Andrew Simon (ch. 2) highlights how certain Egyptian singers such as Umm Kulthum have been favored in official narratives perpetuated by the government, with museums dedicated to those singers, attention drawn to them, and, inevitably, more English scholarship written about them (Simon, this volume; cf. Danielson 1997; Lohman 2010). The focus cast on these singers, however, obscures the importance of other singers associated with counternarratives, such as the singer that Simon writes about. John Lie (ch. 3), in turn, describes how fans favor certain K-pop groups over others based on distinct social values and ideologies that they ascribe to each group (Lie, this volume). These sorts of situations not only highlight certain singers at the expense of others, but also certain *values* at the expense of others.

How a singer is interpreted is also connected to the media through which we encounter them. The iconic Egyptian singer Shaykh Imam from chapter 2, for example, gained traction through informal audiotapes that were recorded, copied, and circulated by individuals. The resulting cassettes enabled Imam's songs to circumvent state censorship, reach a broad audience, and challenge Egypt's ruling regimes. In the process of doing so, Imam came to be seen by many as an artist of the people (Simon, this volume; cf. Simon 2022). The American folksinger Pete Seeger discussed in chapter 1 was similarly able to find a way around McCarthy-era censorship—in his case, being blacklisted from television—by instead releasing records, performing in local concerts, and having his songs covered by other singers, also becoming known as a voice of popular protest in the process (Seeger, this volume; cf. Dunaway 1990). In the contemporary world of K-pop icons described in chapter 3, in turn, social media fandom not only builds up and tears down the status of particular groups and singers but has also evolved into an efficient means of organizing political action (Lie, this volume).

Throughout this volume, we see how different forms of media color the ways we view a singer. We read about a Saturday Night Live parody sketch that highlighted the disjuncture between how different groups of fans interpreted Beyoncé's music in relation to race (ch. 4), how a South African singer's online appearances during the 2020 COVID-19 lockdown contributed to ongoing discussions of diaspora and belonging (ch. 9), how the appearance of a single singer's voice in the soundtracks of nationalistic Indian films became a part of discussions about new ideals of femininity and the role of women in an evolving nation (ch. 10), and so on (Lindsey, this volume; Muller, this volume; Sarrazin, this volume). In each case, the media through which the singers' performances were shared were intrinsically connected to the tenors of the conversations they inspired.

In Jeff Todd Titon's introduction to this first part of the volume, he discusses how singers become iconic figures through authenticating discourses tied to different aspects of identity and life history. Whether a singer's symbolic power draws on their cultural upbringing, musical ability, life experience, perceived emotional expressivity, or some combination therein, such claims to authenticity frequently compete with one another for importance, especially when different singers are compared. In chapter 1, Anthony Seeger writes about various factors that contributed to the American folksinger Pete Seeger's (1919–2014) lifelong career as a musical and political icon. As a member of the Seeger family and Pete Seeger's nephew, Anthony Seeger not only looks at the roles that musicianship, voice, songwriting, economics, and age played in the formation and evolution of an iconic singer who echoed earlier generations of American poet-heroes, but also how his political advocacy was informed by the historical and familial contexts in which he grew up. In chapter 2, Andrew Simon examines the Egyptian singer Shaykh Imam (1918–1995), whose critical compositions boldly challenging the Egyptian government's official historical narrative were spread via an informal network of copied audiocassettes, leading him to become known as an "ordinary icon." Providing counternarratives for, among other things, the state visits of foreign leaders, Imam's artful ability to speak truth to power led the singer and his songs—long after his death—to gain new meaning on Facebook, Spotify, SoundCloud, and YouTube during and since the Egyptian protests that occurred in 2011. In chapter 3, John Lie explores the role that K-pop fans play in building up and tearing down icons. Looking at different claims to authenticity that attract fans to different groups, the chapter highlights ways in which fandom and the worship of idols empowers fans, offering a sense of inclusion and equality for those who feel marginalized and/or excluded, and serving as a powerful network through which the political power of fans can be organized en masse.

Race, Gender, Ethnicity, and Class

In *The Race of Sound: Listening, Timbre, and Vocality in African American Music*, Nina Sun Eidsheim (2019) shows us how listening is "a political act" that "always actively produces meaning" (24), and that "by listening to listening we can trace voice back to ideas" (27). Each of the chapters in the second part of *Social Voices* deal with different ways in which singers are heard and understood by different audiences, in the process becoming focal points for discussions of race, gender, ethnicity, and class.

Singers' gendered performances of different genres of song can provide a means of negotiating race and class identities (cf. Fox 2009; Edwards 2009, 2018; Lott 1997; Lordi 2017), and, at the intersection of ethnicity and gender, singers navigate their "resistance to some stereotypes and . . . compliance with others" (Hellier 2013a, 104; cf. Vargas 2012; Abreu, this volume). Through this process, we find different ways in which identities and the boundaries between identities are constructed and policed (cf. Miller 2010; Stoever 2016; Bachechi 2015; Holmes and Eidsheim 2019). At the same time, we also find that conversations about the cultural politics of gender, race, ethnicity, and able-bodiedness are often tied to narratives of labor and social mobility.

Narratives of overcoming—frequently found in the tellings of singers' life stories—simultaneously challenge and reinforce distinctions between privileged and marginalized identities (cf. Cheng 2017; Dyson 2019; Lordi 2017; Guy 2015). Stories of singers who climb the social ladder through raw talent and hard work give hope to underprivileged groups, yet "a dangerous corollary of rags-to-riches fantasies," notes William Cheng, "is that if you don't succeed, you must have only yourself to blame" (2020a, 70; cf. Sternheimer 2011, 3). Such upwardly mobile singers may use their voices to critique the inequalities of the system, but they do so from positions that belie the immutability of those inequalities. Other singers who stay low, maintaining humbler and/or stigmatized positions, such as the Egyptian singer Shaykh Imam discussed in chapter 2, are able to critique the system in part by embodying the inequality of the system through their own positions, albeit without the benefits of mainstream media (Simon, this volume; cf. Seeger, this volume).

In Eric Lott's introduction to this second part of the volume, he shows how singers of various backgrounds develop performative presences that audiences come to associate with particular subject positions connected to specific communities. In doing so, Lott argues, these singers inspire their audiences with rallying cries that push back against "mainstream" and other groups, while at the same time playing with received understandings of the singers themselves—both utilizing the power of and rejecting the limitations of their representational power. Significantly, all of the singers examined in the chapters in this section are women—resonating with Weintraub and Barendregt's assertion that "female performers, willingly or not, have often taken on a role of the modern woman challenging conservatism, morality, and religion" (2017, 3). As we see in these chapters, in challenging the mainstream and the status quo with "call[s] for changes in attitudes and lifestyle," these singers elicit "attraction and admiration, as well as derision and conflict" (ibid.).

In chapter 4, Treva B. Lindsey looks at how Beyoncé Giselle Knowles-Carter's (b. 1981) oeuvre and the ways in which different audiences understand it reflect underlying discussions about being Black, being a woman, and southern-ness (referring both to the US South and the Global South). The chapter examines how Beyoncé, as a singer who has drawn on and transformed notions of Black female superstardom, has explored and challenged the traditions and limitations of various Black Souths over the course of her career. In chapter 5, Christina D. Abreu shows how the stories and careers of three Afro-Cuban women singers—Graciela Pérez Grillo (1915–2010), Celia Cruz (1925–2003), and Lupe Victoria Yolí (1936–1992)—reflect gender and racial solidarity and shared expressions of Afro-Cuban womanhood, while at the same time highlighting the constraints of the entertainment industry with its racialized and gendered expectations, as well as the complex relationships between the singers and with the men in their lives. In doing so, the chapter addresses a gender gap in the history of Cuban and Latin popular music, allowing "Cuban women performers to speak not from the margins . . . but from the center of the narrative as innovators, pioneers, and agents shaping the popular culture landscape on which they formed their professional careers" (Abreu, this volume). In chapter 6, Nancy Guy examines the American opera icon Beverly Sills's (1929–2007) role in mediating between mainstream and elite tastes—making opera popular through her "down-to-earth demeanor" and appearances on nationally televised talk shows, while at the same time eliciting the scorn of certain highbrow critics. Juxtaposing the online overtures of enthusiastic fans with the critiques of critics and scholars, the chapter highlights class-inspired contradictions present in distinctions between highbrow and popular culture.

Multiplicities of Representations

The third part of *Social Voices* looks at how singers who cross borders come to represent different things to different audiences. In *Women Singers in Global Contexts: Music, Biography, Identity*, Ruth Hellier (2013b) introduces the idea of "multivocality" in discussing how "a singer can adapt to shifting configurations of history, of borders, of politics, of language, of gender, and of memory, altering their singing performance choices to connect with other listeners" (Hellier, this volume). Katherine Meizel (2020 and this volume) describes how singers perform "in multiple vocalities," arguing that the human body is not limited to one voice or one form of representation, although there is the expectation among many listeners that a singer will choose one vocality that represents them as an individual (Meizel, this volume). Many singers in this part of the volume perform in multiple languages, appearing in different ways to different groups of people in different places. Each audience may experience the singer in particular ways while having limited awareness of how other audiences, listening to the singer perform in different languages, may experience and see the singer. And significantly, once again, we find that the singers examined in these chapters are all women, resonating with Weintraub and Barendregt's notion that "female entertainers, positioned at the margins of different intersecting fields of activities" have acted as "artistic pioneers of new music, new cinema, new forms of dance and theater, and new behavior, lifestyles, and morals" (2017, 3). Crossing borders creates new opportunities to try out and present evolving identities with which singers and their audiences can identify, and which they can compare and discuss (cf. Meizel 2020).

In Ruth Hellier's introduction to this third part of the volume, she highlights how singers, songs, and even the concept of singing are always evolving, being recreated, and imagined anew. She stresses the multiple ways in which singers adapt to audiences through different languages, historical eras, political backgrounds, and so on, while also emphasizing the importance of the positionality of the listener—and the multiple identities with which they identify—in the process. She argues that "singers do not generate a single history, but rather create unfolding narratives for multiple listeners that are complex and often contradictory" (Hellier, this volume). In chapter 7, Carol Silverman traces the evolving cultural politics of Balkan Romani song by examining the life of pioneering Yugoslav singer and "Queen of Romani Music" Esma Redžepova (1944–2016). The chapter shows how Redžepova navigated racialized and gendered notions of Romani people, coming to represent a pan-Yugoslav multiculturalism via "multiple performative identities—Romani, Macedonian, Yugoslav, European, Muslim, female, motherly, philanthropic, and her 'rags to riches' life trajectory" (Silverman, this volume). In chapter 8, Michael K. Bourdaghs takes up the career of Taiwanese singer Teresa Teng (1953–1995) in Japan and across East Asia during the 1970s and '80s within the context of Japan's Cold War. The chapter looks at how "multiple, often contradictory, desires could be projected" onto the singer, her music, and her image, offering a discursive site where popular reactions to and interpretations of Teng could be understood as part of her Japanese audiences negotiating the nation's post-World War II identity in Asia and the world. In chapter 9, Carol A. Muller looks at several generations of South African women singers, including Miriam Makeba (1932–2008), Sathima Bea Benjamin (1936–2013), Sibongile Khumalo (1957–2021), Melanie Scholtz (b. 1979), and King Tha/Thandiswa Mazwai (b. 1976), who, during and after apartheid, negotiated various ideas of home and away in their lives and voices amid shifting senses of history, politics, language, gender, and memory. By juxtaposing earlier singers who developed their careers in the United States during the apartheid era with recent singers who have chosen to base themselves in South Africa, the chapter highlights shifting power relations at home and abroad spanning the Global North and the Global South, along with contingent, evolving notions of diasporic identity, belonging, and unbelonging.

Singers and Songs as Interweaving Narratives

The final part of *Social Voices* examines how the meanings read into singers' lives and songs interact and build on one another. By viewing these different strands together as interweaving narratives that exist separately while also infusing one another with synergistic power, we can see how singers' performances gauge the social through the individual (Titon 1998; Rojek 2001) as their life stories "instantiate and in turn are validated by . . . their community's metanarratives" (Titon 2012, 230). For some listeners, a singer's song may gain additional meaning if the audience relates the song's lyrics to what they know or think they know about the personality and life experience of the singer. At the same time, a singer's persona may be reinforced, in the minds of some, by the perceived narrative of a song the singer performs that seems to highlight and express aspects of the singer's identity, further bolstering their image and the power of their iconicity.

And yet, as we will see throughout this volume, singers and songs also act as separate entities, each taking on a life of their own. In some cases where governments and other powerful institutions attempt to silence a singer through imprisonment, denial of recording opportunities and media distribution, and lack of inclusion in institutionalized canons, the songs that the singer composes and performs may find their way through alternative channels to new audiences that the singer cannot reach. Through this dynamic synergy and separability of singer and song, the narrative threads of singers' lives interweave with those of their songs and the life experiences of their listeners, tying otherwise disparate narratives together in ways that enable social conversations that bubble up and dissipate, endure and evolve.

In Kwame Dawes's introduction to this final part of the volume, he examines the ways in which new technologies change how we "apprehend music" and challenge our ideas about what constitutes music. As he introduces the chapters that follow, Dawes highlights the ways in which technology produces global stars who disrupt local values in various ways through their performances. In chapter 10, Natalie Sarrazin examines the impact of Indian film playback singer Lata Mangeshkar's (1929–2022) career, voice, and songs over the course of India's modern history. The chapter highlights ways in which Mangeshkar's unique and highly successful vocal style was not only desired and emulated by other singers, but also played a pivotal role in evoking a new femininity for post-independent India and the nation as a whole. In chapter 11, Katherine Meizel explores how one song, "Ya Toyour" ("Oh, Birds"), has functioned as a bridge between personal and cultural meanings in the lives and performances of two uprooted singers—an American singer, Jennifer Grout (b. 1990), performing on *Arabs Got Talent* in Beirut, and a Syrian singer and refugee of the Syrian civil war, Lubana Al-Quntar, performing at a concert in Ohio intended to foster cross-cultural understanding. The chapter argues that the song both singers sing, originally composed in 1941 as an aesthetic merging across two musical and geographical genres—classical, Arabic-style *tarab* singing and operatic, Italian-style bel canto singing—has continued to take on new meanings as those boundaries have been negotiated, eroded, and reaffirmed amid geopolitical and technological transformations.

Concluding Thoughts

Professional singers' performances bridge the personal and the social, bringing different, sometimes contrasting perspectives and worldviews into conversation with one another through the promise of the singers' representative power. In Elijah Wald's afterword to this volume, he bears witness to the ways singers discussed in this book hold "the power of identification," connecting people to one another. He also emphasizes the dangers that come with that power—the ways singers who evoke communal feelings and nostalgia for a shared past can inspire dangerous nationalisms in both present and future. As a singer who started playing music as a child, Wald went on to travel and make a living as a singer and guitarist for over a decade, and became a musician, writer, and historian who has written books on singers involved in the early blues, Mexican ranchera, and the US folk revival, among others. Both singer and scholar, Wald uses elements of his own life story to highlight the power hierarchies that surround singers in their relationships with others, reminding us that each of us is positioned within "our own power and relationships to power, some chosen, some not," and that therefore, "music is always heard in larger contexts, and the power of song is never just the power of a song itself, or of the singer—there are always infinite powers and relationships shaping its context, its intended and unintended meanings, and our various understandings and relationships to all of that" (Wald, this volume).

In this volume, we see how different claims to authenticity used by singers, together with the media through which their songs reach us as listeners—noncommercial cassettes copied and distributed from person to person (ch. 2), concerts advertised through the social media of fan clubs (ch. 3), live Zoom performances broadcast while the world was on lockdown for the COVID-19 pandemic (ch. 9), songs in nationalistic films shown in theaters across a nation (ch. 10), contestant performances in international televised singing competitions (ch. 11), and so on—are intimately tied to how we come to perceive the singers as symbols, and play into our admiration or critique of the different social values we see them as representing. Professional singers are both empowered and limited by the representative powers we ascribe to them, even as different audiences see the singers in different ways.

In the chapters that follow, we see how singers negotiate their personas and performances toward different audiences: giving voice to communities, even as they critique the stereotypes associated with those representations; pushing back against various powers that be, even as they themselves are empowered over others; and shifting their onstage, sung identities through choices in language and allusions to their own lives and the lives of the songs they sing. By examining the cultural politics surrounding these and other professional singers around the world, we come to address the heart of representation—the ongoing debates about who we are, who we are not, and where we belong.

References

Allaire, Christian. 2021. "Jennifer Lopez Chose Suffragette White for Her Inauguration Day Performance." www.vogue.com, January 20. https://www.vogue.com/article/jennifer-lopez-inauguration-day-performance-chanel.

Azizi, Arash. 2021a. "Jennifer Lopez's Performance at the Biden Inauguration Has a Complicated History." NBC News, January 21. https://www.nbcnews.com/think/opinion/jennifer-lopez-s-performance-biden-inauguration-has-complicated-history-ncna1255168.

———. 2021b. Twitter Post. January 20. 3:15 p.m. https://twitter.com/arash_tehran/status/1351986608635928577.

Bachechi, Kimberly. 2015. "Our Icons: Ourselves. Britney Spears, Justin Timberlake, Kevin Federline, and the Construction of Whiteness in a Post-Race America." *Celebrity Studies* 6(2): 164–77.

Barthes, Roland. 1977. "The Grain of the Voice," trans. Stephen Heath. In *Image-Music-Text*, 179–89. London: Fontana Press.

Betancourt, Bianca. 2021. "J.Lo Wears Suffragist White for Her Inauguration Day Performance." www.harpersbazaar.com, January 20. https://www.harpersbazaar.com/celebrity/latest/a35266177/jlo-wears-all-white-look-inauguration-2020/.

Blair, Elizabeth. 2019. "How 'This Land Is Your Land' Roamed and Rambled into American Life." NPR, March 14. https://www.npr.org/2019/03/14/702792467/woody-guthrie-this-land-is-your-land-american-anthem.

Briggs, Charles L., and Richard Bauman. 1992. "Genre, Intertextuality, and Social Power." *Journal of Linguistic Anthropology* 2(2): 131–72.

Cheng, William. 2017. "Staging Overcoming: Narratives of Disability and Meritocracy in Reality Singing Competitions." *Journal of the Society for American Music* 11(2): 184–214.

———. 2020a. *Loving Music Till It Hurts*. New York: Oxford University Press.

———. 2020b. "The Power of Song: A Response." The Power of Song: The Cultural Politics of Singers Around the Globe. Dartmouth College Conference. December 5.

Danielson, Virginia. 1997. *"The Voice of Egypt": Umm Kulthūm, Arabic Song, and Egyptian Society in the Twentieth Century*. Chicago: University of Chicago Press.

Dawes, Kwame. 2007. *Bob Marley: Lyrical Genius*. New York: Bobcat Books.

Denning, Michael. 1996. *The Cultural Front: The Laboring of American Culture in the Twentieth Century*. London: Verso.

DuBois, Thomas A. 2006. *Lyric, Meaning, and Audience in the Oral Tradition of Northern Europe*. Notre Dame, IN: University of Notre Dame Press.

Dunaway, David King. 1990. *How Can I Keep from Singing: Pete Seeger.* New York: Da Capo Press.

Dyson, Michael Eric. 2019. *Jay-Z: Made in America.* New York: St. Martin's Press.

Edwards, Leigh H. 2009. *Johnny Cash and the Paradox of American Identity.* Bloomington: Indiana University Press.

———. 2018. *Dolly Parton, Gender, and Country Music.* Bloomington: Indiana University Press.

Eidsheim, Nina Sun. 2019. *The Race of Sound: Listening, Timbre, and Vocality in African American Music.* Durham, NC: Duke University Press.

Eyerman, Ron. 2002. "Music in Movement: Cultural Politics and Old and New Social Movements." *Qualitative Sociology* 25(3): 443–58.

Fiske, John. 2011. *Television Culture.* Second Edition. New York: Routledge.

Fleetwood, Nicole R. 2015. *On Racial Icons: Blackness and the Public Imagination.* New Brunswick, NJ: Rutgers University Press.

Fonseca, Felicia. 2021. "For Some Tribal Members, Jennifer Lopez's Inauguration Day 'This Land Is Your Land' Performance Hit the Wrong Note." *Chicago Tribune,* January 21. https://www.chicagotribune.com/nation-world/ct-nw-jennifer-lopez-inauguration-song-native-american-20210121-abxsmrysc5cy3o7hiyobf6chra-story.html.

Fox, Pamela. 2009. *Natural Acts: Gender, Race, and Rusticity in Country Music.* Ann Arbor: University of Michigan Press.

Gibbs, Levi S. 2018. *Song King: Connecting People, Places, and Past in Contemporary China.* Honolulu: University of Hawai'i Press.

———. 2019. "A Semiotics of Song: Fusing Lyrical and Social Narratives in Contemporary China." In *Chinese Folklore Studies Today: Discourse and Practice*, eds. Lijun Zhang and Ziying You, 94–117. Bloomington: Indiana University Press.

Gold, Michael. 2021. "Jennifer Lopez Sang Classic Tributes to America at the Inauguration." *New York Times,* January 20. https://www.nytimes.com/2021/01/20/us/jennifer-lopez-inauguration.html.

Grant, Stan. 2021. "Jennifer Lopez's Inauguration Performance Left Out Key Verses—and Truths about America." ABC News, January 23. https://www.abc.net.au/news/2021-01-24/jennifer-lopez-inauguration-left-out-key-verses-america-truths/13081688.

Gray, Lila Ellen. 2013. *Fado Resounding: Affective Politics and Urban Life.* Durham, NC: Duke University Press.

Greene, Andy. 2021. "Flashback: Bruce Springsteen and Pete Seeger Sing 'This Land Is Your Land' for Obama." *Rolling Stone,* January 21. https://www.rollingstone.com/music/music-news/bruce-springsteen-pete-seeger-this-land-is-your-land-obama-1116187/.

Grossberg, Lawrence. 1992. *We Gotta Get Out of This Place: Popular Conservatism and Postmodern Culture.* New York: Routledge.

Guy, Nancy. 2015. *The Magic of Beverly Sills.* Urbana: University of Illinois Press.

Hadden, Joey. 2021. "Jennifer Lopez Made a Statement by Wearing Head-to-Toe White during Her Inauguration Performance." www.insider.com, January 20. https://www.insider.com/jennifer-lopez-inauguration-style-suffragete-white-2021-1.

Hellier, Ruth. 2013a. "Ixya Herrera: Gracefully Nurturing 'Mexico' with Song in the U.S.A." In *Women Singers in Global Contexts: Music, Biography, Identity*, ed. Ruth Hellier, 92–111. Urbana: University of Illinois Press.

———. 2013b. "Vocal Herstories: Resonances of Singing, Individuals, and Authors." In *Women Singers in Global Contexts: Music, Biography, Identity*, ed. Ruth Hellier, 1–37. Urbana: University of Illinois Press.

Hemmasi, Farzaneh. 2020. *Tehrangeles Dreaming: Intimacy and Imagination in Southern California's Iranian Pop Music*. Durham, NC: Duke University Press.

Holmes, Jessica, and Nina Sun Eidsheim. 2019. "'A Song for You': The Role of Voice in the Reification and De-naturalization of Able-bodiedness." *Journal of Interdisciplinary Voice Studies* 4(2): 131–38.

Hubbard, Madeleine. 2021. "Exclusive: Ed Markey and Squad Sing 'Communist' Song 'This Land Is Your Land.'" *Breitbart*, August 2. https://www.breitbart.com/politics/2021/08/02/markey-squad-socialist-communist-land-your-land/.

Kaufman, Will. 2019. "The Misguided Attacks on 'This Land Is Your Land.'" *The Conversation*, August 20. https://theconversation.com/the-misguided-attacks-on-this-land-is-your-land-121169.

Kennedy, Louise. 2003. "Activists Ask, Where Have All the Peace Songs Gone?" *Boston Globe*, March 17. http://www.sfgate.com/entertainment/article/Activists-ask-where-have-all-the-peace-songs-2662316.php.

Kesler, Sam Yellowhorse. 2021. "The Blind Spot in the Great American Protest Song." NPR, February 3. https://www.npr.org/2021/02/03/963185860/the-blind-spot-in-the-great-american-protest-song.

Kun, Josh. 2005. *Audiotopia: Music, Race, and America*. Berkeley: University of California Press.

Lipsitz, George. 1994. *Dangerous Crossroads: Popular Music, Postmodernism, and the Poetics of Place*. New York: Verso.

Lohman, Laura. 2010. *Umm Kulthūm: Artistic Agency and the Shaping of an Arab Legend, 1967–2007*. Middletown, CT: Wesleyan University Press.

Lordi, Emily J. 2017. "Close-Up: Beyoncé: Media and Cultural Icon: Surviving the Hustle: Beyoncé's Performance of Work." *Black Camera: An International Film Journal* 9(1): 131–45.

Lott, Eric. 1997. "All the King's Men: Elvis Impersonators and White Working-Class Masculinity." In *Race and the Subject of Masculinities*, eds. Harry Stecopoulos and Michael Uebel, 192–227. Durham, NC: Duke University Press.

Meizel, Katherine. 2020. *Multivocality: Singing on the Borders of Identity*. New York: Oxford University Press.

Miller, Karl Hagstrom. 2010. *Segregating Sound: Inventing Folk and Pop Music in the Age of Jim Crow*. Durham, NC: Duke University Press.

Nora, Pierre. 1989. "Between Memory and History: *Les Lieux de Mémoire*." *Representations* 26: 7–24.
Obomsawin, Mali. 2019. "This Land Is *Whose* Land? Indian Country and the Shortcomings of Settler Protest." *Folklife*, June 14. https://folklife.si.edu/magazine/this-land-is-whose-land-indian-country-settler-protest.
Powers, Ann. 2017. *Good Booty: Love and Sex, Black and White, Body and Soul in American Music*. New York: Dey St.
Rojek, Chris. 2001. *Celebrity*. London: Reaktion Books.
Santana, Matthew Leslie. 2020. "Queer Hip Hop or Hip-Hop Queerness: Toward a Queer of Color Music Studies." In *Queering the Field: Sounding Out Ethnomusicology*, eds. Gregory Barz and William Cheng, 185–97. New York: Oxford University Press.
Seeger, Anthony, and Kate Seeger. 2006. "Beyond the Embers of the Campfire: The Ways of Music at a Residential Summer Children's Camp." *The World of Music* 48(1): 33–65.
Seeger, Peter. 1993. "Interview with Anthony Seeger and Ralph Rinzler." In *Pete Seeger, Darling Corey and Goofing-Off Suite*. CD with Booklet. Washington, DC: Smithsonian Folkways Recordings 40018, pp. 2–4.
———, and Bob Reiser. 2009. *Everybody Says Freedom: A History of the Civil Rights Movement in Songs and Pictures*. New York: Norton and Company.
Shaw, Sophie. 2021. "Lady Gaga Masks Up in Custom Suffragette White Alaïa Ahead of Inauguration Day Performance." www.lofficielusa.com, January 20. https://www.lofficielusa.com/politics-culture/lady-gaga-suffragette-white-coat-mask-alaia-inauguration-day.
Simon, Andrew. 2022. *Media of the Masses: Cassette Culture in Modern Egypt*. Stanford, CA: Stanford University Press.
Spitzer, Nick. 2012. "The Story of Woody Guthrie's 'This Land Is Your Land.'" NPR, February 15. https://www.npr.org/2000/07/03/1076186/this-land-is-your-land.
Sternheimer, Karen. 2011. *Celebrity Culture and the American Dream: Stardom and Social Mobility*. New York: Routledge.
Stoever, Jennifer Lynn. 2016. *The Sonic Color Line: Race and the Cultural Politics of Listening*. New York: New York University Press.
Tansman, Alan M. 1996. "Mournful Tears and *Sake*: The Postwar Myth of Misora Hibari." In *Contemporary Japan and Popular Culture*, ed. John Whittier Treat, 103–33. Richmond, UK: Curzon Press.
Taylor, Lori B. 1990. "Introduction." *Don't Mourn—Organize! Songs of Labor Songwriter Joe Hill*. CD with liner notes. Washington, DC: Smithsonian Folkways Recordings SF 40026.
Teitelbaum, Benjamin R. 2017. *Lions of the North: Sounds of the New Nordic Radical Nationalism*. New York: Oxford University Press.
Thompson, William Forde, and Frank A. Russo. 2004. "The Attribution of Emotion and Meaning to Song Lyrics." *Polskie Forum Psychologiczne* 9(1): 51–62.

Titon, Jeff Todd. 1998. *Powerhouse for God: Speech, Chant, and Song in an Appalachian Baptist Church*. Austin: University of Texas Press.

———. 2012. "Authenticity and Authentication: Mike Seeger, the New Lost City Ramblers, and the Old-Time Music Revival." *Journal of Folklore Research* 49(2): 227–45.

Vargas, Deborah R. 2012. *Dissonant Divas: The Limits of La Onda in Chicana Music*. Minneapolis: University of Minnesota Press.

Wald, Elijah. 2012. *Escaping the Delta: Robert Johnson and the Invention of the Blues*. New York: Amistad.

———. 2020. "My Culture, Right or Wrong: Thoughts about Music and Power." The Power of Song: The Cultural Politics of Singers Around the Globe. Dartmouth College Conference. December 4.

Weidman, Amanda. 2021. *Brought to Life by the Voice: Playback Singing and Cultural Politics in South India*. Berkeley: University of California Press.

Weintraub, Andrew N., and Bart Barendregt. 2017. "Re-Vamping Asia: Women, Music, and Modernity in Comparative Perspective." In *Vamping the Stage: Female Voices of Asian Modernities*, eds. Andrew N. Weintraub and Bart Barendregt, 1–39. Honolulu: University of Hawai'i Press.

PART I

The Politics of Authenticity and Iconicity

Introduction
Jeff Todd Titon

Music got ahold of me before ethnomusicology did. My father was an amateur jazz guitarist, and naturally I wanted to be like him. But not exactly: it was the sound of blues that caught me. I was in high school in Atlanta, Georgia, when I saw my first live blues performance: B. B. King and his band at the 617 Club, on the corner of Ashby and Simpson. In college, I tried to play guitar like Etta Baker, Elizabeth Cotten, Mississippi John Hurt, and Muddy Waters. In graduate school, in addition to my studies, I joined a community of blues musicians centered on Black American musicians Lazy Bill Lucas, Jo Jo Williams, and Mojo Buford, eventually joining Bill's blues band. A French promoter produced two LPs of Bill and his friends; the English blues magazine *Blues Unlimited* published interviews I'd done with Bill, Jo Jo, and Mojo about their careers; and after playing locally and in-state, we wound up performing in front of ten thousand people at the 1970 Ann Arbor Blues Festival, along with Muddy Waters, Howlin' Wolf, and many other blues acts. Blues musicians had become icons; blues was having a "revival" and moved into the popular music spotlight in the United States and Europe from the mid-1960s through the early 1970s. I didn't want to try to make a career of blues, though; I loved ideas as well as sounds, and wanted a life that could combine them both; so I finished my PhD and became a professor (Titon 1993).

The record collectors and blues aficionados who fueled the 1960s blues revival determined authenticity on the basis of race: Black Americans had invented the blues, had nurtured it through the years, and held it by birthright. White musicians like me agreed. We also understood that we could become adopted children, as it were, into the blues family on the basis of our musical abilities and our respect for the elders and the tradition. Nevertheless, we would always be without the authenticity of the natural birthright. Pete Seeger made a similar distinction in the early 1960s, referring to himself not as a folksinger but as a "singer of folksongs." Authenticity, then, has had at least two related meanings. One is the traditional difference between the authentic original and the copy. Digital creation and manufacture now troubles this distinction. A second authenticity is personal, where one's word, gesture, and action is thought to arise from one's deep and natural well of truth, uncorrupted by artificiality or the demands of others (Titon 2012).

In their essays, Anthony Seeger, Andrew Simon, and John Lie address the ways Pete Seeger, Shaykh Imam, and K-pop singers became musical icons for vast audiences. We're familiar with icons as images that become symbols in religious contexts: saints, for example. For their audiences, these iconic singers became symbols of authentic cultural values. Their audiences authenticated not only the values but also the singers, weaving their life stories into a larger narrative that included themselves as adherents and of a new society transformed by the power of their songs. Pete Seeger (1919–2014), his nephew Anthony reveals, was driven to sing for the brotherhood and sisterhood of workers, for civil rights, for peace, and for the environment. With his extraordinary talent for leading participatory group singing, he rallied sympathetic audiences into solidarity, enacting cultural democracy on behalf of those transformational movements. Similarly, Andrew Simon shows how the blind singer Shaykh Imam (1918–1995) was turned into an icon during his lifetime and celebrated long after his death for singing lyrics critical of the Egyptian government. Simon offers a case study of the song "d'Estaing" that derided the then-President of France's visit to Egypt in 1975, while the national media promoted the visit and d'Estaing's lofty promises of French aid and friendship for Egypt. Prohibited from appearing in official channels—state-controlled radio and the recording industry—Imam's songs circulated underground on homemade audiocassettes whose recording, manufacture, and distribution were beyond the control of the government. Decades after his death, his songs are still sung, and he is celebrated by the people as a cultural icon of political revolution.

Whereas Seeger and Imam's iconicity was achieved in the last century, K-pop represents a powerful combination of the music industry, fandom, fashion, and contemporary social media. K-pop's authenticity is ambiguous. K-pop artists can be considered inauthentic when regarded as artificially "manufactured idols," actors, and impersonators enjoying great commercial success partly by cultural appropriation of Black American music and dance. On the other hand, the multiple pressures from the music industry and fan idolatry have driven some musicians to express their authentic individuality through "private debauchery" or, tragically, suicide. Moreover, as Lie shows, there is also a way in which their network of fans authenticates cultural narratives such as anti-racism, democracy, and equality in mobilizing their powerful presence on social media and social life itself. Through social media, K-pop fans helped puncture Donald Trump's June 2020 re-election balloon by reducing attendance at an Oklahoma rally from the hundred thousand who were expected, to some six thousand in total. And as I write this, only a few days ago North Korean leader Kim Jong-Un called K-pop a "vicious cancer" corrupting North Korean culture and threatening to make the state "crumble like a damp wall" (Choe 2021). In this regard, K-pop works in the direction of Pete Seeger and Shaykh Imam—when these singers became cultural icons, their followers took inspiration and allied themselves alongside their icons' lives and music, advancing powerful political counternarratives to the cant of official culture and the state.

References

Choe Sang-Hun. 2021. "Kim Jung-Un Calls K-Pop a 'Vicious Cancer' in the New Culture War." *New York Times*, June 10. https://www.nytimes.com/2021/06/11/world/asia/kim-jong-un-k-pop.html.

Titon, Jeff Todd. 1993. "Reconstructing the Blues: Reflections on the 1960s Blues Revival." In *Transforming Tradition: Folk Music Revivals Examined*, ed. Neil V. Rosenberg, 220–40. Urbana: University of Illinois Press.

———. 2012. "Authenticity and Authentication: Mike Seeger, the New Lost City Ramblers, and the Old-Time Music Revival." *Journal of Folklore Research* 49(2): 227–45.

CHAPTER 1

Becoming a "Folk" Icon
Pete Seeger and Musical Activism

ANTHONY SEEGER

Imagine a large college concert hall filled to capacity. The year is 1980. A single tall, slender, sixty-one-year-old man stands on the stage tuning a twelve-string guitar, with a five-string banjo lying on the floor next to him. He wears a cotton shirt his wife made, blue jeans, odd socks, and hiking boots. There is no back-up band, no synthesizer, no drummer—just a bare stage with some of the overflow audience seated in folding chairs behind him. About halfway through the second set, he sings a rousing politically activist song he wrote thirty years earlier called "If I Had a Hammer" (also known as the "Hammer Song"); Pete sings only a few key words and the audience belts out the rest in glorious three-part harmony: "If I had a hammer [...], I'd hammer out danger, I'd hammer out a warning, I'd hammer out love between my brothers and my sisters all over this land." He then introduces the next song, chosen to change the pace. It's a slow love song called "The Water Is Wide." Introducing it, he says, "[This song] means an awful lot to me now, because I keep thinking of the ocean of misunderstanding between human beings. We can sing all kinds of militant songs, but if we can't bridge that ocean of misunderstanding, we are not going to get this world together. [Finishes tuning]. Now, even if you haven't heard this song, you can hum along. It's a nice song to harmonize on. Literally almost any tone works, I've found." He feeds the audience their lines. The wooden walls of the old theater reverberate with the audience's harmonies. Many of those attending will remember this concert for a long time. The singer has transformed an old love song into a political anthem and the audience sings passionately to affirm their hope to cross that ocean and unite the world (P. Seeger 1991a, CD-2, tracks 12 and 13).

Pete Seeger (1919–2014) as a Musical Icon

Pete Seeger was considered a musical icon and moral compass by thousands of people during his lifetime, including many fellow musicians. He was also hated, vilified, and persecuted for his political activism and musical activities by others. He was a socially conscious activist who sought to use music to change people's ways of thinking and mobilize them to take collective action. The specific causes he was involved with changed over the decades from union organizing to civil rights activism to antiwar protesting and peace to environmental issues, local activism, and many other social causes. *The Power of Song* was the title of the 2007 biographical film about Pete Seeger and also the conference that gave rise to this book thirteen years later. Songs can have power.

Pete was a performer, songwriter, and tireless creator of organizations, publications, and musical groups. He was investigated by the House Committee on Un-American Activities in 1955. The FBI assembled thousands of pages of documents on him, and he was effectively banned from radio, television, and large record companies during most of the 1950s and the early 1960s for his political beliefs. But he kept performing and refused to compromise his beliefs. When large venues were closed to him, he sang at colleges and universities, at private schools and summer camps. When major record labels wouldn't record him, he made dozens of LP albums for a small independent label called Folkways Records. He encouraged younger singers, many of whom had sung along at his concerts as children. The music historian Elijah Wald wrote that "it is impossible to imagine Newport, or Dylan, or the folk scene of the 1960s without Pete Seeger" (Wald 2015, 8). Pete's life never took the tragic turn of many touring musicians. He did not drink, smoke, or use drugs, was married to the same woman for seventy years, and died at age ninety-four surrounded by family and friends.

A controversial figure because of his politics, Pete received institutional accolades only late in his life. He was presented with a Grammy Lifetime Achievement Award in 1993 and a Grammy for the album *Pete Seeger at 89* in 2009, five years before he died. He received another for a musical album for children in 2011, and the six-CD set *Pete Seeger, The Smithsonian Folkways Collection* received a Grammy for best historical album in 2019. He was a Kennedy Center honoree in 1994 and was inducted into the Rock and Roll Hall of Fame in 1996 as an early influencer. Long after his voice was too weak to hold sustained notes, he could still play banjo and guitar and lead songs. He performed at countless benefit concerts for causes he supported until just weeks before he died, asking audiences to sing for him. And sing they did—passionately, musically, and with commitment. Many of them still sing for him, years after his death.

Research and Reminiscence

This chapter combines information from some writings about Pete Seeger, especially the well-researched and revised biography by David Dunaway (2008) and works by Pete himself, especially his autobiographical songbook, *Where Have All the Flowers Gone: A Singer's Stories, Songs, Seeds, Robberies* (P. Seeger 1993c). But this chapter is also informed by my growing up in the Seeger family, being Pete Seeger's nephew, listening to many of his recordings, attending concerts and going backstage, and talking with him and other family members over the decades. It is also informed by the work I did as the founding director of Smithsonian Folkways Recordings, the successor to Folkways Records. Pete and his wife Toshi were essential in the label's acquisition by the Smithsonian and served on its advisory board. Since we both have the same last name, I shall refer to him throughout as Pete, rather than Seeger. I am not a scholar of the Seeger family, however, or of Pete.[1] I just happened to be born into it to parents who were themselves musical and principled, but not professional musicians. I am especially interested in the issues raised in this volume about the power of song, where that power comes from, and how musicians use it. I begin this chapter by investigating the evolution of the role of the politically committed singer, and then describe Pete's biography, his voice, instruments, songwriting, and how he made enough money to live on. I conclude with some observations on how his music and his life relate to the central themes of this book.

American Culture and People's Poets and Singers

The power of song derives partly from the abilities of the performers and partly from preexisting ideas that the public has about the role of music, musicians, and sound in American life. Where do the ideas come from that the public uses to evaluate performers and their lives? And where do performers find models for their lives, compositions, and performances? Is there a preexisting model of a musician and songwriter who tries to use music to change the world? There may have been one in the nineteenth-century poet Walt Whitman (1819–1892).

In his book *A Race of Singers: Whitman's Working-Class Hero from Guthrie to Springsteen* (Garman 2000), Bryan K. Garman argues that Walt Whitman's writings and life provided the models for twentieth-century singer-songwriters of topical songs. Whitman promoted the idea of a working-class poet-hero whose poetry could have a political impact. For Walt Whitman, art and politics were inextricably interrelated, and if Americans were to forge a morally responsible society, they would have to replace the courtly traditions of European "art singing" with an aesthetic that subordinated style to substance in the form of "heart singing" (ibid., 81).

If the influence of a nineteenth-century poet on twentieth-century protest music seems unlikely, consider the following: According to Garman, singer-songwriter Woody Guthrie read Whitman's influential book of poetry *Leaves of Grass*. Alan Lomax—a collector, promoter, and influential friend of Pete's—acknowledged the importance of Whitman on his father, John Lomax, their collections of traditional music, and their view of Woody Guthrie. He wrote, "Woody really fulfilled the ideal for a poet who would walk the roads of the country and sing the American story in the language of the people" (A. Lomax in Garman 2000, 89). Pete Seeger quoted from *Leaves of Grass* at some of his concerts (P. Seeger 1958), and Bruce Springsteen "gradually placed himself in the lineage of Whitman's working-class hero" (Garman 2000, 196). Whitman helped shape how singers could understand their lives. He also helped prepare the American public to admire performers who represented his ideal. While neither Guthrie nor Pete had strictly working-class backgrounds, the personae they forged through self-representation—Guthrie's "Okie" rusticity and Seeger's log cabin home, blue jeans, hiking boots, and modest lifestyle—as well as the subject matter of many of their songs represented that status.

In sum, Walt Whitman's ideas that art and politics are intertwined, that poet-heroes are needed to sing about contemporary America, and that "art should be created not simply for art's sake but to inculcate a sense of moral responsibility in the audience" (Garman 2000, 7) may well have influenced what audiences looked for in twentieth-century musicians and how musicians like Pete thought about their lives.

A Life of Political Song

I've often thought I was in the right place at the right time. If I'd been wandering in a different part of the world, I might have ended up being a painter, or a journalist, or a forester. But I happened to be close to this guy [Alan] Lomax, and living in a city called New York, where there were a lot of people saying, "We've got to make a decent world, get rid of fascism, and get rid of racism." Suddenly I began plunging into activities with people I might otherwise never have worked with—Jews, African Americans, and others. So music wasn't just a personal thing, it was something I was getting out and doing with other people. (Pete Seeger in an interview with Anthony Seeger and Ralph Rinzler [P. Seeger 1993b, 4])

The purpose of this brief biographical sketch is to place Pete Seeger in his historical and family contexts. Readers should consult book-length biographies for fuller accounts. Pete Seeger had a long active life performing, organizing, and writing songs. In some ways, this makes his long career more difficult to write about. In other ways, looking at the course of his life, it is easier to highlight consistent features of image, reputation, and composition over the long term.

Pete Seeger was born in 1919, a century after Walt Whitman. He grew up in a family of writers, educators, idealists, and activists that stretched back generations. His father was a composer/musicologist and his mother a concert violinist and violin teacher. Toward the end of his life he told me that one day, when he and my father and their older brother Charles were singing together in the back of the family car, my father—five years older than he—had said, "Peter, you don't have to sing the same note as we do, you can sing different notes." In other words, he could harmonize. It was a lesson the young Pete took to the world during his ninety-four-year life, encouraging generations of ardent fans to join with him in the creation of passionate harmony and political commitment.

The relationship between his parents was tense, and Pete was sent to boarding school starting at age 4. His parents later divorced, and his father eventually married a composer, Ruth Crawford Seeger. In 1933, Pete heard a recording of Appalachian music at a social gathering and it sounded different from anything he had ever heard. He was intrigued. In 1936, he accompanied his father to attend "The Ninth Annual Folk Song and Dance Festival" in Asheville, North Carolina. It changed his life. He would later reminisce, "It's probably impossible to say in words why one person likes one instrument, and another person likes another. I can remember as a thirteen-year-old being tremendously attracted to the sound of the banjo" (P. Seeger 1993b, 3).

Pete dropped out of college after losing his scholarship because he found politics and music more interesting than classes. He wanted to be a journalist, but there weren't any jobs in journalism for college dropouts during the Depression. He joined a puppet theater group that played for union farm workers, making up topical verses to old songs. He later hitchhiked across the country with singer Woody Guthrie. On that trip, he discovered he could make enough money to eat playing the banjo and singing, which was liberating. He also wrote home to borrow my father's guitar because he had broken his instrument jumping off a train. In 1939, Alan Lomax hired Pete as a paid intern at the Library of Congress, where he listened to hundreds of disc recordings collected by the Lomaxes and visited his father and stepmother in the suburbs of Washington, DC.

> My father and Alan Lomax were doing something very important in the 1930s. They wanted America to appreciate its own music. . . . I think Alan Lomax should be given more credit than he is generally given. He is credited with collecting great songs, but Alan also pointed me and others in a direction and said, "Learn this; learn it well. This is great. This is the greatest music in the world. Don't be satisfied until you've got it just right." (Pete Seeger 1993b, 3)

Like his father, Pete joined the Communist Party for a few years because it supported causes that many Americans now endorse and the major political parties at the time did not, such as workers' rights, an end to racism and segregation, peace movements, and reducing economic disparities. He left the Party in 1949, but his commitment to political causes and trying to change the world with song and activism endured for a lifetime, as did his songwriting and performing. However, his ties to the Party and his use of music for social causes would have a profound influence on his career. Whitman was never investigated by the US Congress or convicted for not telling Congress where and to whom he read his poetry; Pete Seeger was.

Just as consistent as his performing over the decades was Pete's drive to join or organize groups around music and political causes. Here is how Mary Jimenez, a member of the topical puppet and music group Pete joined in 1939, remembered him at the age of 20: "Pete had a single-mindedness that belied his appearance . . . Under that painfully shy, modest, seemingly self-effacing exterior was a will of iron. Nobody could make him do what he didn't want to do, though his manner appeared ever so acquiescent and agreeable" (Jimenez in Dunaway 2008, 61). That never changed. It was essential for him to work with others, but he had very strong ideas about how things should go. He formed the Almanac Singers in 1940, started an organization called People's Songs upon returning from the Army in 1945, and, in 1948, started a group called the Weavers to reach larger audiences. He was one of the founders of *Sing Out!* folk song magazine, *Broadside* topical song magazine, and the Newport Folk Festival. He and Toshi founded the non-profit Hudson River Sloop Clearwater, Inc. in 1966. After decades singing to support unions, civil rights, and antiwar movements, Pete continued to think globally but started to act more locally. He worked tirelessly to clean up the waters of the Hudson River from the 1960s on. He was an advisor to numerous musical, political, and environmental organizations over the years.

In 1948, Pete, Lee Hays, Ronnie Gilbert, and Fred Hellerman formed a group called The Weavers. They took their name from a play about an 1844 uprising of weavers in Silesia, a region in Central Europe, protesting automation, exploitation, and wage decreases. The Weavers' rapid rise to national popularity and swift fall due to political accusations and a blacklist provide a dramatic lesson about American music, freedom of speech, and politics (Doherty 2018). The Weavers received public accolades with a song they learned from Huddie Ledbetter, known as Lead Belly, "Goodnight, Irene," which had the Israeli song "Tzena, Tzena" on the other side of the 78-rpm record. The songs stayed at the top of the "hit parade" (the forerunner of today's popular music charts) for thirteen weeks in 1950 and sold over a million copies. But not long after that Pete and Lee Hays were denounced as Communists (Dunaway 2008, 171–83) and Pete was listed in the entertainment industry blacklist publication *Red Channels*. Their record company canceled their contract and deleted their earlier recordings from its catalog. A television contract was never finalized. Their concert bookings were canceled, and the group disbanded in 1952. Although they later reunited, the group never recovered its earlier popularity. Pete returned to a solo career and sang for young children, at summer camps, and for college students, though often in churches or other off-campus venues.

The "Red Scare" and the Cold War affected every member of my family. In 1953 or so, I was playing my father's '78 recording of the Almanac Singers called *Talking Union* on a warm spring day with a cool breeze coming through the window when my father rushed into the room, slammed the window shut, and said, "Never play that music again with the window open!" He had good reason to be concerned. The FBI was watching my family. My grandfather Charles had his passport confiscated by the State Department and had to retire because he couldn't do his job without traveling. My oldest uncle, Charles, could not get a job in the field of astronomy in the United States because of loyalty concerns, and moved his family to the Netherlands. Pete was under FBI surveillance. My aunt Peggy, like Pete a musician and songwriter, had her passport confiscated. My uncle Mike, also a musician, had to be paid through third parties because the bluegrass venue he was playing in didn't want his name on their payment slips. Many of my school friends came from families under suspicion and the previously united folk music community was bitterly divided between those who refused to testify and those who collaborated with the investigations. But Pete was probably the most affected, since he was convicted of contempt of Congress for refusing to answer questions asked him by the House Committee on Un-American Activities on the basis of liberties guaranteed in the First Amendment of the US Constitution.[2] His refusal to answer made him a hero in some quarters and a villain in others. His conviction was later overturned on appeal. But these were very difficult times for him, his family, and many others. My parents tried to shield me from it, but I learned deep in my bones that music is beautiful, powerful, and dangerous. If music has no power, why are so many musicians around the world censored, imprisoned, and even killed for what they perform?

Another constant during Pete's life was his home and family in Beacon, New York. In 1943, he married Toshi Aline Ohta, whom he had met square dancing. She was brilliant, organized, articulate, and shared his commitments. They began to look for a place to live outside New York City, up the Hudson River. Farms in the Hudson Valley being too expensive, Pete and Toshi bought seventeen wooded acres on a hillside overlooking the Hudson in 1949. With hand tools and the help of friends, he built a small log cabin (the outhouse had the best view of any I have used in my life) and lived there until he died. Making and living in a log cabin is also an American trope of self-reliance and honesty, with traces of Thoreau and "honest Abe" Lincoln. Pete and Toshi never moved to a mansion; they never had a gate or security cameras. It was a refuge, a family home, and a kind of pilgrimage site for young musicians who frequently visited them there. It was not a safe refuge, however. Many people were vehemently opposed to his political activism. His name did not appear on a mailbox. You would find his home by looking for a white X painted on a rock next to the highway, taking an unmarked turn a certain distance away, and driving up a famously long, steep, and rutted driveway.

Visitors who made it to Pete and Toshi's house were usually greeted warmly, fed, and put to work. Music might be exchanged, and stories told. Many collaborations were planned from there. Pete often performed with other artists to introduce his audiences to them and their music. Among these were Odetta, Kim Lee Wong, and the Freedom Singers. He played at Carnegie Hall with Sonny Terry, at the Village Vanguard with Memphis Slim and Willie Dixon, and with many others at multi-artist events called "hootenannies." One of the objectives of the Newport Folk Festival was to give audiences a chance to hear and interact with artists from different parts of the country and different musical traditions and languages. Throughout his career, Pete worked to give other people's songs and voices a way to be heard by his audiences.

Pete's Instruments

In discussions of Pete's politics and his singalongs, his musicianship is often ignored. Let there be no doubt, he was a consummate musician. There are musical subtleties in his melodies and performances that are often lost by those who cover his songs. He was also intensely and genuinely interested in other people's music. He would sometimes stop everything to sit next to a musician and listen to their performance. He often gave generous praise and sometimes would take out an instrument and play along while those with him would have to wait to get to their destination.

Pete was a multi-instrumentalist and tuneful whistler. He played wind instruments like the recorder and flutes. But he most frequently played the five-string banjo, the six-string guitar, and the twelve-string guitar. The banjo can be loud and percussive, and he developed a rhythmic strum that turned it into a perfect song-leading instrument. He learned the banjo by studying recordings, listening to banjo players, and experimenting. His more traditional banjo playing is featured on his first album on Folkways Records, the 1950 *Darling Corey*, an homage to the musicians and recordings he learned from. But he was an experimenter as well, as his 1955 *Goofing Off Suite* Folkways Recording shows—it includes his banjo arrangements of pieces by Bach, Beethoven, Irving Berlin, and a variety of other sources. Both albums were reissued on the same CD (Seeger 1993b).

Pete didn't just play the banjo, he wanted other people to play it too. He wrote an instruction manual, *How to Play the Five-String Banjo,* which he sold from his home for many years and then passed on to a commercial publisher (P. Seeger 2013 [1948]). It was profoundly influential for generations of young urban banjo players, including banjo superstars like Bela Fleck. I can hear the influence of the book in the playing of many musicians in the Folk Revival of the 1960s and beyond. He also made a Folkways Recording to illustrate the lessons, and eventually a video instruction DVD (P. Seeger 1991b).

Pete learned to play the six-string guitar as a youth, but he learned the twelve-string guitar from Lead Belly, who called himself the "King of the 12-String Guitar." Lead Belly had a driving, rhythmic, and virtuosic way of playing the instrument. With twelve strings, the bottom four pairs tuned in octaves and the top two pairs tuned in unison, the sound shimmers, rich with low notes, high notes, and overtones. Lead Belly could make it sound like a barroom piano. Pete used the thick, rich, and sustained sound of the twelve-string to lead songs, as he did at the concert described in the opening paragraph.

Like many professional musicians, Pete had instrument makers craft custom instruments to fit his hands and the sounds he wanted to produce.

His banjos had wider fingerboards and necks that were three frets longer than standard banjos. For a few years, the Vega banjo company made a Pete Seeger-model banjo with the extended neck.

Pete Seeger's Voice

Pete had a distinctive vocal performance style, free from vibrato and sometimes characterized as "untrained." He did not have formal vocal training, but he did learn from the styles of the Appalachian musicians he admired. His stepmother, Ruth Crawford Seeger, had painstakingly transcribed Library of Congress recordings for a book by the Lomaxes. She wrote an introductory essay to their songbook that included an important discussion of the folk performance style she discerned from the recordings (R. C. Seeger 1941 [abridged version] and 2001 [unabridged]). The sixteen instructions she gives to readers of the book who might want to sing the songs from her transcriptions are a good characterization of the vocal style and performance practice of a lot of American vernacular music, often called "folk music." It influenced many members of her family, including Pete and his half-siblings Mike and Peggy:

> (1) Do not hesitate to sing because you think your voice is not good. (2) The songs are better sung in a natural voice than a bel canto voice. (3) Do not sing "with expression"—maintain a level of more or less the same degree of loudness or softness from the beginning to the end of the song. (4) Do not slow down at ends of phrases, stanzas, or songs. (5) Do not hesitate to keep time with your foot [and] unless otherwise indicated sing with a fairly strong accent. (6) Do not "punch" or typewrite out each tone, when two or more tones are to be sung to one syllable of text. (7) Do not make too much difference between major and minor degrees in songs containing both. (9) Do not feel, in group songs, that these songs require harmonizing. (10) Do not hesitate to sing without accompaniment, and (11) when doing so, do not make noticeable pauses between stanzas. (12) When accompaniment is required, a guitar or banjo is to be preferred. (13) When singing with accompaniment, the voice should rest occasionally between stanzas to allow for instrumental interludes. (14) Remember that most songs begin with the chorus and end with the chorus. (15) Do not "sing down" to these songs. Theirs are old traditions, dignified by hundreds of thousands of singers over long periods of time. (16) Listen to phonograph recordings of these songs and others like them. (adapted from R. C. Seeger 1941, xxxi–xxxiii)

Pete didn't follow all these rules—he adapted them to his own style. When he was a young man, his tenor voice could reach high harmonies, and rang out when singing with groups. He did not mimic the vocal qualities of the singers whose songs he introduced to his audiences. He didn't try to sound like a blues singer or an Appalachian farmer. He kept his own intonation and speaking accent across genres. He was not faithfully repeating, he was adapting songs to his musical and vocal styles and audiences.

Pete's Songwriting

In his autobiographical songbook, *Where Have All the Flowers Gone*, Pete starts his comments with "On both sides of my family, I come from people used to putting pen to paper. Letters, diaries, speeches, essays, journalism, occasionally poems or books" (P. Seeger 1993c, 11). To this list, he and his half-sister Peggy added songs.

Much of Walt Whitman's poetry emulated the rhythms of everyday speech. This may have been another influence on American songwriting. My aunt Peggy suggested in a conversation that a key to understanding the stylistic continuity in American protest song is the use of vernacular speech patterns in the songs. The rhythms and melodies of the songs often follow those of spoken English (Peggy Seeger, personal communication). Pete remarked to me that "a good protest song has to be above all a good *song*. It can't be a treatise set to a melody."

Pete sang many old songs that had been sung for hundreds of years. He frequently added new verses to old songs to make them apply to contemporary situations. He introduced recently composed songs to his audiences. But he also composed new songs himself, or in collaboration with others. Because of the blacklist, Pete's performances of his songs were heard only by small audiences. But other singers popularized them, often making some musical changes in the process. "If I Had a Hammer" became a major hit for Peter, Paul, and Mary in 1962, Trini Lopez in 1963, and was later covered by dozens of artists and in several languages. "Turn, Turn, Turn" was popularized by the Byrds and was number one on the *Billboard Hot 100* chart in 1965. "Where Have All the Flowers Gone?," written in 1955, was performed by Peter, Paul, and Mary. It became a hit for the Kingston Trio and was later performed by other artists in different styles. The blacklist slowly faded after Pete's acquittal of contempt of Congress, and his recordings on Columbia Records, starting in 1961, reached larger audiences. Appearing on television was much more difficult and took longer. An effort to create his own TV show, *Rainbow Quest*, using his money and musical friends failed for lack of stations willing to carry it.

Pete also performed and composed songs and stories for children. During the blacklist, Pete taught music at elementary schools and gave many concerts specifically for children. The songs he sang for them were often about farmers, railroad workers, and animals, in addition to some action songs and stories.

Moses Asch, the founder of Folkways Records, asked many of the artists who recorded for him to also record albums for children. Pete's LPs for children were among his most popular recordings on the label. His stepmother compiled several collections of songs for children from recordings at the Library of Congress, among them *American Folk Songs for Children*, *American Folk Songs for Christmas*, and *Animal Folk Songs for Children*. Pete recorded some of the songs from those books, along with others, on a series of children's albums, among them *American Folk, Game, and Activity Songs for Children* and *Birds, Beasts, Bugs and Fishes, Little and Big*. The most popular of them all was *Abiyoyo and Other Story Songs for Children*. On it, Pete tells a long story, adapted from a Bantu tale, about a noisy boy and his magician father who, ostracized by their community, save everyone from a cannibal giant by first making him dance and then making him disappear. The story of Abiyoyo, and a lullaby on the same record, "One Grain of Sand," were later turned into award-winning children's books. Pete even coauthored a book of stories with advice to parents and grandparents on storytelling techniques (P. Seeger and Jacobs 2000).

Making a Living

Musicians make music for a variety of reasons, but unless they only do it part-time, they need to receive enough money to live on. Some musicians have "day jobs" that pay them salaries and they perform after work. Others give music lessons to help support themselves. I don't know how much money Pete made, but I do know that it came from several sources and that he lived a very modest lifestyle. His wife Toshi, his music publishing company The Richmond Organization (TRO), and his long-term manager Harold Leventhal managed the money. Pete did not. Some of his income came from solo concerts, though most of them were in small venues. He probably didn't make much money from his audio recordings for Folkways Records, but he made more from Columbia Records after he started recording for the label in 1961. Pete earned money from his songwriting and arranging even when his own performances were not played on the radio or on television and his records sold few copies.[3] When other singers recorded his songs, his publishing company would get paid a few cents for every copy of a recording. These are called "mechanical" royalties, or composer's royalties. TRO would keep a commission and send the rest to Toshi. Even one penny a track adds up: one million records sold is ten thousand dollars. Composers also receive a share of money paid for the use of their compositions on film or TV soundtracks, television shows, advertising, and other purposes. In his songbook, *Where Have All the Flowers Gone*, Pete mentions that TRO kept asking for new songs that could become popular and fewer obscure ones. His most popular songs, like "If I Had a Hammer," "Turn, Turn, Turn," and "Where Have All the Flowers Gone?," were performed by many artists, and he received composer royalties for all of them. In the 1990s, Pete told me that a week or two performing with Arlo Guthrie gave him enough money to live on for a year, allowing him to give benefit concerts for causes he supported the rest of the time. This was possible partly because he was a man of few extravagances. In 1939, he had written in his journal: "A person shouldn't have more property than he can squeeze between his banjo and the outside wall of his banjo case" (Dunaway 2008, 62). That changed with marriage and three children, of course, but only to a degree.

From the early 1950s on, Pete and Toshi lived in the same place, though they added plumbing, a barn, and a larger log house next to the first log cabin. Pete didn't travel with an entourage, but by himself or with Toshi or his grandson Tao as his driver and companion. Toshi managed the sound checks at the venue, the money, and the travel. According to Toshi, after Pete and Bruce Springsteen sang at a concert for Obama's inauguration, Pete went to the Amtrak station to wait hours for the first train toward home the next morning. Bruce Springsteen apparently heard about this and offered him a ride in his private airplane. Pete had no airplane, no driver, no roadies to carry his instruments, and only occasionally a secretary to handle his voluminous correspondence. This fit his ethical stance and the role of a people's poet: singing for America, not amassing wealth. His simple lifestyle and financial modesty were among the reasons he was called an "icon."

A Lifetime of Performing Takes Its Toll: Pete in the 1980s and Beyond

Many musicians discussed in this book are still young, so it is worth looking at how performers deal with the effects performing has on their bodies and their music. Touring alone can be hard on musicians, with long nighttime drives between gigs, hazardous flights in small airplanes, stress, and the temptations of alcohol, drugs, and fans. Later in life, Pete gave more concerts closer to home. But musicians' bodies are also affected by repetitive stress and the passage of time. The most obvious of these was in his voice. Pete's singing style is identifiable in his earliest recordings and photographs. He sang with his head back, not a good position for saving vocal cords, and often forced his voice to high registers to sound out above the audience. While his voice changed over the years, his banjo and guitar styles remained much the same, but he suffered from pain in his wrists. In his seventies, he would say, "I'm fine from the neck down," and ruefully describe his growing deafness, his worsening eyesight, and his failing voice. His hearing aids gave him trouble, and he needed glasses.

The combination of deafness and years of abuse of his vocal cords made it difficult for him to hold sustained notes later in life. His voice would quaver uncontrollably. He dealt with these changes in several ways. Starting in his late sixties, Pete began touring with his grandson, Tao Rodríguez-Seeger. Their voices were similar in timbre and Tao would double Pete's weakening voice and also provide the lyrics if Pete failed to remember them. Since Pete could sing short notes but not sustain them, he performed more songs that didn't require sustaining long notes. He added more stories to his concerts. Most of all, he counted on his admiring audiences to sing for him. He would start a song and then speak or sing the first word or next line of the verse as they sang the melody. In his later years, he did fewer entire concerts on his own, but would play a few songs at concerts with other people. Many of his appearances were at benefit concerts for causes he supported. His name on a list of performers would draw large audiences of fans. Performing kept him young and rejuvenated him as he aged. In the years before his death, he sometimes looked like an old and tired man off stage, but he would straighten up and drop a decade or two when he stepped out before an audience and asked them to, once more, sing for him.

Conclusion

I have suggested, following Bryan K. Garman, that Walt Whitman's ideas about the relation of politics to the arts and the figure of the poet-hero helped to shape the attitudes of twentieth-century Americans about singer-songwriters and topical song. So did his idea that poets should teach a moral code that opposed the ethos of acquisition and exploitation (Garman 2000, 10). Whitman's writings thus provided a model for performers to embody. I have enumerated a number of things Pete Seeger did—consciously or not—that made him a model for that role. He was a poet speaking truth to power and also a DIY person who could build his own house, split his own firewood, publish his own books, clean up after events, and work with others to get things done.

I have suggested that Whitman may also have influenced American ideas about singing style and the choice of the American southern mountain vernacular music as a model for topical songs. These vocal qualities were described by Ruth Crawford Seeger in 1941, drawn from field recordings made in Appalachia. There were other influences on Pete's music as well, of course. His choices of genre and singing style had special meaning as models for songwriting and the selection of songs for performances.

What is the difference between a poet and a singer, a poem and a song? Whitman himself appears at times to identify poetry with song. But does singing add anything in terms of symbolic power compared to speech? Labor songwriter Joe Hill had part of the answer in 1914: "A pamphlet, no matter how good, is read only once, but a song is learned by heart and repeated over and over" (Hill in Taylor 1990, 1). Melodies are sneaky. They can get into your head even before you know what the lyrics are about. That's partly what Pete referred to when he said a protest song had to be above all a good *song*. But Pete also quoted jazz writer Charles Edward Smith's definition of a song: A song is "a living poetry to be molded to the singer, the voice, [and] the instrument to be fused with them in the fire of singing so that words and music, are, for that moment of creation, inseparable" (Smith in P. Seeger 1993b, 18). That's probably the best definition of a song I have ever seen.

When we talk about singing, it is important to consider *who* is singing. Pete lamented the decline of group singing during his lifetime. More and more musicians sing *to* their audiences rather than *with* them. Pete didn't sing *to* audiences so much as sing *with* them. He could hear his audiences and together he and the audience would create sounds and experiences neither could create on their own. Singing together can forge a haphazard group of individuals into a united group (A. Seeger and K. Seeger 2006, 53–54) and I think this was what Pete intended to accomplish in his concerts.

Pete's life was so long, and his composed songs so numerous and varied that one could create many narratives with them. They "called out a warning" ("If I Had a Hammer") but with Ecclesiastes, suggest that there is a season for everything ("Turn, Turn, Turn") and wonder whether people will "ever learn" ("Where Have All the Flowers Gone?"). Or maybe music will cause a problem to disappear (the story of Abiyoyo). But the song Pete wrote with Lee Hays, "If I Had a Hammer," was one of his iconic compositions and expresses part of his role in twentieth-century music. In the last verse, he sings, "We have a hammer! And a bell! And a song! It's the hammer of justice, it's the bell of freedom, it's the song about love between my brothers and sisters." Pete sang in the morning; he sang in the evening; he sang all over this land. He sang out for justice, he sang out for freedom, and he sang out for love between his brothers and his sisters, all over this land.

Notes

I am very grateful for the conceptual and editorial assistance of my wife Judith Seeger and for comments by Elijah Wald on an earlier draft of this chapter. I alone, however, am responsible for the result.

1. When people ask me about my family, I usually refer them to the excellent biographies written about many of them. Among these are Werstein (1967) and Dickon (2017) on Pete's poet uncle Alan Seeger; Pescatello (1992) on his father Charles; Tick (1997) on his stepmother Ruth Crawford Seeger; Freedman (2017) and Peggy Seeger (2017) on his half-sister Peggy; and Malone (2011) on his half-brother Mike. The bibliography about Pete Seeger is too extensive to include here. His grandfather also wrote 800 pages of memoirs (Charles Louis Seeger Sr. MS), and part of Toshi Seeger's father's dramatic life is fictionalized in Ohta and Sperry (1929).

2. Pete stated his position in his responses to the Committee: "I am not going to answer any questions as to my association, my philosophical or religious beliefs or my political beliefs, or how I voted in any election or any of these private affairs. I think these are very improper questions for any American to be asked, especially under such compulsion as this" (Dunaway 2008, 213). Dunaway gives a full description of this period of Pete's life in chapters 7–9.

3. Songwriting and arrangement royalties are very complicated, especially with respect to folk or traditional public domain material, and space does not allow me to go into the details here.

References

Dickon, Chris. 2017. *A Rendezvous with Death: Alan Seeger in Poetry, at War.* Wickford, RI: New Street Communications, LLC.

Doherty, Thomas. 2018. *Show Trial: Hollywood, HUAC, and the Birth of the Blacklist.* New York: Columbia University Press.

Dunaway, David K. 2008. *How Can I Keep from Singing? The Ballad of Pete Seeger.* Updated and revised edition. New York: Villard Books.

Freedman, Jean R. 2017. *Peggy Seeger: A Life of Music, Love, and Politics.* Urbana: University of Illinois Press.

Garman, Bryan K. 2000. *A Race of Singers: Whitman's Working-Class Hero from Guthrie to Springsteen.* Chapel Hill: University of North Carolina Press.

Malone, Bill C. 2011. *Music from the True Vine: Mike Seeger's Life and Musical Journey.* Chapel Hill: University of North Carolina Press.

Ohta, Takashi, and Margaret Sperry. 1929. *The Golden Wind.* New York: Charles Boni Paper Books.

Pescatello, Ann M. 1992. *Charles Seeger: A Life in American Music.* Pittsburgh: University of Pittsburgh Press.

Seeger, Anthony, and Kate Seeger. 2006. "Beyond the Embers of the Campfire: The Ways of Music at a Residential Summer Children's Camp." *The World of Music* 48(1): 33–65. JSTOR stable URL: http://www.jstor.org/stable/41699678.

Seeger, Charles L., Sr. MS. *Memoirs of Charles Lewis Seeger, Sr.* Manuscript covering the years 1860–1938. Available in the Seeger collection at the Library of Congress.

Seeger, Peggy. 2017. *Peggy Seeger, First Time Ever, A Memoir.* London: Faber and Faber.

Seeger, Pete. 1958. *Pete Seeger and Sonny Terry at Carnegie Hall.* Notes by Pete Seeger. LP record. FW02412 track 202. The poem is not listed in the record contents but was recited following the song "The Good Reuben James."

———. 1991a. *Pete Seeger Singalong, Recorded Live Sanders Theatre, Cambridge, MA, 1980.* 2-CD box with notes with booklet. Washington, DC: Smithsonian Folkways Recordings SF 40027/8.

———. 1991b. *How to Play the 5-String Banjo.* DVD. Woodstock: Homespun Video SGR-BJ21-DVD.

———. 1993a [1955]. "How I Composed (Swiped) the Goofing-Off Suite" footnote. CD booklet to Smithsonian Folkways SF 40018, p. 19.

———. 1993b. "Interview with Anthony Seeger and Ralph Rinzler." In *Pete Seeger, Darling Corey and Goofing-Off Suite.* CD with Booklet. Washington, DC: Smithsonian Folkways Recordings 40018, pp. 2–4.

———. 1993c. *Where Have All the Flowers Gone: A Singer's Stories, Songs, Seeds, Robberies.* Bethlehem, PA: Sing Out Corporation.

———. 2013. *How to Play the 5-String Banjo.* Third Edition. Woodstock, NY: Homespun Music Instruction.

———, and Paul DuBois Jacobs. 2000. *Pete Seeger's Storytelling Book.* New York: Harcourt.

Seeger, Ruth Crawford. 1941. "Music Preface." In *Our Singing Country: Folksongs and Ballads*, Collected and Compiled by John A. Lomax and Alan Lomax, xxix–xxxv. Minneola, NY: Dover Publications.

———. 2001. *"The Music of American Folk Song" and Selected Other Writings on American Folk Music*, eds. Larry Polansky and Judith Tick. Rochester, NY: University of Rochester Press.

Taylor, Lori B. 1990. "Introduction." *Don't Mourn—Organize! Songs of Labor Songwriter Joe Hill.* CD with liner notes. Washington, DC: Smithsonian Folkways Recordings SF 40026.

Tick, Judith. 1997. *Ruth Crawford Seeger: A Composer's Search for American Music.* Oxford: Oxford University Press.

Wald, Elijah. 2015. *Dylan Goes Electric! Newport, Dylan, and the Night that Split the Sixties.* New York: Dey Street Books.

Werstein, Irving. 1967. *Sound No Trumpet: The Life and Death of Alan Seeger.* New York: Thomas Y. Crowell.

Multimedia Playlist

Brown, Jim, Michael Cohl, William Eigen, Pete Seeger, Sam Pollard, Jason L. Pollard, Bob Dylan, et al. 2008. *Pete Seeger, The Power of Song*. DVD. 58 minutes plus bonus films. The Weinstein Company.

Musselman, Jim (executive producer). 1998. *Where Have All the Flowers Gone: The Songs of Pete Seeger*. 2-CD tribute album of other artists singing songs by Pete Seeger. West Chester: Appleseed Recordings.

Place, Jeff, and Robert Santelli. 2019. *Pete Seeger: The Smithsonian Folkways Collection*. 6 CDs in 200-page illustrated book. Washington, DC: Smithsonian Folkways Recordings SFW40225.

Seeger, Anthony. 2019. *America's Musical Heritage*. Twelve 30-minute lectures. Survey of 200 years of musical sounds and styles that are linked to the history of the USA. Chantilly: The Great Courses. Course 7244.

CHAPTER 2

An Ordinary Icon
Cassettes, Counternarratives,
and Shaykh Imam

ANDREW SIMON

On the evening of June 10, 2012, hundreds of Egyptians, spanning multiple generations, gathered in front of *Dar Merit*, a publishing house committed to freedom of expression and thought, in downtown Cairo. Assembling only a short distance from Tahrir Square, the epicenter of Egypt's most recent revolution, the crowd convened to honor the memory of Shaykh Imam (1918–1995), an iconic artist who set the colloquial poetry of Ahmad Fu'ad Nigm (1929–2013) to song and whose tracks traveled on noncommercial cassettes created and circulated by individual listeners in the mid-to-late twentieth century. Musicians in attendance paid tribute to Imam's acoustic legacy by performing a number of his compositions, which state-controlled Egyptian radio refused to broadcast, while students, reveling in the bygone artist's rhythms, distributed placards decrying the present state of political affairs preceding the second round of presidential elections to replace the freshly ousted Husni Mubarak (r. 1981–2011), who had ruled over Egypt for three decades. Local and regional news outlets covering the sonorous event reported singing and shouting in the streets. Shaykh Imam's songs, accompanied by calls criticizing military rule, filled the air after the sun set. And the swell of sounds, generated by those present, led journalists to conclude that what had begun as a "cultural celebration" had turned into a "revolutionary demonstration."

But who was Shaykh Imam? Why did Egyptians gather to perform his songs years after he passed away? And what could explain the artist's lasting resonance? Taking these questions as a starting point in this chapter, we will explore the making of Shaykh Imam, an "ordinary icon" whose critical compositions boldly challenged the Egyptian government and its hold on history. After beginning with a brief introduction to Imam's life, we will address the centrality of audiotape technology to his career, recognizing the productive power and circulatory potential of cassettes at a point in time when Egyptian radio was state-controlled. Then, we will pay particular attention to a single song that serves as the informal soundtrack of a historic event: French President Valéry Giscard d'Estaing's visit to Egypt in 1975. In "d'Estaing," Imam openly mocks the politician's promises, offering one of several counternarratives that angered Egyptian authorities and found an especially attentive audience among the Arab left in a time of Islamic revival. Turning to Imam's performances online, where YouTube, Facebook, and other social media sites serve as informal archives, we will next explore Imam's afterlife and recent resurgence during the Arab Spring. Ultimately, we will conclude by considering the politics of preservation when it comes to iconic artists and how Imam's inclusion in this edited volume may constitute a subversive act from the perspective of Egypt's cultural gatekeepers and political authorities.

Shaykh Imam: A Very Short Introduction

On June 8, 1995, Egypt's leading newspaper, *al-Ahram*, announced the death of Shaykh Imam. In sharp contrast to the lengthy eulogies celebrating the artist's state-sanctioned peers, the brief notice simply acknowledges Imam's departure. Buried in the back of the state-controlled periodical, amid advertisements for consumer goods, the publication reduces Imam's life to a single bullet point. One of several "Morning News" items, it relays how the "blind singer" passed away the day prior at the age of seventy-eight after suffering from diabetes, and how Imam gained fame following the 1967 War, when he introduced several "critical songs" penned by Ahmad Fu'ad Nigm. The exact nature of these critiques is unknown, but Imam, we are told, received a "Platinum Record" from the "International Union for Song." Based on this remarkably unremarkable obituary, Imam, it seems, merited little mourning, much less recognition as an "iconic" artist.

In a second text, the *Encyclopedia of Singing in Egypt* (2006), Muhammad Qabil, an Egyptian artist, broadcaster, and writer, documents the lives, careers, and contributions of more than seven hundred musicians. Among the individuals to surface in this compendium is Imam, a "singer" and "composer" whose entry begins with the titles of some of his songs, from "Guevara Is Dead" ("Jifara Mat") to "Haha's Cow" ("Baqara Haha"). After noting these numbers, the item pivots to the voice behind them. According to the account that follows, Imam was born blind in the village of Abu al-Numrus in 1917 and went on to memorize the Qur'an and serve as a paid reciter until 1962. It was at this point in time when Imam crossed paths with poets whose words he set to song. Imam's relationship with one poet, Nigm, proved to be particularly productive and resulted in a number of politically charged compositions. The duo's collaborations reportedly found an especially receptive audience among students, with one number becoming "an anthem for students, workers, peasants, and the political opposition" in the period following 1967. Neither Imam's repertoire nor his audience, however, were limited to Nigm and Egypt. The artist, Qabil acknowledges toward the end of the entry, animated the writings of multiple poets and performed in Europe as well as across the wider Arab world prior to his passing in 1995.

Yet who exactly was Shaykh Imam before he joined forces with Ahmad Fu'ad Nigm? What was Imam's upbringing like, his education, and his life prior to 1962? And how did he become an artist in the first place? Moreover, why did others find meaning in Imam's music? How might he have told his own story? And what experiences shaped him? On these fronts, *al-Ahram*'s obituary and Qabil's encyclopedia entry provide little in the way of answers. To begin to address these questions, it is necessary to look elsewhere. In the spirit of developing a better grasp on Imam as an individual, his trajectory, and his status as an "ordinary icon," let us turn to a third source, one of the most extensive engagements with Imam to date—his memoir. Recorded by Ayman al-Hakim, a writer for the Egyptian weekly *al-Kawakib*, in 1993, and published in Cairo in 2001, *Years of Art, Prison, and Tears: The Memoirs of Shaykh Imam* provides a unique window onto the icon's evolution.

Born Imam Ahmad Muhammad 'Isa on July 2, 1918, in a small village outside of Central Cairo called Abu al-Numrus, Imam was the only one of eight boys to survive more than a few days past birth. Shortly thereafter, he lost his sight on account of a rural medicine administered by his mother to cure an eye infection. Like other children, Imam enrolled in the local *kuttab*, or primary school, where he learned to recite the Qur'an at the hands of the village shaykh (a title often granted to public figures possessing religious knowledge). Outside of these religious lessons, Imam recalls sitting with the women of the town. He mentions the "sweet songs" they sang while kneading wheat in preparation for village-wide gatherings celebrating a new marriage or the annual Islamic pilgrimage (*Hajj*). It was at the former where Shaykh Mahmud Sulayman, a singer employed by an Islamic philanthropic organization to "revive" rural celebrations along Islamic lines, first noticed Imam. In need of a few backup singers, he enlisted the boy and, after hearing his voice, recommended Imam be sent to Cairo to complete his religious studies. After memorizing the Qur'an by the age of twelve, Imam left Abu al-Numrus for Egypt's capital, which he had visited with his uncle by foot, at least once prior, to pray at the Fadil Pasha Mosque in the neighborhood of Sayyida Zaynab. It was there, Imam recalls, where he first heard Muhammad Rifa'at, a figure of some renown, recite the Qur'an during Friday prayers.

Imam's adoration of Shaykh Rifa'at, whose "magical" voice reportedly enchanted Muslims and Christians alike in Cairo's cafes, ultimately led to Imam's dismissal from the Islamic institute where he was studying and residing. After being expelled for listening to one of Rifa'at's recitations over the radio—a technology that was a gateway to "unbelief, immorality, and disobedience," according to the establishment's administrators—Imam, now homeless, found his way to al-Ghuriyya, a working-class neighborhood. There, he scraped out a living by reciting the Qur'an in houses and stores, and singing at weddings and religious festivals. During one such performance, Imam piqued the attention of Shaykh Darwish al-Hariri, who invited him to be his pupil. After studying the essentials of "Eastern music" with one of its authorities, who previously instructed well-known artists like Zakariyya Ahmad and Muhammad 'Abd al-Wahhab, Imam added the oud (a pear-shaped, short-necked, stringed instrument resembling a lute) to his musical arsenal and committed himself to his artwork on a full-time basis by 1945. In the years to follow, Imam continued to sing at local events and enjoyed a brief stint with Ahmad's troupe, before later meeting Nigm, who had recently emerged from prison following a three-year sentence for forging papers, in 1962.

In addition to highlighting a few of the more formative moments in Imam's life before Nigm, this snapshot directs our attention to the artist's hardships, religiosity, and simple lifestyle, which, along with his later outspokenness, would endear Imam to listeners and play a key part in his evolving legacy as an artist and his standing as an "ordinary icon." This image, to be certain, was one endorsed by Imam. As he states at the very outset of his memoir: "I am one of the sons of this country. I was born poor, I lived with the poor, and I sang to them." In these regards, Imam's relationship with Nigm only further solidified his "ordinary" status. By performing Nigm's vernacular poetry, Imam often sided with "the people" against those in positions of power and sang to listeners in a manner they could understand, minimizing the distance between lyrics and the language used by his compatriots on a daily basis. The resulting songs, which, in the words of one Arab listener, were "so dangerous" because they were "so singable" (Petric 1980, 18), inspired the ire of Egypt's ruling regimes, landing Imam and Nigm in prison multiple times. But how did Imam go about popularizing Nigm's poetry and reaching a wider audience? And what may the artist have meant when he once said, "My mass media are the masses" (Booth 1985, 21)?

State-Controlled Radio and Noncommercial Cassettes

Early on in *Halim* (2006), a biopic revolving around one of Egypt's most beloved artists, a young ʿAbd al-Halim Hafiz (played by Ahmed Zaki) appears before a four-person panel in a dimly lit room. Up until now, the singer has yet to make it big, but his fortunes are about to change. With the approval of those present, ʿAbd al-Halim's voice will soon sound over the radio, a medium whose reach extended well beyond Egypt's borders to the wider Middle East. This scene, which lasts less than a minute in the film, recalls a key moment in its subject's career. Following ʿAbd al-Halim's graduation from a state-sponsored conservatory in Cairo in 1948 and a brief stint as a music teacher, he auditioned as a singer at the radio. While ʿAbd al-Halim was certainly an extraordinary artist on many fronts, his experience before the radio's inspectors was decidedly less so. Screening committees, comprised of artists, broadcasters, and sound engineers, routinely ensured that only select voices enjoyed wider audiences over state-controlled Egyptian airwaves. Collectively, these local gatekeepers strove to determine who created Egyptian culture and what shape it assumed, elevating individuals like ʿAbd al-Halim, who would go on to sing in support of ruling regimes, and suppressing others like Imam, who criticized those in positions of power.

Radio in Egypt, to be certain, was not always a state-controlled enterprise. Although relatively short-lived, radio stations run by amateurs relayed a wide array of content from the late 1920s to the mid-1930s. Often times, these independent stations adopted the names of their operators and broadcast out of a single room or lone apartment to surrounding residences. According to one estimate, around a dozen such stations existed in Egypt. The owners of these private programs presented any content they saw fit. As one historian recalls, some hosts went so far as to report that a "bomb" had exploded on al-Muski Street, or a "fire" had set al-Shubra Street alight, in order to grab the attention of listeners before announcing a toy shop's sales in Islamic Cairo or the opening of a new tavern north of the capital's center (Shalabi 1995, 20). The great freedom enjoyed by these novice broadcasters, however, was not destined to last.

In October of 1932, Tawfiq Dus, Egypt's Minister of Transportation, informed local journalists that one could no longer set up a radio and a receiver without a license. Shortly thereafter, the minister met with radio entrepreneurs and presented the government's plan to establish a state-operated station, at which point all other channels would be compelled to close. Over the course of the next two years, many Egyptians vigorously resisted this state-imposed silence. Station owners petitioned politicians, broadcast pleas for public support, and made their case to remain alongside a government station in the national press. These efforts, nevertheless, were in vain. By May 29, 1934, amateur airwaves reportedly fell quiet in Egypt. Forty-eight hours later, on May 31, the Egyptian government's station, with the support of the British Marconi Company, issued its first broadcast, marking the official start of state-controlled Egyptian radio.

With the invention of the audiocassette in 1963, Egyptian radio's gatekeepers would soon face a new challenge. Cassette technology, which gained traction in Egypt in the 1970s and continued to be an influential medium well into the early 2000s, enabled its users to produce and circulate cultural content, from pop songs to Islamic sermons (Hirschkind 2006). No longer relegated to the role of cultural consumers, an unprecedented number of Egyptians harnessed cassettes to become cultural producers and distributors for the first time, much to the dismay of radio officials, state censors, and other cultural gatekeepers (Simon 2022). In these regards, Imam was no exception. He harnessed the creative power and circulatory potential of cassettes to reach a wider audience in the absence of state-controlled Egyptian radio, which refused to broadcast his critical compositions, including a number of songs that forcefully undermined the "official stories" told by Egypt's ruling regimes. Cassettes, accordingly, facilitated the construction of counternarratives and the decentralization of state-controlled Egyptian media long before the advent of the internet. To begin to gain a better sense of the ease with which Imam's voice traveled on audiotapes, it is useful to consider a home video.

Uploaded to YouTube, the private video offers some clues as to what Imam's performances looked like in practice in Egypt. In the footage, the artist sits and strums his oud on a couch in someone's home. He converses with those around him and laughter fills the air in what is clearly a joyous affair. As Imam begins to play, those present clap in unison, and as the camera zooms out, a cassette player appears. The boombox sits on a nearby table and a microphone extends toward the guest of honor. Imam proceeds to sing the opening to "d'Estaing," a song that sharply ridicules French President Valéry Giscard d'Estaing's visit to Egypt in 1975. Those in the room do not sit by silently. Instead, they participate in the performance, repeating the number's opening refrain, as Imam playfully interjects in French. This concert, notably, is not unique. Other videos, circulating on social media platforms, similarly

Figure 2.1. Two of Imam's Noncommercial Cassettes: The first (left) reads "First Meeting with Shaykh Imam," while the second (right) records a Shaykh Imam performance in Shubra, Cairo. Source: Author's archive.

showcase Imam singing in informal settings alongside cassette players, which lent his live acts a greater degree of longevity (Figure 2.1). But why was Imam performing in people's homes as opposed to national venues in the first place? To answer this question, let us now turn to the subversive song at the center of this video: "d'Estaing."

Valéry Giscard d'Estaing Visits Egypt

On December 10, 1975, Egypt's president, Anwar Sadat (r. 1970–1981), welcomed Valéry Giscard d'Estaing (r. 1974–1981) of France with open arms. The primary purpose of the historic visit was to strengthen relations between the two countries. The timing of the five-day trip, the first of its kind for a French head of state, was propitious. Under Sadat, Egypt was moving away from the Soviet Union toward the West. Material evidence of this political shift was evident at Cairo's airport. Shortly after d'Estaing's arrival, the Egyptian Air Force flew overhead in French Mirage fighters. Soviet-built MIGs, which usually soared above, were nowhere to be found. From the very moment d'Estaing touched down in Egypt, his welcome played out as an extravagant affair. A red carpet blanketed the runway, where an honor guard and cameras awaited, while Sadat accompanied his guest of honor in a jet-black Cadillac convertible to Qubba Palace, a decadent site renowned for its lavish events. French and Egyptian flags flew from lampposts in the capital's streets and crowds of cheering Egyptians greeted the measured motorcade with signs, banners, and mass-produced portraits of the two presidents. Holding onto a specially designed bar in the open-air car, a smiling Sadat and d'Estaing stood, side-by-side, waving at those around them (Figure 2.2).

Figure 2.2. Sadat and d'Estaing's Motorcade in Cairo (1975). Source: Jean-Claude Deutsch/Paris Match Archive via Getty Images.

D'Estaing's celebratory sojourn culminated in the signing of a joint statement. Coined the "Cairo Communique," the document outlined a myriad of promises made by the French to the Egyptians. What the written agreement lacked in depth, it made up for in breadth. In addition to aiding Egypt and other Arab countries in assembling a defense-minded arms industry, d'Estaing pledged to support economic development in Egypt and confirmed the readiness of France to assist in the local construction of nuclear power plants. The assurances, however, did not end there. France promised to contribute to countless other initiatives. These projects included the creation of a Cairo metro system, a telecommunications cable connecting the cities of Suez and Port Said, and plants for the production of steel, aluminum, and polyester fiber. French expertise, in short, would remake Egyptian society. Shaykh Imam, needless to say, was less than impressed by d'Estaing, his guarantees, and the fanfare surrounding his reportedly "successful" visit, which one Egyptian periodical, within days of d'Estaing's departure, went so far as to proclaim, succeeded in "strengthening friendship, supporting the economy, exchanging culture, and defending peace."

If d'Estaing's trip was a triumph in the press, it was the subject of derision on cassettes. In "d'Estaing," Imam runs with the theme of promises (see Appendix). He praises the French politician, albeit to ludicrous ends, and recognizes all of the ways by which Egypt will benefit from d'Estaing's support. He begins by acknowledging how d'Estaing and his wife will "grab the wolf by its tail," or do the impossible. In the "fabulous" world that awaits, he elaborates, "we're going to be spoiled rotten." Color TV, new service clubs, and perfume-powered cars would become a reality. Egyptians, moreover, would finally be worth something when it came to culture. "We'll make it big," Imam humorously boasts, "on the stage and screen, or, even, at the zoo," a clear jab at d'Estaing's pledge to support cultural exchange between Egypt and France, especially in the domain of theater. As for politics, Egypt would work with Europe. "Who needs Syria or Libya?" Imam wryly asks, singing, "We'll make an Arab Union with London and the Vatican." These changes, the artist concludes, would all be "courtesy of my magnanimous friend, d'Estaing, the romantic." Often in dialogue with contemporary coverage of the French President's visit, Imam's song subverts the state's official narrative of the event and counters one of the government's most powerful tools—its stories. In challenging Egypt's ruling regimes, Imam found a particularly receptive audience among the left, keeping the flame of resistance alive in the 1970s and 1980s.

Leftist Politics and the Islamic Revival

In the spring of 2019, the *International Journal of Middle East Studies* published a series of short essays on the Arab left. The contributions span less than twenty pages, in total, and cover everything from the circulation of ideas, people, and objects in an increasingly interconnected world to the limits of area studies and the nation-state as an analytical paradigm to the perils and promise of critical biographies, global histories, and local fieldwork. Collectively, these reflections raise no shortage of questions. What insights might interdisciplinary scholarship on the Arab left offer into the making of the modern Middle East? How might histories of this overlooked topic unfold on different planes, from the micro to the macro? And what shapes might an archive of the Arab left assume in and outside of the Arab world? Such inquiries, no doubt, promise to inspire different responses, but similarly stand to expand our understanding of an era, which, in the case of Egypt, is often narrated not through the lens of leftist politics, but the Islamic revival.

Following the 1967 War, which resulted in not only the loss of territory for Egypt but an existential crisis across the Arab world, Islam came to play an increasingly important role in public life and political discourse in the Middle East. For some seeking to make sense of the humiliating defeat dealt to Egypt, Jordan, and Syria by Israel, Islam provided an answer. In Egypt, Islamic dress, print culture, and banking, along with previously repressed Islamists, gained ground in the 1970s and 1980s. It was during this time, too, when Imam came into greater contact with the local left. Here, the artist's involvement with the student movement, which led the way in criticizing the Egyptian government's inaction toward Israel after its resounding victory, stands out. Alongside Nigm, Imam performed on college campuses, and in one song, "Return of the Students" ("Rajaʿu al-Talamidha"), he commends student activists and their commitment to "the cause"—ending Israel's occupation of Egyptian and Arab land—despite the best efforts of others to distract them. Later, in 1977, when Sadat cut subsidies on bread and other staples, resulting in protests, Imam once again sided with those taking the government to task. In "Who Are They?" ("Humma Min?"), he echoes contemporary protest slogans and draws a clear divide between "the people" and those in power. As we will see, this song would resound once more in Egypt decades later.

In addition to circulating locally, most often on informal cassette recordings, Imam's music crossed Egypt's borders, where it resonated with a wider audience, including leftists elsewhere. Among Nigm and Imam's many collaborations is "Forbidden" ("Al-Mamnuʿat"). The song's lyrics, which open with a series of prohibited actions, from traveling to singing, draw on the duo's lived experience. Penned by Nigm in the mid-1970s and performed by Imam shortly thereafter, it introduces an Egypt where repression is all too commonplace and continues to intensify, day by day, alongside one's love of the country. Although this oppression, in many ways, would endure, Imam's ability to travel changed. In 1984, Mubarak's regime permitted him to venture abroad for the first time. Accompanied by Nigm and Muhammad Ali, a mutual friend and fellow artist, Imam performed before boisterous crowds in amphitheaters and small gatherings inside people's homes across the Middle East, where his noncommercial cassette recordings often reached listeners well before he appeared in person. On this international tour, Imam also encountered and engaged Arab communities residing in Europe at a distance from their homelands. Such was the case with one concert in England, where some two thousand "Middle Eastern exiles" welcomed the artist with the opening lines of Egypt's national anthem and "several hundred, mainly left-wing, self-exiled Egyptians in the audience wept" as he sang (Darwish 1995). Imam's music, clearly, struck a chord in and outside of Egypt.

Although often inspired by Egypt, the content of Imam's songs was not limited to it. At times, his compositions recognized individuals who resisted repression worlds away. In addition to criticizing western leaders like d'Estaing, Imam extolled icons of the global left, foreign revolutionaries fighting familiar struggles. This is perhaps no more evident than in the case of "Guevara Is Dead." Released in the aftermath of Che Guevara's execution in Bolivia in 1967, the track ponders the combatant's final moments, praises him as the "ideal fighter," and calls upon "workers, the deprived, and the chained" to take up arms to enact change. A broadcast team traveled all the way from Cuba to Cairo to record the song, while an Italian record company released it on an album, adopting Guevara's name, in 1971. There is then "Ho Chi Minh," a second production memorializing the late President of North Vietnam, who passed away from a heart attack in Hanoi in 1969. In the number, Imam recognizes Ho, a life-long revolutionary, as a selfless ruler whose legacy presents a pathway forward for those opposing oppression. Like "Guevara Is Dead," this recording, too, would make its way further afield, appearing on a record in France in 1982. Collectively, these works invite us to revisit leftist politics in a time of Islamic revival and to reconsider the intersections of art, activism, and solidarity on local, regional, and global scales. At the same time, Imam's songs crossed not only national borders, but also historical eras. Decades after Imam first raised his voice, it sounded once more during the Arab Spring.

Imam's Resurgence and Egypt's Revolution

In the days leading up to Mubarak's downfall and in the years following the end of his rule, Shaykh Imam's compositions experienced a revival. From the very start of mass demonstrations in Cairo in 2011, Imam's voice accompanied citizens in the streets. A YouTube video capturing protestors marching toward Tahrir Square on January 25 confirms the presence and enduring resonance of Imam's music. In the short clip, spanning little more than a minute in length, a young man addresses the vast disparities that exist between the "haves" and "have nots" in Egypt. "They eat pigeon and chicken," he calls out to the crowd behind him, which loudly echoes the chant, "while we eat beans until becoming nauseated." This statement, one of a few the man makes, may be traced back to a song first performed by Imam decades earlier: "Who Are They?" In the number, the artist draws a stark distinction between "the poor and the oppressed" and rulers whose lives "move along pleasantly." He positions himself squarely on the side of the people and encourages listeners to question where power truly resides, an invitation accepted by those in the video, who collectively played a part in Imam's resurgence.

If protestors mobilized Imam's songs in and outside of Tahrir Square to take aim at Egypt's ruling regime and galvanize those rising up against it, others have also contributed to the artist's acoustic afterlife since the start of 2011. One of the individuals who has been instrumental to Imam's revitalization is the independent Egyptian singer and songwriter Maryam Saleh. Saleh first met Imam, a family friend, at a young age, when her parents, who both worked in the arts, invited him to perform at their house. Inspired by what she heard, Saleh went on to breathe new life into Imam's oeuvre. Over the past decade, Saleh has refashioned Imam's tracks across multiple genres, from rock to triphop, performing creative covers of his songs in Egypt, Jordan, Lebanon, and Palestine. On SoundCloud, Saleh's rearrangement of "d'Estaing" has amassed over 100,000 plays, while her rendition of "Nixon Baba" has been heard more than 200,000 times since it surfaced on the site nine years ago. Both of these songs appear on Saleh's 2015 album *Clown* (*Halawella*), a collaboration with Lebanese producer Zeid Hamdan that draws heavily on Imam's repertoire. More recently, in 2018, Saleh organized a workshop in Egypt where participants had the opportunity to learn more about "Shaykh Imam's world" and develop a greater appreciation of his art, which continues to evolve not only on the ground in the Middle East but also online.

In cyberspace, Imam's specter spans multiple platforms. On Spotify, a playlist titled "This Is Sheikh Imam" features nearly five hours of the artist's "essential tracks," while on SoundCloud, one may listen to Imam as well as other singers, like Saleh, perform several of his songs. On YouTube, countless individuals have made Imam's original cassette recordings available to a global audience, together with grainy videos of Imam singing before "live" audiences in Egypt, Europe, and elsewhere. Through these social media sites, which contain an astounding amount of archival material, Imam's legacy takes the shape of a communal enterprise and an interactive exercise to which anyone with an internet connection may contribute. Perhaps nowhere is the collective nature of Imam's virtual footprint clearer than in the case of Facebook, where the singer is the focal point of several posts, pages, and groups. Here, one need only consider "Shaykh Imam," a Facebook page with over 275,000 followers for "fans of committed art wherever they may be." In addition to posting photographs of Imam and archival footage of his concerts, the site showcases many people performing his songs closer to the present in videos that evidence the late icon's lasting importance and inspire no shortage of engagement on the part of those who watch them. One node in a far more expansive digital network, sites like "Shaykh Imam" have played a key part in the artist's recent revival by providing internet users the world over with a space to preserve his memory, celebrate his life, and experience his music.

Nearly one year to the day protestors first took to Tahrir Square in 2011, Egyptian filmmaker Ahmed Manawishi introduced a new project on his

YouTube channel. The video, a trailer to an upcoming documentary titled *El Shaykh vs. Imam* (*'Indama al-Shaykh Wajh Imam*), begins with a cassette tape turning before recognizing Shaykh Imam's birth in an Egyptian village, his struggle against oppression, and the artist's recent resurgence. "Sixteen years after his departure," the production proclaims, Imam "returned to participate in a revolution." Footage from that revolution and Imam's earlier performances abroad follow, while various speakers address who Imam was and what he meant to them. The icon that emerges is a multifaceted one—a "blind man," a "shaykh," an "oudist," and a "rebel" whose songs "were elided from Egypt's memory." Manawishi's film strives to capture this complexity and counter Imam's historical erasure. In these regards, the project seems to share much in common with this chapter. Whether or not the filmmaker succeeds on either of these fronts, however, is difficult to determine. The documentary, to this day, has yet to be released. The causes for this near decade long delay are not entirely clear, but one thing is beyond any doubt. Much more work on Imam remains to be done.

Conclusion: The Lives and Afterlives of Iconic Artists

Five years prior to Shaykh Imam's passing in 1995, Egypt's Ministry of Culture published a poster based on a painting by Salah 'Inani, an Egyptian artist who, at the time, directed a government-sponsored gallery in Cairo. Titled "A Hundred Years of Enlightenment" ("Mi'at 'Am Min al-Tanwir"), the mass-produced print pays tribute to Egypt's cultural "renaissance" and features no shortage of important figures (Armbrust 1996, 190). Among these individuals are writers, such as Naguib Mahfuz, actors, such as Yusuf Wahbi, and singers, including Umm Kulthum. Of all these subjects, it is Umm Kulthum who enjoys pride of place. Standing in a red, floor-length dress atop a platform in the scene's center, the performer strikes a familiar pose and rises above many of her compatriots. At the same time, the colorful composition is noteworthy not only for who it recognizes as a cultural icon, but also who it omits. Shaykh Imam, notably, is nowhere to be found.

The Ministry of Culture's poster directs our attention to the politics of preservation when it comes to iconic artists. It is but one of many examples of the Egyptian state elevating certain voices and marginalizing others. These efforts, which assume multiple forms, extend beyond the lives of public figures to their legacies. Here, one need look no further than Umm Kulthum. State institutions have taken numerous steps to celebrate and commemorate the late singer. State-controlled media continued to broadcast Umm Kulthum's songs long after her death, while the government named a street after her, minted a coin in her memory, and issued a stamp in her honor. In 2001, a museum devoted exclusively to Umm Kulthum opened in Egypt, while two years later, an Umm Kulthum memorial surfaced near her former home in Cairo. Most recently, Umm Kulthum performed before a live audience forty-five years after her passing. With the support of the Ministry of Culture, and courtesy of advancements in the arena of virtual technology, Umm Kulthum appeared on stage as a hologram at the Cairo Opera House in 2020.

In sharp contrast to Umm Kulthum and other state-approved singers who enjoyed close relationships with Egypt's rulers and who have merited no shortage of attention from scholars (Danielson 1997; Lohman 2010), Shaykh Imam was neither circulated on currency nor sacralized on stamps in Egypt. His name was not emblazoned on street signs, his career has yet to merit the establishment of a museum, and his literary footprint is surprisingly limited. State-controlled media refused to broadcast Imam's critical compositions both before and after his passing. There are no monuments to remind onlookers of his impact, and Imam has not performed posthumously as a hologram at national venues. Despite being forgotten by the Egyptian state, Imam has been remembered by ordinary Egyptians, who are responsible for his preservation. It was at the hands of non-state actors that Imam's songs witnessed a revival during Egypt's revolution and continued to resonate after Mubarak's historic fall on February 11, 2011. Online and on the ground, in Egypt and at a distance from it, Imam's legacy continues to evolve in the absence of state support.

This chapter, ultimately, builds upon efforts to write Imam back into Egypt's historical memory. Indeed, Imam's very inclusion in this edited volume, especially in a part on "icons," may constitute a subversive act. Much like Imam's music, the artist's presence on these pages is not something Egyptian gatekeepers would endorse. This exploration, then, is both an inquiry into Imam and an invitation to look beyond him to other artists on the margins of national narratives. Who else might have been forgotten by states but remembered by citizens? What other performers were popular but not praised by political authorities? And what insights might the overlooked lives and legacies of these icons offer into the past and present? Such questions are worth asking lest we end up assigning importance to the same performers deemed important by ruling regimes.

Appendix

"D'ESTAING" (1975)[1]

Valéry Giscard d'Estaing[2]
And his lady-love, too
Will grab the wolf by its tail[3]
And feed every hungry mouth in town.

Oh man, you *guys*
Check out all the *gentleman* people walking around
We're going to be spoiled rotten
And life will just be fabulous
We'll have color T.V.
And new service clubs galore
And rather than running on gas, cars will run on *parfan*.[4]

Behold, a great cultural renaissance awaits
We'll make it big
On the stage and screen
Or, even, at the zoo
Life will be sweet like zalabiyya[5]
Who needs Syria or Libya?
We'll make an *Arab* Union[6]
With London and the Vatican.

The poor will eat sweet potatoes
And strut down the street with swagger
And instead of calling their kids Shalata[7]
They'll name them *Jean*.

All of this is courtesy of my magnanimous friend
d'Estaing, the Romantiki[8]
And not one of you will be able to keep up
With me, my neighborhood, and my crowd.

Notes

1. Lyrics by Ahmad Fu'ad Nigm. This translation is my own.
2. Imam performs parts of this song in a French accent, particularly the *italicized* words.
3. To "grab the wolf by its tail" means "to do the impossible" in Arabic.
4. "Perfume" in French.
5. A type of fried dough ball soaked in syrup.
6. Imam pronounces "Arab" (*Arabiyya*) with a French accent, stressing the *alif* instead of the 'ayn.

7. A common Egyptian name with lower class connotations.
8. The "Romantic" in Arabic.

References

Al-Hakim, Ayman. 2001. *Sanawat al-Fann wa al-Sijin wa al-Dumuʻ: Mudhakkirat al-Shaykh Imam* (*Years of Art, Prison, and Tears: The Memoirs of Shaykh Imam*). Cairo: Dar al-Ahmadi lil-Nashr.

ʻArafa, Sharif, dir. 2006. *Halim*. Egypt: Al-Sharika al-ʻArabiyya lil-Intaj wa al-Tawziʻ al-Sinimaʼi, 155 min.

Armbrust, Walter. 1996. *Mass Culture and Modernism in Egypt*. New York: Cambridge University Press.

Booth, Marilyn. 1985. "Sheikh Imam the Singer: An Interview." *Index on Censorship* 14(3): 18–21.

Danielson, Virginia. 1997. *"The Voice of Egypt": Umm Kulthūm, Arabic Song, and Egyptian Society in the Twentieth Century*. Chicago: University of Chicago Press.

Darwish, Adel. 1995. "Obituary: Sheikh Imam." *The Independent*, June 9. https://www.independent.co.uk/news/people/obituary-sheikh-imam-1585763.html.

Hirschkind, Charles. 2006. *The Ethical Soundscape: Cassette Sermons and Islamic Counterpublics*. New York: Columbia University Press.

Lohman, Laura. 2010. *Umm Kulthūm: Artistic Agency and the Shaping of an Arab Legend, 1967–2007*. Middletown, CT: Wesleyan University Press.

Petric, Faith. 1980. "Speak Out Freely, Speak Out! Egypt's El Sheikh Imam." *Sing Out!: The Folk Song Magazine* 28(5): 16–19.

Qabil, Muhammad. 2006. *Mawsuʻat al-Ghinaʼ fi Misr* (*Encyclopedia of Singing in Egypt*). Cairo: Dar al-Shuruq.

Shalabi, Hilmi Ahmad. 1995. *Tarikh al-Idhaʻa al-Misriyya: Dirasa Tarikhiyya (1934–1952)*. Cairo: Al-Hayʼa al-ʻAmma al-Misriyya lil-Kitab.

Simon, Andrew. 2022. *Media of the Masses: Cassette Culture in Modern Egypt*. Stanford, CA: Stanford University Press.

Multimedia Playlist

ʻABD AL-HALIM HAFIZ, "Ya Gamal ya Habib al-Malayin" ("Gamal, Beloved of Millions"), 1958.
"SHAYKH IMAM" (*Al-Shaykh Imam*), Facebook Page, n.d.
SHAYKH IMAM, "d'Estaing," 1975.
AHMAD FUʼAD NIGM, *Al-Aʻmal al-Kamila* (*Complete Works*), 2002.
JEHANE NOUJAIM, *The Square* (film), 2013.
MARYAM SALEH, "d'Estaing," 2012.
PETER SNOWDON, *The Uprising* (film), 2013.

CHAPTER 3

Idolatry and Iconoclasm in K-Pop Fandom

JOHN LIE

President Donald Trump's rally in Tulsa, Oklahoma, on June 20, 2020, imploded to the tune of his enemies' ecstatic schadenfreude. With over a million registered electronically and expecting perhaps 100,000 supporters to show up, only 6,200 went through the turnstiles at the BOK Center, which can accommodate nearly 20,000 people. Were leftist protesters blocking the entrance, as some in the Trump camp alleged? Did Oklahomans and their neighbors worry about COVID-19 transmission? Surely there were numerous variables at play, but a factor that contributed to the chasm between the Trump re-election campaign team's high expectations and the cold reality of low turnout was a most unlikely source: K-pop fans and especially the BTS fan group, ARMY (see Y. Kim 2019; Sprinkel 2019).

How can South Korean popular music and its fans have anything to do with US politics? To answer this question, it is crucial that we do not, as K-pop fans are wont to say, "columbus": that is, to think that we have discovered something that has been there (and discovered by others much, much earlier). For interested but novice readers, however, I discuss the sheer presence and force of K-pop fandom and the nature and contours of K-pop (see also Lie 2015; Choi 2017; S. Kim 2018). After treading the ground familiar to K-pop fans, I stress the centrality of K-pop fandom in the constitution of the musical genre called K-pop. In so doing, I touch on the issue of individuality and authenticity before discussing idolatry and iconoclasm. Idolatry is a core phenomenon of K-pop, but it has its dark double in iconoclasm: forces that destroy idols, most spectacularly via suicide. The dialectic of idolatry and iconoclasm provides a window onto the lightness and the darkness that enshroud the passionate world of K-pop fandom. Although US politics is a mere sideshow for the majority of K-pop fans, it is but one sector that experiences their largely unintended consequences from their loyalty and commitment, passion and devotion.

As a social media phenomenon par excellence, to research K-pop and its fandom perforce requires a deep dive into YouTube, Twitter, Instagram, and related sites, as well as fan (and some anti-fan) interactions on the internet. It is not that there aren't written and published materials, but the world of analog information and communication remains an afterthought. A partial exception is attendance at K-pop concerts and events, where I talked with K-pop fans (and some detractors). One critical caveat is that English seems like the lingua franca of K-pop, but in fact national fan groups rely disproportionately on their native tongues and the monolingual approach obfuscates national and cultural differences (for example, the relative political quiescence of BTS's Japanese fans). Needless to say, the vast majority of K-pop performers (and almost all K-pop producers and managers) are South Koreans who by and large only speak Korean. Nevertheless, the locus of the politically active segment of ARMY is the United States and thereby the US fans' site attracts more politically minded fans than their counterparts in South Korea or Japan. Therefore, this essay tilts toward the goings-on in the United States and therefore is US-centric.

The Unlikely Ascent and Impact of K-Pop

A prescient observer in the 1980s—the dark decade of authoritarian rule in South Korea but also a period of rapid industrialization (Lie 1998)—may have been able to foresee the global success of Hyundai automobiles or Samsung smartphones in the twenty-first century, but no one, as far as I know, predicted the global dissemination of South Korean popular culture in general and popular music in particular. What South Koreans listened to back then was, needless to say, differentiated across demographic and taste groups and ranged from classical Western music to national folk music, but the most popular genre was what then was called *kayo* and what has retrospectively become categorized as *trot*: a congeries of pop music genres that stitched Western, Japanese, and domestic threads into slow, often mournful, ballads. Their descendants remain popular in 2020, especially among older South Koreans, but it would be fair to say that they have extremely few followers outside the country. At least according to younger, urban listeners, it is a genre that was already behind the times in the 1980s, and something that would have been about as palatable to Japanese or North American ears as the South Korean breakfast staple of the time, the pungent miso soup with rice and kimchi, would have been in their mouths.

Since its inchoate beginnings in the late 1990s, K-pop emerged as export-oriented popular music that combined the latest trends in Black American-inspired popular music and dance, the explicit reliance on the internet and social media to disseminate songs and videos, and the active cultivation of participatory fandom (Lie 2015). Initially making inroads into neighboring China and Japan in the late 1990s, it had become a global sensation by the late 2010s. It is part and parcel of South Korea's export-oriented cultural industry, ranging from television dramas to popular music, which is collectively known as *Hallyu* or the Korean Wave (Hong 2014).

To gauge the popularity of K-pop, consider the group BTS, K-pop's most spectacular manifestation. Already by 2018, the BBC had called the group "the Beatles for the 21st Century" (Jackson and Browne 2018). As of the writing of this chapter, BTS has been number one for over 180 straight weeks on the popular music trade journal *Billboard*'s Social 50 that ranks the most active musicians on the leading social media. BTS fans—called ARMY (Adorable Representative M.C. for Youth)—claim 48 million unique accounts (active fans number in the hundreds of thousands). From their preferred perch on Twitter—one thing they shared with President Trump—they have meandered across the digital landscape and made their presence known on Instagram, Facebook, TikTok, and other popular digital hangouts. They are not mere truants, however. They not only engage in involuted discussions of all matters BTS and K-pop but they have also sought to spread the word. At over six billion tweets in 2019, K-pop was the most tweeted popular music topic, and BTS was the most tweeted popular music act. Social media, as any self-respecting marketer knows by now, is not just cat videos and idle gossip but big business. To get a sense of BTS's commercial impact, it was involved in ten out of "101 times brands went viral" in 2019. For the hardheaded materialists, consider that when Big Hit Entertainment, the agency that represents BTS, went public in September 2020, its valuation topped $8 billion (Song 2020). To gauge the scale of this achievement, consider that the total global music revenues in 2019 amounted to $20 billion (IFPI 2020).

How does K-pop fandom go from cultivating cult-like devotion with commercial implications to becoming a political player? We shouldn't look to K-pop producers or artists. They are no Taylor Swifts enjoining their followers to vote Democratic. They tend to be resolutely non-political; they are out to please fans and make money, not to change the world. However, like Dr. Frankenstein's Monster, K-pop fans are not passive automatons. Intense online exchanges are not just about recherché debates on who has the most adorable hair style but also to disperse K-pop knowledge: most importantly their favorite group in particular and K-pop in general. In so doing, some of them are acutely aware of outsiders' criticisms—such as that K-pop has illegitimately appropriated Black music—and ongoing social, cultural, and political topics seep into their chats and tweets. Furthermore, it's not just about words but also deeds. Gifts to charity and non-profit organizations with good causes have been ongoing for years.

The shocking video of George Floyd's painful death sprung some ARMY and other K-pop fans into action. They spammed #WhiteLivesMatter and the online birthday card for President Trump (with K-pop videos no less). BTS ARMY raised $1 million for Black Lives Matter groups. Many fans who responded to the call are not white, to be sure, but one consequence of a generation's worth of multicultural education is Generation Z's widespread, almost reflexive anti-racist sentiments. Some K-pop fans, in addition, are sensitive to the debt that K-pop owes to Black music in particular and the general ethos of woke culture in general: a generational consensus on the evils of racism, sexism, and homophobia. It is far from the case that the majority of BTS or K-pop fans are political activists, but given the large fan base even a small minority can make a huge impact. And one thing K-pop fans—most of them digital natives—know how to do is to elevate their favorite groups' likes and followers and to generate upward trends and things going viral. They have also made meaningful gestures on behalf of good causes, as noted. Their repeated successes have empowered them. For most fans, it's not much of an effort to click and push a few times and to enjoy the reward of recognition both for K-pop and K-pop fandom for a good cause.

Almost exactly a year before the Tulsa rally, President Trump visited South Korea, and President Moon Jae-in duly welcomed him and his entourage by bringing a popular K-pop boy group Exo in tow. The choice expresses the outsized role that K-pop plays in South Korean life. We don't know what Trump thought of Exo, but we know what Exo fans thought of Trump: somewhere between indifference and hostility. Their negative reactions should have alerted him to the potential peril of K-pop fandom for his re-election campaign.

The Making of K-Pop

After Theodor W. Adorno (and Max Horkheimer), who wrote a pioneering analysis of the intersection of capitalism and popular culture, it is difficult to talk about popular music without invoking the concept of the culture industry (see Horkheimer and Adorno 2002). Technologically reproducible music, now widely heard through smartphones and associated ear buds, cannot be discussed apart from the institution of industrial capitalism. In this regard, K-pop is no different, if not just more so.

Precisely because the first two decades of K-pop were dominated by three major entertainment agencies—SM Entertainment, JYP Entertainment, and YG Entertainment, all founded in the mid-1990s—their family resemblances writ large become characteristics of K-pop. Rather than relying on the bottom-up emergence of musical talent—the proverbial garage band that does gigs, gets airtime, cuts a promo tape, and signs a contract—K-pop has pursued a top-down approach. All three agencies recruit very young performers—usually via auditions—and train them for five to ten, sometimes more, years before releasing them as professional, potential K-pop stars. Relying on an extensive division of labor, K-pop performers almost never make artistic decisions or engage in musical composition or choreography. Instead, they are trained to be K-pop stars: not just the expected singing and dancing, but also language training and fan interaction. They are shaped physically, too, as evinced by rigorous training regimes and the widespread use of plastic surgery. K-pop stars are thus manufactured idols.

Almost polar opposite to the idealized image of an American rock star, K-pop stars are redolent of produced goods that are conceived and executed by K-pop agencies. As fine-tuned and fine-brushed as they are, they find it difficult to escape the charge of being automatons, or at least of enacting inauthenticity. Well-crafted and well-executed as their songs and dance routines may be, K-pop seems the ne plus ultra of manufactured idols, following the footsteps of past sensations, such as the New Kids on the Block or the Spice Girls.

Beyond exemplifying and extending the culture industry, there are three innovations that K-pop has advanced, and the innovations in turn have contributed to their global expansion. First, K-pop is an export-oriented product. In the history of popular music, there are numerous acts and songs that have transcended national borders. US popular music is heard around the world, for instance. Yet popular music remains a robust national phenomenon; most pop stars are *national* sensations. How many people outside of China and the Chinese diaspora can name a single Chinese singer? Or French or Argentinian, for that matter? Even American acts do not set out to become global superstars, but rather as a star born, reared, and celebrated in the United States first and foremost; their transnational stardom is almost always an afterthought, an unintended consequence of their American success.

K-pop is different. It was intended from the outset to be a transnational product. At first focusing on the neighboring countries of Japan and China,

K-pop agencies sought to craft their talent to fit foreign markets. This is especially striking at the very start of K-pop. SM Entertainment Agency shaped BOA and Dongbang Singi (the latter also known as TVQX among other names) initially to be *Japanese* stars, passing as any other Japanese acts including attaining native fluency in Japanese. When H.O.T. became an unexpected sensation in the late 1990s in littoral Chinese cities, K-pop agencies duly sought to advance to that large, but piracy-ridden, market. American and global expansion, in turn, has been K-pop agencies' vaunting ambition in the twenty-first century. K-pop's export orientation is embedded in the larger and deeper South Korean business and government penchant for export and expresses a widespread consensus that the domestic market is small and unprofitable. K-pop compresses the half-century of South Korea's export-oriented industrialization, however unlikely popular music was a candidate for global consumption.

Second, K-pop surfed the tidal wave of the digital revolution. The received business model of popular music has been to get gigs at ever larger venues and to peddle records and CDs or their digital manifestations as downloads or part of a subscription package, such as Spotify. K-pop has embraced the post-thing economy from the beginning. Rather than seeking to sell physical products or focusing on digital downloads, all the major K-pop agencies have made songs and videos available for free on the internet and social media. Money is to be made from selling concert tickets, advertising revenues, fan-related events, and other means not directly related to the sale of physical products and digital downloads. To be sure, it is the case that in Japan, the largest export market in the first two decades of K-pop, the sale of physical products, such as CDs and DVDs, are critical and provided major revenue streams for the K-pop industry. Furthermore, K-pop agencies are increasingly focusing on generating revenues from social media and subscription venues. Nevertheless, K-pop is enmeshed in the digital revolution and its global expansion followed the transnational spread of social media platforms ranging from Facebook to YouTube, Twitter, and TikTok.

Finally, dictated in part by its innovative business strategy, K-pop agencies have relied heavily on fan clubs and fandom to execute business functions normally undertaken by talent agencies and record companies (G. Kim 2019; Lee 2019). Needless to say, fans are critical to any popular music; without fandom, no popular music. Fans have also been crucial in disseminating the crucial information about record releases and concert dates. From fanzines to groupies, the history and sociology of popular music cannot be told apart from fandom. Nevertheless, K-pop fandom is in another league, or inhabits an altogether distinct dimension. Rather than paying heavily for advertisement in traditional or social media, K-pop agencies have worked with fan clubs to spread the news and information about K-pop acts and their activities. It is not an accident that K-pop songs and videos accumulate millions and millions of hits and downloads on the day of their release; fan clubs are apprised of the date and ready themselves to click away and distribute the information to the wider social media public. As noted above, BTS's ARMY is ready to reward companies that employ BTS to promote their products. Fandom plays the role of traditional marketing and advertising departments. Put simply, K-pop fandom is a critical and essential component of K-pop's business strategy.

In summary, K-pop as a culture industry has several extra-musical innovations: its insistent export orientation, its embrace of the digital revolution, and its reliance on fandom. The extra-musical dimension of K-pop is revolutionary in the world of the popular music industry.

Individuality and Authenticity

K-pop may do pop well, so goes a strong strand of opinion, but has serious shortcomings. The most oft-repeated criticism is that K-pop is manufactured and K-pop stars are performing automatons. In other words, K-pop is perceived as an inauthentic, market-oriented, and mass-produced product. It is particularly this question of authenticity that rankles defenders and critics alike. As Jeff Todd Titon writes in his introduction to this section of the volume, there are at least two ways in which authenticity is invoked. On both counts, K-pop is found guilty: On one hand, it is not original, but emulation (and, worse, an illegitimate appropriation of Black American popular music). On the other hand, it is fake, artistically and emotionally.

Why all the fuss about authenticity? Pop songs are often experienced as embodying and expressing meaning in and of themselves, relating to individual listeners—however connected they may be to other fans—directly. Although scholars such as Martin Stokes (2010) have shown how pop songs can serve to animate feelings of connection among imagined communities (cf. Anderson 1983; Herzfeld 2016), any collective signification they produce is accumulated through the way they resonate with individual listeners. To be sure, all manners of group identification are sensitized and mobilized from time to time, from generational to national. However, the place of individuality and authenticity becomes all the more important in works of the culture industry (Benjamin 1977). Without authenticity, pop songs become indistinguishable from advertising jingles; no one has shed a tear upon listening to ditties that promote an industrial product, but many have their favorite pop tunes etched, indelibly it seems, in the very fiber of their being. That is, the performer is singing to you the listener; direct and unmediated, not for money or fame but to communicate from one heart to another. No one can quite expunge the cash nexus that lies at the heart of the culture industry, but there is a necessary misrecognition that popular songs relate musicians and listeners, soul to soul, and therefore the urgency of authenticity remains rife in and crucial to popular music.

As criticisms of inauthenticity mounted, K-pop agencies have sought to counter and supersede them. They have imbued individuality and quirkiness in their top acts, but the greatest breakthrough in K-pop emerged in the form of the aforementioned BTS. It is symptomatic that the group was not represented by the three major agencies but was the first and still the only blockbuster group from a nascent entertainment agency, Big Hit Entertainment. BTS marked a major advance from earlier K-pop groups not so much in superseding their perfectionism, whether in appearance, singing, or dancing, but rather in expressing individuality and authenticity. Unlike their K-pop counterparts, they participate in artistic decisions and at times air their opinions publicly, sometime to the detriment of their popularity. They therefore can be seen as authentic in both senses of the word; original and real. Their ideology of "love yourself" is a kinder and gentler version of Lady Gaga's "born this way," and an appeal to and an affirmation of individuality and authenticity not only of BTS but of their fans as well. Whatever the intentions of BTS members or the judgments of ARMY acolytes, there is no question that the package sells, and individuality and authenticity remain an indisputable element of not just BTS and K-pop but of contemporary popular music.

To be sure, fans of other K-pop groups would balk at the charge that their idols lack individuality or authenticity. After all, there are no objective guidelines of individuality or authenticity. An idol may merely be performing authenticity, acting or speaking in such ways to resonate with what the audience wants or expects, which is surely the case for some recent K-pop acts (Blackpink, for instance, retains the form of received K-pop but infuses its performance and identity with claims of individuality and authenticity). In contrast, folk musicians who celebrate their counter-cultural credibility and thereby their individuality and authenticity from the conformist majority may merely constitute a *herd* of like-minded and like-looking independent musicians. Alternatively, individuality and authenticity may be in the eyes of the beholder. Like Emperor Qin Shi Huang's terracotta warriors in Xi'an, some viewers initially see them as homogenous and homologous. Upon closer inspection, the same viewers may note the warriors' distinct, individual characteristics. Upon yet more extended observation, however, they may see the same few patterns recur. In the case of K-pop, one ardent and longtime fan of Super Junior told me that she knows all their back stories, has seen them grow and mature, and feels that she knows them better than her own siblings. For her, individual members of Super Junior are irreducibly and irreplaceably individuals, replete with unique characteristics and authentic selves: as unique and unforgettable as friends and family members she grew up with. There is an epistemic principle at work that familiarity and intimacy generate recognition of individuality and authenticity. Who can believe that her lover, however ostensibly boring and a type to boot, is not without individuality and authenticity?

Be that as it may, BTS's claim to authenticity rests on the broad backdrop of K-pop groups that have been enjoined to avoid controversial statements and personal revelations and exist as performers without artistic inputs. It may be that BTS's initial controversies had more to do with a lack of managerial professionalism (and therefore the agency having less firm a grip over the group than with other K-pop idol groups), but its blunders and scandals merely accentuated a sense of BTS's individuality, authenticity, and expressiveness. The young men were said to be original and real, autonomous and creative. We should also not forget that BTS began as a hip-hop group but softened its edges to garner popularity as a pop music group with strong hip-hop elements. Again, there are no indelible aesthetic or epistemic chasms that separate BTS from the rest of K-pop, but there is also no doubt that BTS stands out for its stress on individuality and authenticity.

We are now ready to explore the world of idols and iconoclasts that animates the universe of K-pop.

Idols and Icons

Idolizing charismatic characters must be something close to a cultural universal in complex societies. Important religious figures, for example, are crystallized as icons, to be gazed at, admired, and worshipped. Although there are proscriptions on idolatry, or excess adulation of mortal, and therefore ephemeral, idols, certain individuals become objects of visual production and reproduction that are in turn sanctified. Idols, moreover, resist outside interpretation, which perforce violates the integrity and the sanctity of idols and icons (cf. Panofsky 1939). They are, in other words, sui generis entities that repose in the fundamental embrace of followers or fans. In contemporary societies, religious idols are in decline—part and parcel of the process that we call secularization, though we should not underestimate the salience of cults and other charismatic movements—and tend to be associated with less developed societies, and have been superseded by popular culture stars, ranging from the world of sports to that of music. Enter any teenager's room in the United States or South Korea, and one is likely to encounter a veritable shrine to one or another popular culture icon.

The existence of pop music idols and icons is uncontroversial; few escape teenage years without succumbing to the temptation to festoon their personal space with posters or photos (even if now on their smartphones). Popular music stars—the stock figure of the rock star, for instance—have occupied an outsized role in the secular constellation of stars and idols: from at least the time of Elvis and Sinatra to the Beatles and the Doors. Whose grave is garlanded more with bouquets and offerings than Jim Morrison's in the fabled Père Lachaise cemetery in Paris? Put simply, popular music and the phenomenon of idols and icons have been inextricably intertwined. These intuitions are axiomatic.

K-pop idols are therefore only the latest development of pop music idols and of idol music. Idol music is a genre geared consciously to target a younger, usually teenaged, audience by combining accessible, upbeat music with attractive visuals. K-pop entertainment agencies took inspiration from the US idol groups, such as the New Kids on the Block, and Japanese variants, such as Shōnentai, in the 1980s. To be sure, the contemporary fanbase of BTS, for instance, spans a wide age range, but the fundamental rudiments of idol music apply to BTS in particular and K-pop in general.

Like their foreign counterparts, idols elicit adulation and desire, albeit in a highly circumscribed fashion. Fans subscribe to the prevailing norm of idol worship. They cannot, for example, possess their object of desire symbolically or physically. Indeed, K-pop stars, in spite of their physical attractiveness and sexual desirability, maintain a veneer of public virginity; they expunge private passions and physical relations and publicly express and exercise their fealty to fandom. Not surprisingly, there are no married K-pop stars (as of 2020). Desire and its denial are constitutive of both religious and pop music idols, who in principle refrain from close entanglements with their followers. Needless to say, rock stars notoriously have their groupies and charismatic cult leaders have been known to engage in sexual dalliances with their followers. It is also certainly not the case that the temptation is never breached, but the basic condition of the possibility of idol pop music is the regulated distance between idols and fans, and the denial of desire unbound on the part of both stars and fans. Just as Jesus and Mohammad, for instance, are not clouded by rumors of sexual adventures—the mere murmur will raise the ire of the faithful—K-pop stars studiously avoid taints of sexual advances and forays.

The denial of desire makes possible the seemingly unstable state of one or a few stars who enjoy the adulation of many fans. Idols exist for all the fans, and the fans, in turn, live without the fantasy of monopolizing their idols.

The idol-fan relationship, as well as the dialectic of desire and its denial, are generic, though the particulars retain their historical and cultural variability. Although rock stars in the West may marry and even revel in rumors of sexual debauchery, the same cannot be said of pop star idols. Some religious idols marry, after all, but the fundamental dynamics of the idol-follower relationship, including a systematic curb on desire, remain robust generalizations. But what makes K-pop distinct is the intensification and expansion of idolization and iconization.

Intensification stems from the primacy of fandom in K-pop's constitution. As noted, it is not that earlier idol groups or pop music stars in general didn't engage in interactions with fans, from signing records to affairs with fans. But K-pop stars' lives are enmeshed with those of their devotees. Constant meetings not only generate revenues but also entrench fans' commitment and loyalty. For example, there are events in which K-pop fans can exchange high fives with their favorite stars and groups. A flash of physical intimacy becomes for some fans an indelible experience. As one fan told me: "I couldn't wash my right hand for two days. I felt that [my idol's] imprint remained in the fading reddish tone of the palm of my right hand." A shorter, less intense version of stigmata enjoined her and her friend to redouble their devotion to the group as they purchased posters and towels as physical tokens of their ephemeral but memorable encounter.

Expansion is a consequence of the digital revolution. The internet and social media colonize many people's waking moments from dawn to dusk and into the small hours. Tweets, chats, breaking news: all these and more are readily accessible from a smartphone or a laptop and with an internet connection provide steady sources of information about their favorite icons. It is possible to devote hours, for example, to the nature and significance of a particular K-pop star's favorite color or preferred dish. There is constant jockeying for knowledge and information: access to the trivia and the secrets of their idols. As a self-identified recovering fanatic recalls: "I couldn't get my mind off [my idol]. A free moment allowed me to delve into fan-club chats or to check on the latest news about other aspects of the world of K-pop. I breathed K-pop day and night." In the past, thinking about idols was precisely a matter of recall and reflection; in the post-digital world, virtual interaction expands to fill any vacuum, to fill one with idol matters and idle chatters.

The intensification and expansion of fan interaction provide a distinct character to K-pop fandom: true to its etymological roots, a whiff of fanaticism. Intense, obsessed, and crazed are some of the adjectives bandied about by K-pop fans themselves. K-pop occupies a preeminent place in fans' cognitive space. They are devoted not merely to K-pop stars but to preserving and disseminating their iconic presence. Hence, there are constant efforts to spread the word, and to brighten and burnish the image of their idols (and to a lesser extent that of K-pop in toto). Missionaries for their idols, they seek to enhance their idols' image and reputation. Devotion manifests itself, for instance, in the sort of activities that ARMY engages in, whether to promote the products that BTS endorses or to donate money to causes that resonate with BTS's value commitments, such as the Black Lives Matter movement. As some Christians seek to do God's work in this fallen world, some BTS fans take their interpretation of BTS's message and enact it in the unjust world. Most Christians are nominal believers and may even miss weekly services; similarly, most BTS fans are fair-weather fans and will go for weeks without visiting ARMY sites. But both groups have their core devotees, and ARMY has its avant-garde born of the intensification and expansion of fan interaction and fanaticism who spread what they take to be BTS's message in words and deeds.

Fanaticism evokes negative traits associated, for example, with terrorism, but K-pop fandom's fanaticism tends to work within the realm of reason. When asked to account for their devotion, K-pop fans routinely and predictably discuss their idols' beauty and talent, among other manifest and obvious attributes. In addition, non–South Korean fans talk about how involvement in K-pop has expanded their cultural horizon, whether in gaining introductory knowledge of Korean language and culture or other, wider cultural and political matters. "K-pop opened a new world for me. I discovered Korean dramas and movies well before they became mainstream. I learned about Korean food and culture. I feel I have gotten to know a fascinating part of the world," recalled a US fan in her thirties. For some, it is learning about the minutiae of music or searching for cultural allusions to K-pop lyrics; for others, it is emulating the dance moves and riffing on the choreography or belting out their favorite tunes in a local karaoke joint. Cognitive or physical enhancement may be a post hoc rationalization, but K-pop fans are surely sincere in their appreciation of their expanded cultural horizon because of their participation in K-pop fandom.

Another striking dimension of idol worship is that a fan not only becomes knowledgeable or skilled but also that the experience of fandom is itself empowering. This is manifestly the case for followers of religious idols. Icons provide comfort and relief, and proffer hope and salvation. K-pop offers the same range of emotional support and courage. A Palestinian woman in her early twenties, who looked very much the conservative, religious woman, gushed: "Girls' Generation [a popular K-pop group] are just like me: good on the outside but a little bit naughty inside." Baffled by the scantily clad Girls' Generation being like the almost fully covered woman, she explained: "It's not what's on the surface; that doesn't matter. What matters is that I feel free when I listen and follow their songs and dance routines" (cf. Otmazgin and Lyan 2013). Empowerment is a constant theme in K-pop fandom, especially for ARMY with its mantra of "love yourself."

An oft-remarked sociological aspect of K-pop fandom outside of eastern Asia is the genre's appeal to members of ethnic and other minority groups. The existence of a non-normative pop star—neither white nor Black—may have an understandable appeal to co-ethnic or co-racial individuals, but their attraction spreads wider. In appealing to those who have felt marginalized or excluded, K-pop is in part a salve, not unlike some religious groups that spread the gospel of inclusion and equality. Idolization in this sense is less blind worship and more reasoned, however enthusiastic, embrace. To be sure, ARMY is inclined to underscore BTS's universal appeal. Does Jesus have ethnicity? Sure, but his appeal is universal. The same train of logic accounts in part for BTS's global attraction.

In short, K-pop has intensified and expanded the nature of idols and icons in the realm of popular music. Whether in gaining knowledge or in feeling empowered, K-pop fandom functions not unlike religious idols and icons for their followers.

Heretics and Iconoclasts

Nothing commands universal adulation; no pop music idols are without their nay-sayers. The rise of K-pop has generated a steady supply of K-pop bashers and critics, for reasons ranging from being fake and inauthentic to lack of originality and creativity. But it is less the existence or the content of criticisms that are of interest—for they exist for anyone beyond middling fame—but rather how those criticisms work as counterpoints to being idols and icons. There are at least two sources worth considering.

There are people who are not fond of K-pop in general or a particular K-pop act. External critics are easy to dismiss because it remains neither here nor there that there are those who are indifferent to or dislike K-pop. It is not as if K-pop detractors are physically obstructing chat groups or the downloading of songs. The closest that detractors come is to create a climate in which open admission of being a K-pop fan is difficult, as is the case from time to time in Japan where anti-Korean bloggers and populists spew hateful messages and occasionally demonstrate their sentiments (for example, by complaining about the airing of a K-pop tune at a café). K-pop has enemies, but they are not quite heretics and heathens who endanger the world of K-pop fandom. There are no crusades nor fatwas against K-pop.

Nevertheless, a tempest in a teacup spills over from time to time and creates a climate of, if not anti-idolatry and iconoclasm, surveillance and shakedown. If BTS is authentic precisely because its members speak out on their own—in contradistinction to their tighter-lipped and better disciplined K-pop counterparts—then it is also liable to a public uproar and even censure from time to time. In 2018, BTS members wore an "atomic bomb shirt" that appeared to celebrate the bombings of Hiroshima and Nagasaki, presumably because they contributed to Japan's defeat and Korea's liberation from Japanese colonial rule. The ensuing brouhaha led to a much-publicized cancellation of BTS's appearance on a Japanese TV program and even led the venerable *Bulletin of the Atomic Scientists* to issue a notice (Nguyen 2018). Something as seemingly innocuous as Blackpink stars stroking a panda bear became a global news as some took offense that the K-pop sensations had put a panda cub at risk (Zhuang 2020). Trivial in nature and significance as each scandal may be, taken together they constitute an omnipresent dark cloud ready to rain on K-pop's parade.

Much more significant, paradoxically, is K-pop fandom. Precisely because of the expansion and intensification of star-fan interactions in K-pop, K-pop idols are subject to constant surveillance and discipline. It is as if they inhabit a panopticon that has been turbocharged and upgraded: It is not quite the world of *The Truman Show*, in which the life of a protagonist is a constantly streamed reality TV show, but hundreds and thousands of fans view and discuss almost every aspect of K-pop stars' lives—what they eat, how they dress, and so on. When I was in Jerusalem, some Israeli and Palestinian fans were chasing a K-pop star strolling in the Old City with a young woman (the star was visibly surprised and shaken that he would be recognized halfway around the world). The fiercest critics are almost always the most ardent fans who find the tension, or the contradiction, between their idealized imagery and the inevitably imperfect reality unbearable.

The inevitable chasm between the idealized figure of the idol and the inevitably imperfect reality of the star generates constant pressure on K-pop stars. They are shorn of privacy, and the demand of exposure makes the desire for it difficult, if not impossible. The meaning and sense of privacy surely vary across time and space, but K-pop stars have been reared in affluent, Westernizing South Korea that valorizes personal space and time (if not to the same extent as their North American counterparts). Idols and icons, in other words, live in constant fear of being exposed as frauds and iconoclasts who undermine the fiction that they have sought to create and sustain. Some inevitably crack under the pressure: auto-iconoclasm (Choe and Lee 2019). Most commonly, they erupt as one or another scandal, such as some K-pop stars' sexual forays and misadventures. Far from hewing to the standards of public virginity, their private debauchery threatens to undermine the fiction and the misrecognition that K-pop survives and thrives upon. The recent spate of suicides, along with scandals, is an unfortunate yet unavoidable byproduct of K-pop stars' sanctified existence. The revenge of the repressed is a constant undercurrent in the world of K-pop fandom.

Conclusion

K-pop is far from exhausted as a genre and its global expansion continues apace. Facing predictions of their imminent demise from the outset, we would be remiss to underestimate its capacity to persist and transform. As South Korea's leading export and representative product, K-pop is as good a barometer as any for understanding the country, but it can also tell us a great deal about the culture industry in general or the nature of fandom and the logics of authenticity and of idol worship.

K-pop's constitutive reliance on fandom—and the attendant dialectic of idolatry and iconoclasm—remains an immanent source of its instability and possible decline. Iconoclasm within and without remains an ever-present threat to the glitter of K-pop and the unstable tension between desire and its denial. Along with the debate over authenticity, K-pop is also good to think with if one wishes to make sense of the culture industry and fandom in the twenty-first century.

References

Anderson, Benedict. 1983. *Imagined Communities: Reflections on the Origin and Spread of Nationalism*. London: Verso.

Benjamin, Walter. 1977 [1936]. "Der Erzähler." In *Gesammelte Schriften*, vol. 2, 438–64. Frankfurt am Main: Suhrkamp.

Choe Sang-Hun and Su-hyun Lee. 2019. "Suicides by K-Pop Stars Prompt Soul-Searching in South Korea." *New York Times*, November 25.

Choi, JungBon. 2017. *K-Pop*. Abingdon, UK: Routledge.

Herzfeld, Michael. 2016. *Cultural Intimacy: Social Poetics and the Real Life of States, Societies, and Institutions*. London: Routledge.

Hong, Euny. 2014. *The Birth of Korean Cool*. London: Picador.

Horkheimer, Max, and Theodor W. Adorno. 2002. "The Culture Industry: Enlightenment as Mass Deception." In *Dialectic of Enlightenment: Philosophical Fragments*, ed. Gunzelin Schmid Noerr, trans. Edmund Jephcott, 94–136. Stanford, CA: Stanford University Press.

IFPI. 2020. "Global Music Report 2020—The Industry in 2019." https://www.ifpi.org/wp-content/uploads/2020/07/Global_Music_Report-the_Industry_in_2019-en.pdf.

Jackson, Marie, and Kesewaa Browne. 2018. "BTS and K-Pop: How to Be the Perfect Fan." BBC News, October 9. https://www.bbc.com/news/uk-45800924.

Kim, Gooyong. 2019. *From Factory Girls to K-Pop Idol Girls*. Lanham, MD: Lexington Books.

Kim, Sul-Young. 2018. *K-Pop Live*. Stanford, CA: Stanford University Press.

Kim Yông-dae. 2019. *BTS*. Seoul: RH Korea.

Lee, Hark Joon. 2019. *K-Pop Idols*. Lanham, MD: Lexington Books.

Lie, John. 1998. *Han Unbound: The Political Economy of South Korea*. Stanford, CA: Stanford University Press.

———. 2015. *K-Pop: Popular Music, Cultural Amnesia, and Economic Innovation in South Korea*. Oakland: University of California Press.

Nguyen, Viet Phuong. 2018. "BTS, the 'Atomic Bomb Shirt,' and South Korean Attitudes Toward Nuclear Weapons." *Bulletin of the Atomic Scientists*, November 19.

Otmazgin, Nissim, and Irina Lyan. 2013. "Hallyu across the Desert: K-Pop Fandom in Israel and Palestine." *Cross-Currents: East Asian History and Culture Review* 9: 68–89.

Panofsky, Erwin. 1939. *Studies in Iconology*. New York: Oxford University Press.

Song Jung-a. 2020. "BTS Agency's Shares Soar Up to 160% on Market Debut." *Financial Times*, October 15.

Sprinkel, Katy. 2019. *The Big Book of BTS*. Chicago: Triumph Books.

Stokes, Martin. 2010. *The Republic of Love: Cultural Intimacy in Turkish Popular Music*. Chicago: University of Chicago Press.

Zhuang, Yan. 2020. "Blackpink Coddled a Baby Panda. Not Cute, the Chinese Internet Said." *New York Times*, November 12.

Multimedia Playlist

BLACKPINK, "As If It's Your Last," 2017
———, "Lovesick Girls," 2020
BTS, "I Need U," 2015
———, "Blood, Sweat, and Tears," 2016
———, "Spring Days," 2017
———, "Idol," 2018
———, "Love Myself," 2018
———, "Dynamite," 2020
GIRLS' GENERATION, "Mr. Taxi," 2009
SEO TAIJI AND BOYS, "I Know," 1992
SUPER JUNIOR, "Sorry Sorry," 2009

PART II

Race, Gender, Ethnicity, and Class

Introduction
Eric Lott

As I began to think and write about Black American culture and politics in the 1980s, I began too to wonder about the pre-history of white interest like mine in the aesthetic urgencies of Black Americans. Such cross-racial interest seemed to me then (and still does) to have crystallized if not begun in the blackface minstrel show of the 1830s, '40s, '50s, and beyond, which led to the publication of my first book, *Love and Theft: Blackface Minstrelsy and the American Working Class* (1993). I was interested there (and still am) in the way even grotesquely problematic forms of popular performance like blackface—white men singing and dancing in "black" makeup and costume making racist fun of Black Americans for sport and profit—raise to view public cultural concerns and organize audience constituencies in ways that bear importantly on the social and political life of their times.

Researching my book, I came across a brief but remarkable 1922 essay by famed poet T. S. Eliot on the British music hall singer Marie Lloyd. Elitist Anglophile Eliot nonetheless celebrated the massively popular Lloyd and her expression of working-class feelings and values in a fashion that resonates with this section's three essays and the five singers they discuss. Eliot refused to see Marie Lloyd's popularity as an achievement of mere commercial success. "It is [rather] evidence of the extent to which she represented and expressed that part of the English nation which has perhaps the greatest vitality and interest"

(659). Lamenting the "listless apathy" characteristic of middle and upper-class fans of other entertainments, Eliot—in curiously Whitmanesque tones—suggests that the "working man who went to the music-hall and saw Marie Lloyd and joined in the chorus was himself performing part of the work of acting," engaged as he was in "that collaboration of the audience with the artist which is necessary in all art" (662). Eliot's key assertion about Lloyd is that it was "her understanding of the people and sympathy with them, and the people's recognition of the fact that she embodied the virtues which they genuinely most respected in private life, that raised her to the position she occupied at her death" (662). These remarks could easily extend to Beyoncé Giselle Knowles-Carter (b. 1981), Graciela Pérez Grillo (1915–2010), Celia Cruz (1925–2003), Lupe Victoria Yolí (1936–1992), and Beverly Sills (1929–2007) as depicted in the following essays by Treva B. Lindsey, Christina D. Abreu, and Nancy Guy; these singers occupy similar relations with their respective audiences and express similar values alongside them, often against the grain of prevailing standards and cultural demands.

In each case study, these artists summon at once a subject position, a community commitment, and an aesthetic profile with which audiences passionately identify, and in so doing align themselves with a cultural-political worldview that brings singer and audience as a constituency into being. The Deep South/Global South Blackness affirmed by Beyoncé; the female-identified Afro-Cuban alliances variously brought forth by "queens" Graciela, Celia Cruz, and La Lupe; and the broad middling commitments of new opera lovers solicited by the pop-friendly Beverly Sills all have cultural impacts well beyond the particular performance contexts that launched them. All these singers push back against not only dominant artistic and political tendencies but also, very often, conventional understandings of these artists themselves. And they do it more often than not by mindfully working crossover changes on format, a category different in kind from genre, tradition, roots, and so forth (Weisbard 2014). It is no secret in these performers that soul, salsa, and soprano are variously the bottom line; what is at stake is the *way* those weapons are wielded.

Beyoncé's way, argues Treva B. Lindsey, has been to engage ever more deeply the "Blackness, womanhood, and southern-ness" of her persona that Lindsey importantly insists were there all along. A singer who Lindsey terms a "multi-talented glitch in a system primed for disposing of artists on a whim," Beyoncé exists both within and outside a tradition that affords superstardom. That outside is in part an insistence on her native Texas—a US South connection that Beyoncé has brought to everything she does, both with Destiny's Child and after, up to and including the music video *Formation* (2016) and expanded across diasporic scales on the visual albums *Lemonade* (2016) and *Black Is King* (2020). As Lindsey puts it, Beyoncé has always bet on Black sound, and however crossover her appeal, her iconicity depends on its particular southern resonances—an archive and vocal citational home so crucial as to be itself a featured character in her work (hot sauce, anyone?).

For their part, the Latin jazz and salsa royalty described by Christina D. Abreu emerged from the color and gender "double erasure" of male-led bands to cut diva-like figures of Afro-Cuban prominence. Abreu's canny account of these performers' intramural adjacencies and rivalries illuminates the industry predicaments in which they found themselves. Conventional strictures on female respectability were sometimes followed, sometimes flouted; flirting with those strictures was itself part of the act, whether in Cruz's straight-laced persona or La Lupe's performative intimations of occult mysticism and orgiastic excess. This was a struggle carried out in public and on behalf of the fans the singers represented, and Abreu's attention to audience responses (as in certain staged crownings of this or that "queen") shows how multiple, simultaneously available performance strategies cunningly resisted the challenges they faced.

Beverly Sills took her immense talents to the people, won their loyalty and what T. S. Eliot calls "collaboration," and in the process offended plenty in the opera world proper. Her lower-class and Brooklyn Jewish origins made her at once totem and target. As Nancy Guy shows, Sills graced not only stages but very soon television talk shows, game shows, and even phone book covers; like Marie Lloyd, she became a household name. Guy's crucial reliance on reviews, blog posts, fan statements, and other sources reveals the kind and intensity of Sills's broad-based audience embrace. In reaching beyond the opera house, she organized a self-conscious and discerning constituency of so-called "Beverly Sillsbillies" who relished their circumvention of elitist cultural sacralization. Fandom, multi-media affiliation, personality, and vocal intelligence, argues Guy, need not occupy discrete zones of cultural impact, and Sills conjoined them in a mode reminiscent of nineteenth-century opera popularity.

It is always the way with stars such as these: in cultivating terrestrial alliances, they don't stand still in the sky.

References

Eliot, T. S. 1922. "London Letter." *The Dial* 73(6): 659–63.
Kelly, Karen, and Evelyn McDonnell. 1999. *Stars Don't Stand Still in the Sky: Music and Myth*. New York: New York University Press.
Lott, Eric. 1993. *Love and Theft: Blackface Minstrelsy and the American Working Class*. New York: Oxford University Press. Second ed., 2013.
Weisbard, Eric. 2014. *Top 40 Democracy: The Rival Mainstreams of American Music*. Chicago: University of Chicago Press.

CHAPTER 4

All On They Mouth Like Liquor

TREVA B. LINDSEY

Beyoncé Giselle Knowles-Carter (b. 1981) is one of the most well-known popular artists of the late twentieth and early twenty-first centuries. A beholder of many monikers—Queen Bey, King Bey, Baddie Bey, Yoncé, and Mrs. Carter—she can drop an album with no notice and cause the entire pop music world to stop and listen. Her loyal fans and fiercest critics are passionate in their resolve around their respective love and disdain for this Black girl from Houston, Texas. Depending on who you ask, she is either the greatest living performer in popular music or a "terrorist" (hooks 2014). It often appears that it is difficult to simply like or dislike Beyoncé. Discussions about her artistry can be stifled by uncritical adoration or by unabashed contempt. Wherever you land on your read of her, however, doesn't deter the notoriously private artist from publicly relishing in her ubiquity. Quite frankly, that's perhaps why I continue to find her compelling, or better yet, why I remain intrigued by the reactions this Black girl from the deep US South inspires.

Beyoncé achieved international acclaim in a world in which anti-Black racism and misogyny converge to render Black women distinctly vulnerable to violence, poverty, premature death, food and housing insecurity, and criminalization (Lindsey 2022). So while anyone becoming a consistently charting and top-billed artist across multiple decades defies incredible odds, Black women achieving at the highest level in mainstream pop music bulldoze through additional barriers on their respective journeys. This chapter explores Beyoncé's career to grapple with how her Blackness, womanhood, and southern-ness show up in her body of work as well as the reception to it. Moving from her time as the lead singer of Destiny's Child to her 2019 musical film and visual album, *Black Is King*, I assess the cultural impact of her career and offer a Black feminist reading of the contours of her multi-sited trajectory as an artist. More specifically, I contend that to comprehensively understand Beyoncé's music, one must contend with the US South and, to a lesser extent, the Global South as a point of entry. "The Souths" provide a lens through which we can wrestle with her discography and its enduring popularity. Her emergence as one of the greatest living entertainers in pop music defied even the highest expectations of industry insiders when she burst onto the scene in the late 1990s as the lead singer of Destiny's Child (Sanneh 2003).

Beyoncé's star quality as a lead singer was palpable even as teenager, and yet her rise to iconicity was not inevitable. As a Black woman from Houston, Texas, introduced in a moment in which a growing lack of interest in Black female vocalists anchored in the rhythm and blues tradition began to decline, Beyoncé and the members of Destiny's Child found a way to achieve pop culture ubiquity (Leight 2017). She tapped into a tradition of Black women's popular music performance that as African American performance studies scholar Daphne Brooks asserts "made the modern world" (Brooks 2021, 2). Beyoncé, as both the lead singer of one of the bestselling female groups of all time and as a solo artist, crafted a distinct path upon which she became a twenty-first century global icon. Her iconicity, whether celebrated or abhorred, too often misreads the core elements of her sound. Although her legacy continues to unfold, her first three decades as a popular singer illuminate both the possibilities and the limitations of an industry still struggling with wholly valuing and generatively engaging the talent of Black women. Her exceptional success is by no means illustrative of popular music's handling of Black women and femmes as mainstream artists—rather she is a multi-talented glitch in a system primed for disposing of artists on a whim. As Brooks notes, more often than not Black women singers have been "overlooked or underappreciated, misread and sometimes lazily mythologized, underestimated and sometimes entirely disregarded" (ibid.). Beyoncé's omnipresence in the pop music landscape, however, doesn't fully eliminate misreads or mythologizing.

She exists both within and outside of a tradition in which Black women and femmes can and do achieve superstardom. Comparisons to legendary artists such as Tina Turner and Diana Ross pervade debates about Beyoncé's position within the elite echelons of popular music superstardom. With each televised performance and headlining tour, she re-inserts herself into conversations about top-tier entertainers in modern pop music history. Her performances of her wide-ranging catalog, in particular, prompt questions such as: Is she the greatest performer alive or is she the greatest performer ever? (Easter 2018). No matter how one responds to these questions of comparative greatness, her career warrants our critical consideration. Fans and critics alike grapple with what her still-forming legacy will be. And what role will The Souths play in how we assess and explicate her iconicity?

Contending with racism, sexism, regionalism, and misogynoir—a distinct form of racialized misogyny directed toward Black women, girls, and femmes—Black women face distinct barriers in becoming powerful forces in the mainstream music industry (Mahon 2020). Beyoncé's journey is at once unprecedented and reminiscent, while also providing a somewhat inimitable blueprint for newer artists striving for enduring popularity. People have strong opinions about this Black xennial from Houston (Chambers 2019). Her storied career has prompted countless articles, books, panels, conferences, symposia, and viral social media moments. So what more is there to say about the woman who "stays all on they mouth like liquor?" Furthermore, what is there to say about her as a musician after over twenty years in an industry where most artists become one-hit wonders? And last, what does it mean that a Black woman from the Deep South has achieved such a remarkable level of success in both a national and global sociopolitical context that systemically devalues and marginalizes Black women?

A Black Girl from Texas

When Saturday Night Live featured a segment in February 2016 titled, "The Day Beyoncé Turned Black," I remember laughing (Saturday Night Live 2016). The segment poked fun at white people's reactions to Beyoncé's latest song, "Formation," and her Black Power-themed Superbowl performance. The song lyrics, coupled with the vivid imagery in the music video, signaled a connection to and a longing and affinity for a Black southern heritage (Caramanica et al. 2016). Journalist Jenna Wortham called the swag of the song "the blackest of Black" (ibid.). "Formation" has numerous nods to what journalist Wesley Morris describes as "gloriously specific" markers of Blackness and southern-ness (ibid.). Arguably, there's a deliberate illegibility to non-Black audiences that Beyoncé and the creative team behind "Formation" sought.

My laughter at the SNL skit came from a place of pondering if her Blackness had become more knowable and legible to non-Black people in these specific cultural moments. Certainly, audiences read her as a Black woman (maybe from the South) prior to this point—but was this new song coupled with the Superbowl performance signaling something different to them, and maybe, for her? The SNL segment, although not explicitly, touched upon the inherent racism of a colorblind approach to popular culture consumption by laying bare the absurdity of people evacuating Beyoncé's Blackness to embrace their fandom (Kooijman 2019, 432). The premise of the segment: many white people didn't see her as Black or as embracing her Blackness prior to her proclaiming, "I got hot sauce in my bag." While hilariously executed and comedically exaggerated, I couldn't help but wonder if her more overt engagement with cultural markers of Blackness, southern-ness, and politicized topics such as police brutality would in fact affect her status as a global icon.

To assess the impact of this song, it's important to examine the roots and routes of Beyoncé's meteoric rise single-named phenom. As the lead singer of one of the most successful "girl groups" of all time, Beyoncé formally entered the pop music lexicon with soulful pop singles and albums (Lipshutz 2017). While initial singles such as "No, No, No" and "Bills, Bills, Bills" didn't push the envelope on the sonic possibilities of pop music, her singing style stood out because of her well-executed trills and staccato approach to many mid-tempo and upbeat songs (Critic of Music 2021). The staccato approach, although not unusual for artists trained within a soul tradition, also indicated an affinity for rap music. Her breath control, something she's maintained throughout her career, permits her to almost rap-sing while performing (Lindsey 2019, 187). Listening to Destiny's Child's first major hit, the remix of "No, No, No," listeners are introduced to a singing style that undeniably taps into a hip-hop-adjacent delivery. The song resonates as sonically Black with its percussive elements and lyrical execution, while supplying a catchy, pop vibe.

Destiny's Child struck their first hit in a pop culture moment in which youthful, pop music reigned the charts à la boy bands and solo pop princesses. Late 1990s and early 2000s pop, however, relied heavily upon Black sonic elements. At the turn of the twenty-first century, a form of contemporary R&B also emerged that included Black artists like D'Angelo, Erykah Badu, and Maxwell. Music industry entrepreneur Kedar Massenburg labeled this emergent form "neo-soul" (Okoth-Obbo 2017). The mainstream breakthrough of artists who resisted a more producer-driven approach to rhythm and blues signaled a revival of something that some felt had been lost in recent years in soul music. The "neo" indicated a turn toward exploring new facets of an enduring Black musical tradition. As Dimitri Ehrlich noted in an interview with Vibe magazine in 2002, neo-soul "breathed presence into time-tested formulas," and the result was commercially viable rhythm and blues (Ehrlich 2002).

Destiny's Child was by no means a group associated with neo-soul. Although the group's sound merged rhythm and blues and pop, the all-girl group existed as a contemporary of the Black artists whom cultural studies scholar Mark Anthony Neal identified as contributing to the redefinition of "the boundaries and contours of black pop" (Neal 2003, 117). Beyoncé's voice, in particular, however, had something distinct in it that went at least partially untapped as the lead singer of one of the bestselling women's groups of all time. It seemed inevitable that a solo project was on the horizon from this stand-out voice among the highly talented singers who populated the group throughout its tenure. Destiny's Child perfectly nailed "girl empowerment" anthems, but there was something perhaps more soulful and more conspicuously Black in the realm of possibility for where Beyoncé could grow and develop as a solo artist.

Leaning into Black sound, nevertheless, was risky. By the time Beyoncé went solo in 2003, so-called neo-soul and, more broadly, rhythm and blues music confronted dwindling commercial viability and attention from major labels. Beyoncé also had to contend with high expectations stemming from her belonging to such a successful group. Questions circulated as to whether she would largely maintain a sound and vibe similar to that of Destiny's Child or branch out in new directions. Would the talented singer attempt a more soulful project? Or would she dig deeper into the evolving depths of Black pop to anchor her solo sound?

Dangerously in Love (2003), her first solo album, brought together quite a few Black elements for a commercially successful and critically acclaimed debut project. Collaborations with rap artists such as Big Boi of Outkast, Missy Elliott, and her future husband, Jay-Z, showed Beyoncé's fuller embrace of hip-hop bravado and vocal aesthetics. She paired with Sean Paul for her hit "Baby Boy," which tapped into the heightened popularity of dancehall music in the United States in the early to mid-2000s (Platon 2017). Beyoncé paired with Black pop legend Luther Vandross for a remake of Donny Hathaway and Roberta Flack's "The Closer I Get to You." The album also featured samples from songs by artists such as Donna Summer, the Chi-Lites, Bootsy's Rubber Band, Whitney Houston, Shuggie Otis, and DeBarge. The range of samples and collaborations convey a deep affinity for a decidedly Black musical archive. There's funk, disco, Black pop, blues, jazz, rhythm and blues, hip-hop, and dancehall. Without question, *Dangerously in Love* unveiled an affinity for soul music in its multitude of genres. Attempts to divorce Beyoncé from a soul-singing tradition and locate her as just another pop starlet seemed misguided in the face of an album indebted to such a rich archive of Black sound.

The incorporation of various Black musical genres into her music alongside an anchoring in what Daphne Brooks identified as a "voice of black female discontent" have been key elements across the entirety of Beyoncé's solo discography (Brooks 2008, 184). Over a decade before SNL made light of white people "confronting" Beyoncé's Blackness, Beyoncé explicitly aligned herself with a tradition of Black women using their music to express their discontent, whether it be more sociopolitical in the vein of Nina Simone and Abbey Lincoln or romantic and intimate like Millie Jackson or Chaka Khan (ibid., 185). The overtly sociopolitical came later in Beyoncé's repertoire, but there's never been a point in her solo career in which she wasn't testifying about her desires, autonomy, and personal struggles as a Black woman.

She didn't need to outright say, "this is about my journey as a Black woman," for it to be legible to other Black women and girls listening to her. Her articulations of dissatisfaction and pleasure resonated with many Black late gen-xers and millennials who felt our pain and ecstasy in Beyoncé's songs. She's always been someone who as Brooks notes is "actively and consistently producing a public record of cultural expression that affirms the intersecting personal and political questions and concerns of women of color in the early twenty-first century" (Brooks 2008, 201). The fact that she did this on frequencies largely undetectable to some of her white fan base for as long as she did is quite astonishing. I can't imagine fully appreciating *Dangerously in Love* without knowledge of at least some of the soul references. In an attempt to distance herself from the more pop-oriented and highly successful girl and women's empowerment anthems offered by Destiny's Child, her debut solo album bet on Black sound—past and present. Distinguishing herself as a solo artist, and not only as a lead singer of a girl group, Beyoncé topped the charts and won numerous industry awards (Purvis 2004). She proved to be a force in the industry and did so with an album filled with an array of Black musical elements, many of which derived from the US Black South.

Beyoncé's career trajectory drew further comparisons to incredibly successful artists like Diana Ross. Assessing Beyoncé's performance style, people drew comparisons between her and Tina Turner. Unsurprisingly, comparisons to other Black female artists, whether as foremothers or contemporaries, followed Beyoncé throughout her career as well. A thread connecting these artists and how people compared them is the idea of transcending race and, more specifically, transcending Blackness to become "universally acclaimed." The "crossover," if you will, always points toward non-white artists garnering a substantial white fan base (Lindsey 2020, 29–30). Crossing-over also seemingly only occurs in one direction as people gesture toward "deracialized appeal" as the reason for the favorable reception of Black artists by non-Black audiences (ibid., 30).

When folks identify Black artists, particularly Black female artists, as "crossover," they tend to intimate that these artists left behind "musical categories connoted as Black such as soul and rhythm and blues" (Kooijman 2014, 305). In this figuration, the presumptive evacuation of traces of Blackness from their sound allegedly propels them to greater superstardom than if the artists took a more soulful route. The prevailing problems with this figuration, however, are its erasure of Black musicians who were primary architects in US pop music and its analytical whitewashing of the actual bodies of work produced by an artist such as Beyoncé Knowles-Carter who has more than a few pop hits in her discography—but what if we located those hits within a longer tradition of Black women's pop music? What do we miss in sweeping her into the category of mainstream pop in the twenty-first century?

We miss all of the moments prior to the more explicit ones of the *Lemonade*, *Homecoming Live*, and *Black Is King* chapters of Beyoncé's career if we listen for the possibility of transcendence versus the actualization of a form of soulful pop anchored in co-extant Blackness, southern-ness, and womanhood. These co-constitutive elements were there from *Dangerously in Love* through her 2013 self-titled, visual album, *Beyoncé*. These projects dropped prior to mainstream assessments of her music as becoming more resoundingly Black. "Formation" and the visual imagery from that music video exemplified elements already present in her body of work but overlooked by many. Without question, Beyoncé strove for mass appeal; nevertheless, she didn't veer too far from Black soundscapes to cultivate her sonic imprint on popular music at any point in her solo career.

Responses to Beyoncé's second solo album, *B'Day*, varied. With a lead-off single "Déjà Vu," she once again tapped into funk, 1970s soul, and more contemporary R&B. With primarily live instrumentation and an emphasis on the horns and bass guitar, Beyoncé commandingly sang about constantly being reminded of an ex-lover. The song met with mixed reviews, despite its charting in the Top Five on the Billboard Hot 100 (Cinquemani 2006). The album as a whole was more up-tempo and to some critics felt reminiscent of her time as the lead singer of Destiny's Child (ibid.). What's intriguing about that read of her sophomore project is that it implies a move away from the soulfulness of *Dangerously in Love* back to the more pop-friendly sound that music critics felt Destiny's Child offered their fans. There was little attention paid to a distinct brand of soulful pop enlivened through the voices, sound memories and archiving, and intergenerational exchanges of southern, Black women.

Few if any of Beyoncé's most memorable solo hits prior to "Lemonade" are devoid of soulfulness—although to varying extents. What has always been clear to me, as a Black woman listening, is her deep appreciation of soul music. The citational practices in her music don't just come from the production—it's the choices she makes as a singer. Breathy tracks like "Naughty Girl," "Dance for You," and "Speechless" channeled Donna Summer and sultry sounds of both 1970s disco and funk songstresses. On the album *I Am . . . Sasha Fierce*, Knowles-Carter brought together vulnerable pop ballads, hip-hop-influenced rhythm and blues, and a Black woman-centered bravado that echoes singers such as Chaka Khan and Patti LaBelle. Not quite as raw and sexual as a Millie Jackson just yet, Beyoncé began to flirt with a more libidinous approach to her music by her third album. Each album dove deeper into a robust Black blueswoman tradition of exploring sexual desires and fantasies (Davis 1999, 4). As Beyoncé solidified her status as a superstar, her explorations of love and sexuality in her music intensified.

It's in those explorations where we find that powerful combination of Blackness, southern-ness, and womanhood. The sounds of the Black South informed Beyoncé's evolution as an artist. The blues notes, the incorporation of zydeco, chopped and screwed (which originated in Texas), and eventually country music, as well as her affinity for deeply affective melisma, rendered, as Robin M. Boylorn asserts, "the South as a main character in her work" (Boylorn 2019, 195). Describing Beyoncé's Black southern sensibilities, Boylorn argues that,

> Beyoncé, like me, always stayed close to home, metaphorically if not literally. Conspicuous sonic signifiers of the south seeped out in the Southern drawl of her speaking voice, the Houstonian accent in her spoken words on tracks, her collaboration with down South hip hop heads like Andre 3000, Bun B, and Slim Thug . . . Shout-outs and subtle Southern innuendoes had always been present in her work. (Boylorn 2019, 194)

Boylorn's assessment of Beyoncé points to the absurdity of reads of her artistry that erase her southern-ness, her Black southern-ness. There's an insistence on including the US Gulf region that birthed her, blues women, and so many Black female artists for generations. Her "crossover appeal," even if undetected by a sizable portion of her adoring fans, encompassed Black/woman/southern sensibilities. It was with *Lemonade*, however, that Beyoncé let those sensibilities propel an entire album. It was also the project on which Beyoncé made more connections to the Global South in both her sonic and visual performances. With her three albums from the latter part of the 2010s, Beyoncé relinquished what L. H. Stallings calls a "dis-ease" with funkiness, deviance, explicitly sexual content, unabashed and raw emotion, and fiery interiority (Stallings 2020, 11). In succession, *Lemonade*, *Homecoming Live*, and *Black Is King* call upon Black Souths (Bradley 2021, 4–5).

They Don't Love You Like I Love You

While much of the discussion around Beyoncé's second visual album, *Lemonade*, pivoted around questions and commentary about the presumptive depiction of Beyoncé and rapper Jay-Z's storied marriage, less attention was paid to the sonic landscape of the audiovisual offering. Admittedly, a visual album lends itself to interrogations that largely overlook what the music and lyrics are saying and how they operate as texts. The core of the album is multi-sited and necessitates both an integrative and a textually specific exploration. Since the eponymously titled *Beyoncé* album, the songstress has released albums with a visual component for each track. These include two visual albums, a concert film and accompanying live album, and a musical film. Teasing out what the sonic and musical elements distinctively offer is perhaps more challenging in this era of her work.

With *Lemonade*, however, each track dives into the Black Souths for its sonic resonances. From brass band to rock to country to fuzz-tone guitar psychedelia to reggae, the album nimbly moves between and among genres, many which were cultivated in the Black Souths. Blending styles and genres, Beyoncé and the creative time behind *Lemonade* anchors in the US South as a distinct point of departure for storytelling and evocation. Even without the accompanying visuals, it becomes apparent from the first song through the last that the US South, and more specifically, the US Black South, is the point of origin for the soul of the album. The Global Black South, although not as pronounced on *Lemonade*, appears in the form of samples and cultural exchanges between the US, Latin America, and the United Kingdom. The album traverses the Black Atlantic culture through melodic memories and rhythmic routes. As conceptualized by historian Paul Gilroy, Black Atlantic culture absorbs and combines elements of US, African, British, Caribbean, and Latin American cultures (Gilroy 1993). *Lemonade* epitomizes Black Atlantic culture, while being particularly attuned to sonic traditions of the US South.

The Black South *Lemonade* lays claims to is one that identifies Black people as innovators of genres such as rock and roll, the blues, zydeco, and country. Whereas there's widespread acknowledgment of Black people creating hip-hop, which is featured in collaborations, samples, and production on the album, country and rock and roll are genres often marked as "white," despite their respective historical origins in Black musical communities (Hamilton 2016, 3; Hughes 2017, 1–7). *Lemonade* sonically reclaims these genres not only as Black at the root, but as a province in which Black women exist and have existed since the birth of these genres. This reclamation took Beyoncé to the 2016 Country Music Awards to perform her song "Daddy Lessons" with country music band The Chicks (then-named The Dixie Chicks). On country's "biggest night," Beyoncé performed her zydeco, bluesy, and country-inspired track with "bonafide" country artists. Despite some pushback, the performance was widely lauded and once again confirmed Beyoncé's status as a pop star with wide-ranging appeal.

The performance of "Daddy Lessons" at the Country Music Awards without equivocation was an act of firmly situating the song within a musical tradition not often associated with Black women singers. With references to guns, an opening shoutout to Texas, and a mention of The Bible, the song evokes place with a sense of familiarity and longing. Through the intimacy conveyed in the lyrics, coupled with a blending of musical genres popular in both Texas and Louisiana, Beyoncé reintroduces herself yet again as a daughter of the US Black South. This South isn't wholly separate from other racialized figurations of the region. Nevertheless, the album centers Blackness as both place and space.

The reclamation of rock and roll on the hard-hitting "Don't Hurt Yourself" ties Beyoncé to Black women pioneers of the blues-rooted genre (Mahon 2020, 2). Black music scholar Maureen Mahon notes that the history of Black women in rock and roll, particularly at its inception, has been "marginal to the dominant narrative" (ibid.). Beyoncé and her creative team dive into the power of this understudied archive and reemerge with a track that is delightfully ferocious and pulsating with a kinetic energy. That she uses rock and roll to score her anger, her declarations of exhaustion, her refusal of humility, and her full-throttled embrace of self-possession in a song capturing the aftermath of infidelity is telling. She taps into a blues and rock and roll tradition among Black women singers who tell stories of scorned lovers and heartbreak. "Don't Hurt Yourself" evades the longing often found in rhythm and blues. The choice of rock and roll gives Beyoncé a space for unfiltered rage. There's nothing pristine here. It's messy and unpolished—adjectives not typically used to describe Beyoncé's flawless image.

"Don't Hurt Yourself" nods to her southern roots while expanding how we read who Beyoncé is as a singer. She's someone capable of moving among multiple genres, but with an acute sense of the ways Black women have always moved within and beyond these musical categories. As a Black woman singer from the US South, she reveals the porousness of these categories. She's not dabbling in the unfamiliar, she is extracting from the traditions that shaped her. While the sound of *Lemonade* may feel like a departure from her earlier work as both a member of Destiny's Child and as a solo artist, it's a bringing forth of what was always there and perhaps not seen as commercially viable.

It's home. She isn't visiting or even revisiting. Beyoncé gives listeners a forty-five-minute-and-forty-five-second glimpse into the sonic worlds that birthed and nurtured her. She lives here, and with this album, she offers her home(s) as a place in which her audience can briefly dwell. For those already deeply familiar with, residing or raised in, or ancestrally tied to the places in which the music of *Lemonade* is birthed, *Lemonade* can resonate as a homecoming of sorts. The sounds of the US Black South—in its multitudes—welcome visitors, ex-pats, and those who never left with a knowing smile of its depths.

"I'm the First Black Woman to Headline Coachella . . . Ain't That a Bitch?"

Two years after *Lemonade*, Beyoncé headlined Coachella 2018. Affectionately renamed "Beychella" by her adoring fans, Beyoncé strove to create her own historically Black college/university Homecoming with her performance, which would eventually become both a concert film and a live album. Those who watched it live at the festival or via livestream on YouTube got the first taste of a project that included music genres go-go, brass band, Afrobeat, Latin pop, and chopped and screwed music. She took it to the Black Souths. During the concert, music samples included that of Black artists like Fela Kuti, Dawn Penn, Gudda Gudda, Sister Nancy, Pastor Troy, Juvenile, C-Murder, and Crucial Conflict. Sounds from places such as Abeokuta, Nigeria; Kingston, Jamaica; Atlanta, Georgia; and New Orleans, Louisiana, can be heard on the live album. Once again, she travels across the Black Atlantic to craft the album.

The US Black South played the most prominent role on *Homecoming*. Beyoncé sampled and covered artists from numerous cities with distinct Black music cultures, including those in which she has direct ties like Houston and New Orleans. The inclusion of music from Black musical cultures outside of the United States is a powerful reminder of the roots and routes of Black musical traditions. The exchanges among those in the African diaspora, especially those in the Black Atlantic, are integral to understanding the vastness of Blackness on a global level. Black musical cultures are iterative and are at once anchored in and unbound by place-based factors. The sonic finds a way to permeate geopolitical boundaries and form syncretic relationships.

The US Black South is her center and the Global Black South is where she ventures in search of familiar and unfamiliar sounds with ancestral and contemporaneous resonance.

This search ultimately leads her to *Black Is King*, which is both an album and a musical film. The Global Black South takes centerstage on this album in which Beyoncé collaborates with artists from across Africa. She brings with her the US Black South, with a deliberate intent to foreground Black artists based outside of the United States. The result of these collaborations and their placed-based anchoring in a fictional Africa makes this arguably one of Beyoncé's most ambitious projects thus far in her career. She relies upon musical traditions that are not home spaces for her. Although she doesn't abandon her Black southern girl disposition or approach on this album, she does place it alongside an array of genres created by Black people outside of the US. Whether she achieved a decentering or if that was even necessary is debatable; however, it is indisputable that the collaboration with numerous Black artists from countries such as Nigeria, Cameroon, Ghana, and South Africa showcased the bounty of sonic possibility found within the Black South.

Through genres such as Afro-pop and reggae dancehall, Beyoncé once again creates from a space of reclamation. In this iteration, it's a reclaiming and lauding of a heritage historically disrupted by the forceful dispersal of peoples of African descent throughout the Black Atlantic via the transatlantic slave trade. Although slavery and colonization aren't overtly addressed on the album or in the musical film, their presence as historical realities are subtly gestured toward by calls to "remember who you are" throughout the album/musical film. Beyoncé sings about heading back to the South on this collaborative album. The South invoked here, however, has baobab trees—a species primarily native to mainland Africa. *Black Is King* is an attempt to more fully engage the Black Souths.

The inclusion of Black Souths on *Black Is King* resounds as a logical progression of her musical explorations of heritage, tradition, and ancestral practices. She's something other than a visitor or interloper. She doesn't fully belong either. The songs on the album more often than not exhibit a blending of the Black Souths without an attempt to subsume the differences extant among the genres on the album. *Black Is King* basks in the ease with which it moves among a range of musical cultures within the Black Souths to produce something that is at once cohesive and discrete. The album reminds or perhaps newly informs her audience of the musical conversations among the Black Souths. What she does on this album isn't novel per se, although it does signal the existence and continued need for a generative space for artists across Black Souths to work together. For Beyoncé, in this album, the more she digs into the musical cultures of the Black Souths, the more she seems to find her voice as a singer.

"I Am a Whole Mood"

Beyoncé's albums of the latter part of the 2010s reflect an evolving audacity to proclaim the power of music that is affixed to her willingness to explore the Black Souths. Whether read as cocky, self-possessed, or simply playful, this lyric from Beyoncé's 2019 song "Mood 4 Eva" from *Black Is King* aligns with a trend that emerged in her music during the 2010s. Although her discography spans decades, the lyrics from the 2010s radiate a particular kind of playful self-assuredness, a delighting in being a Black girl from the South who sees herself as derived from the Black Souths. From "I'm the number one chick, I don't need no hype" on the 2013 track "I Been On" to "mad cause I'm so fresh, fresher than you" on her 2014 song "7/11," Beyoncé unapologetically celebrates her own greatness. Her refusal to perform humility defies expectations that women, and particularly Black women, adhere to gendered conventions that deem bragging or boasting as unladylike and distasteful. Furthermore, it departs from a distinct southern feminine performance often demanded of southern women in which propriety, modesty, and unpretentiousness are trumpeted. Her immodest lyrics offer a distinct point of departure for exploring Knowles-Carter's superstardom and the responses to her ascent to pop royalty status. More specifically, her defiance of regionalized gender norms regarding "appropriate" feminine performance catapults her into the global consumptive imagination in a seemingly intractable way.

It's befitting that Beyoncé more fully stepped into unapologetic performances of self-possession through her more explicit exploration of the Black Souths. The Black Souths are not just places from which she pulls inspiration or collaborators—these places shaped her. Beyoncé albums from the latter part of the 2010s cue us into how Beyoncé identifies her sonic home. She does this without relinquishing her pop star iconicity. It's a broadening of how we can understand her as a singer and as a musical collaborator. The borrowing, citations, and covers of sounds from the Black Souths give us insight into how she sees herself as a Black woman singer. She may be singular in her numerous accomplishments as an artist, but it is her growing insistence on incorporating the musical landscapes of the Black Souths that reminds us of the expansive well from which she draws. The Black Souths indeed have something to say.

References

Boylorn, Robin M. 2019. "Meridional: Beyoncé's Southern Roots and References." In *Queen Bey: A Celebration of the Power and Creativity of Beyoncé Knowles-Carter*, ed. Veronica Chambers, 193–99. New York: St. Martin's Press.

Bradley, Regina N. 2021. *Chronicling Stankonia: The Rise of the Hip-Hop South*. Chapel Hill, NC: University of North Carolina Press.

Brooks, Daphne. 2008. "'All That You Can't Leave Behind': Black Female Soul Singing and the Politics of Surrogation in the Age of Catastrophe." *Meridians* 8(1): 180–204.

———. 2021. *Liner Notes for the Revolution: The Intellectual Life of Black Feminist Sound*. Cambridge, MA: Harvard University Press.

Caramanica, John, Wesley Morris, and Jenna Wortham. 2016. "Beyoncé in 'Formation': Entertainer, Activist, Both?" *New York Times*, February 6. https://www.nytimes.com/2016/02/07/arts/music/beyonce-formation-super-bowl-video.html.

Chambers, Veronica, ed. 2019. *Queen Bey: A Celebration of the Power and Creativity of Beyoncé Knowles-Carter*. New York: St. Martin's Press.

Cinquemani, Sal. 2006. "Review: Beyoncé *B-Day*." www.slantmagazine.com, August 29. https://www.slantmagazine.com/music/beyonce-bday/.

Critic of Music. 2021. "Vocal Range and Profile: Beyoncé (Updated 2021)." https://thepopsmarts.com/vocal-range-and-profile-beyonce/.

Davis, Angela. 1999. *Blues Legacies and Black Feminism: Gertrude "Ma" Rainey, Bessie Smith, and Billie Holiday*. New York: Vintage Books.

Easter, Makeda. 2018. "Is Beyoncé the Greatest Performer . . . Ever? We Took an Informal Poll." *Los Angeles Times*, April 22. https://www.latimes.com/la-et-ms-beyonce-greatest-performer-20180421-story.html.

Ehrlich, Dimitri. 2002. "Young Soul Rebels: Neo-Soul Isn't Just a Subgenre Tailored to the Dread Set. It's a Sublime Paradox, Too." *Vibe*, February: 72–73.

Gilroy, Paul. 1993. *The Black Atlantic: Modernity and Double Consciousness*. Cambridge, MA: Harvard University Press.

Hamilton, Jack. 2016. *Just around Midnight: Rock and Roll and the Racial Imagination*. Cambridge, MA: Harvard University Press.

hooks, bell. 2014. "Are You Still a Slave?" https://livestream.com/TheNewSchool/Slave.

Hughes, Charles. 2017. *Country Soul: Making Music and Making Race in the American South*. Chapel Hill, NC: University of North Carolina Press.

Kooijman, Jap. 2014. "The True Voice of Whitney Houston: Commodification, Authenticity, and African American Superstardom." *Celebrity Studies* 5(3): 305–20.

———. 2019. "Why I Too Write about Beyoncé." *Celebrity Studies* 10(3): 432–35.

Leight, Elias. 2017. "R&B's Changing Voice: How Hip-Hop Edged Grittier Singers Out of the Mainstream." *Rolling Stone*, October 13. https://www.rollingstone.com/music/music-features/rbs-changing-voice-how-hip-hop-edged-grittier-singers-out-of-the-mainstream-195201/.

Lindsey, Treva B. 2019. "King Bey." In *Queen Bey: A Celebration of the Power and*

Creativity of Beyoncé Knowles-Carter, ed. Veronica Chambers, 185–92. New York: St. Martin's Press.

———. 2020. "Fuck the Grammys: The Conundrum of 'Transcending' Race and the Politics of Excellence." In *Culture as Catalyst*, ed. Isolde Brielmaier, 28–33. Saratoga Springs, NY: The Frances Young Tang Teaching Museum and Art Gallery at Skidmore College.

———. 2022. *America, Goddam: Violence, Black Women, and the Struggle for Justice*. Berkeley, CA: University of California Press.

Lipshutz, Jason. 2017. "Top 10 Girl Groups of All Time." www.billboard.com, July 11. https://www.billboard.com/articles/pop-shop/girl-group-week/5901266/top-10-girl-groups-of-all-time.

Mahon, Maureen. 2020. *Black Diamond Queens: African American Women and Rock and Roll*. Durham, NC: Duke University Press.

Mervis, Scott. 2004. "R&B Diva Beyonce Wins Five Grammy Awards." *Pittsburgh Post-Gazette*, February 9. http://old.post-gazette.com/ae/20040209grammy0209p1.asp.

Neal, Mark Anthony. 2003. *Songs in the Key of Black Life*. New York: Routledge.

Okoth-Obbo, Vanessa. 2017. "Where Neo-Soul Began: 20 Years of Erykah Badu's *Baduizm*." pitchfork.com, February 10. https://pitchfork.com/thepitch/1440-where-neo-soul-began-20-years-of-erykah-badus-baduizm/.

Platon, Adelle. 2017. "The 12 Best Dancehall and Reggaeton Choruses of the 21st Century." assets.billboard.com, April 28. https://assets.billboard.com/articles/columns/latin/7776734/best-dancehall-reggaeton-choruses-21st-century.

Purvis, Jennifer. 2004. "Grrrls and Women Together in the Third Wave: Embracing the Challenges of Intergenerational Feminism(s)." *NWSA Journal* 16(3): 93–123.

Sanneh, Kelefa. 2003. "The Solo Beyoncé: She's No Ashanti." *New York Times*, July 6. https://www.nytimes.com/2003/07/06/arts/music-the-solo-beyonce-she-s-no-ashanti.html.

Saturday Night Live. 2016. "The Day Beyoncé Turned Black." NBC Universal, February 13.

Stallings, L. H. 2020. *Dirty South Manifesto: Sexual Resistance and Imagination in the New South*. Oakland, CA: University of California Press.

Multimedia Playlist

BEYONCÉ, *Lemonade*, 2016
———, *Homecoming: A Film by Beyoncé*, 2019
———, *Black Is King*, 2020
JULIE DASH, *Daughters of the Dust*, 1991
SATURDAY NIGHT LIVE, "The Day Beyoncé Turned Black," 2016

CHAPTER 5

Compromise and Competition
The Musical Identities of Afro-Cuban Women Singers

CHRISTINA D. ABREU

During the second half of the twentieth century, three Afro-Cuban women singers held royal court on the Latin popular music landscape. To be dubbed "queen" (or "king") by fans, music promoters, and record executives signaled an achievement, that you had made it on the music scene, having been recognized for your musical talent as well as your ability to command profitable concert ticket and record sales. Genre and style differences earned Graciela Pérez Grillo (1915–2010), Celia Cruz (1925–2003), and Lupe Victoria Yolí (1936–1992) unique royal titles that, according to the gimmick, best characterized each woman's dominion within the larger Latin music sphere.[1] These women would not be contained or constrained by these nominal limitations. Graciela earned the moniker "Queen of Afro-Cuban Jazz" and "Queen of Latin Jazz," although she was on occasion simply referred to as the "Queen" ("Mario Bauzá's Legacy"). Celia held the title of "Queen of Salsa," but her popularity breached the salsa boundary line and earned her a reputation as the "undisputed queen of Latin music" ("Hispanic Rhythms"; Pareles 1983, 1989). On that broader terrain, Celia came head-to-head with La Lupe. Billed most often as the "Queen of Latin Soul" and the "Queen of Spanish soul music," La Lupe also earned titles that indicated far wider reach, including "Queen of Latin American song," "Queen of Latin Song," "Latin Music Queen," and "Queen of Sabor" (Wilson 1969; Gourse 1969; Zimmerman 1969; D. Moore 1971; Dove 1973; "'Black Music'"; "Tito Puente"; Rockwell 1973; Kirby 1969; "Latin Festival"; González-Wippler 1984; Advertisement 1968, 1973; "Teleprograma"; "Arderá el MSG"). Adding some formal flair to the naming bit was La Lupe's "official" crowning ceremony in 1968 during a concert in New York City; it was there, shortly after her split from Tito Puente, the bandleader known as the uncontested "King of Salsa," that she was crowned the "Queen of Salsa" in front of an audience of several thousand fans (Salazar 2000). One might easily dismiss such—sometimes overlapping—descriptors as nothing more than the marketing schemes of savvy music promoters and record executives. But doing so would miss the fact that this was the discursive and performative terrain on which these Cuban women of color crafted their musical identities and competed for audiences.

Historical, literary, and cultural studies of Cuban, Puerto Rican, and other Latinx singers and musicians have generally given less attention to women and their roles in the male-dominated Latin music scene. This chapter builds on more recent studies that have recognized the need for feminist intervention and the analysis of sex and gender in music and popular culture studies (Aparicio 1998, 2002; Aparicio and Valentin-Escobar 2004; Poey 2005, 2014; Cepeda 2010; Pacini Hernández 1995; Vazquez 2013; Fiol-Matta 2017). It offers a social and cultural history that is purposefully comparative and intersectional in its attempt to recover the professional careers and musical contributions of Afro-Cuban women performers from the backstage of the historical record. What follows is a story of similar, overlapping, and shared experiences and memories as well as key differences and divergences in perspectives and lived realities. By charting these similarities and differences, this study begins to reconstruct a more complete and thick history of Cuban and Latin popular music that allows Cuban women performers to speak not from the margins—as exotic sidepieces and gimmicky accessories to the "real work" being done by men—but from the center of the narrative as innovators, pioneers, and agents shaping the popular culture landscape on which they formed their professional careers. The stories told here reflect gender and racial solidarity and shared expressions of Afro-Cuban womanhood, but also point to the realities of inclusion within the entertainment industry: compromise and competition, among each other and with the men in their lives.

This study spans the mid-twentieth century, examining the lives and careers of Graciela, Celia, and La Lupe from the early 1950s to the late 1970s, a period that marks an uneven shift from the golden age of Latin music characterized by the sounds of the rumba, mambo, and cha cha cha to the development and growing popularity of the "new" sound of salsa, a genre that has long defied classification (Fernández 2006; Boggs 1992; Leymarie 2002; Waxer 2002; Flores 2016). This period also coincided with the dramatic increase in the number of Puerto Ricans and Cubans in the United States, especially in New York City and Miami. By 1960, the number of Puerto Ricans in New York City had risen to over 610,000 from a little over 61,000 in 1940. Nearly 250,000 Cubans arrived in south Florida in the early 1960s in the wake of Fidel Castro's Cuban Revolution, and most of these exiles were whites of the middle and upper classes. A popular image soon developed that characterized the Cuban exile experience as "white" and "elite" and, in the process, obscured the visibility of, and, to a certain degree, denied the existence of Cubans of color in both symbolic and lived spaces (D. García 2010; M. García 1997; Benson 2016). It was on the terrain of popular culture that Cubans of color, especially Cuban women of color like Graciela, Celia, and La Lupe, confronted this erasure and became representatives of (Afro-)Cuba and (Afro-)Cubanness for other Cubans as well as for broader publics of Latinxs and North Americans.

Musical Migrations from Havana to New York City

The case can certainly be made that Graciela, Celia, and La Lupe were of different generations, both in terms of age and music or genre. Graciela was born in 1915, Celia in 1925, and La Lupe in 1939. Consider that by the time Celia joined the band La Sonora Matancera in 1950, Graciela had already toured Paris and New York City with Cuba's first all-woman band, Orquesta Anacaona, and made a name for herself as lead vocalist for Machito y sus Afro-Cubans (Castro 2007). Joe Conzo, Latin music insider and biographer of Tito Puente, remarked in an oral history interview that Graciela was the only notable Latin woman singer of the 1940s and 1950s; she was succeeded, in his view, by Celia and La Lupe (Interview, March 20, 2010). Each woman achieved vastly different levels of stardom and celebrity throughout her career, but to say that each existed in isolation of the other or that there was little overlap in their careers overlooks the synchronicity that marked their personal experiences and professional achievements.

It was in New York City that all three women established themselves as singers and entertainers. Contemporary and historical accounts have often attributed the fame and celebrity of these women to the men—family, singers, bandleaders, promoters, and record company executives, among others—who "discovered" them, mentored their musical development, or otherwise provided the opportunity for them to perform. The implicit (and sometimes explicit) claim has been that their entry into the entertainment world depended on an introduction from these men, without which they would not have become popular, gotten recording contracts, or developed their own following with Latinxs and, to varying degrees, white North American audiences. Missing from these accounts is an acknowledgment of these women's agency and their ability to create for themselves the opportunities that brought them success in the music business. One needs to place these gendered accounts within the context of contemporary racialized discourses that credited white men for introducing and popularizing rhythms and musical genres created by Afro-Cuban and Afro-Latino men. What plays out in contemporary reporting and subsequent historical assessments is the multilayered marginalization of performers who were women of color. Emphasis on their dependence on men—Graciela's on Machito and Mario Bauzá; Celia's on Tito Puente, Johnny Pacheco, and Jerry Masucci; and La Lupe's on Mongo Santamaría and Puente—yields an interesting consequence: these narratives and discursive moves elevate the status and contributions of Afro-Cuban and Afro-Latino men, performers whose talents and innovations were often marginalized in the entertainment industry, as they were commonly relegated to the status of raw materials repackaged for popular consumption by white performers for mostly white audiences. In the process, however, women of color face a double erasure on the basis of both their race and gender. The point here is not to discredit musical influences or the significance of musical partnerships with men but to pay attention to the historical conditions and processes that have obscured these women's roles as musical pioneers who acted with purpose as they navigated the racial and gender constructs that diminished their efforts.

The story of Graciela's early career reinforces the notion that women relied on men to make it in the music world. Graciela could not entirely break from this pattern, despite the fact that her professional career began when she joined the all-woman Orquesta Anacaona in 1933 at the young age of seventeen. Accounts of her involvement with the band highlight the role of her brother, Machito, whom she credited for introducing her to the band and teaching her the popular songs of the period. But Graciela wasn't entirely demure on the matter, insisting that while singing with the band in the open-air cafes of Havana, she "wasn't at all scared of the public," even though large crowds would gather to see them perform (Pérez, interview with Fernández and López, 1998; Ortiz 1979; Pérez, interview with Salazar, 1985). She reflected on her time with Anacaona later in life, acknowledging that "being an all-woman orchestra was quite an attraction back then" (Varela 2005). It seems that men advanced and intervened in her professional career at key moments. It was, after all, Mario Bauzá who "summoned" her to New York City to fill in for Machito when he left the band during the Second World War. Bauzá remained involved in her career even into the 1960s and 1970s. Graciela described an episode when a lawyer for Fania Records approached her with a contract: The "bandit," as she called him, offered her an unfair contract, and it was Bauzá who countered that "if he wanted to sign me he had to come up with 'a deal worthy of someone like me'" (Varela 2006). The story doesn't end there. Graciela and Fania never reached an agreement, but what she recounted next seems a strategic move to elevate her own status and perhaps explain her waning presence on the Latin music scene in the late 1960s and 1970s. According to Graciela, when Fania was unable to sign her, the company settled for Celia: "Do you know why she recorded for Fania? Because I wouldn't. She wasn't doing much, so she took the offer" (ibid.).

At the height of her popularity with the Machito orchestra in the 1940s and 1950s, Graciela generally appeared as a side note in the popular press, rarely cited as key to the attention or commercial success achieved by the band and often dismissed as the "maestro's sister" (*Billboard* 1950, 118). Most descriptive comments about Graciela hinged on her physical appearance and performative sexuality. Reviewers dubbed her "good-looking" and "fiery" and noted that she "charm[ed] the public which admires and closely follows Machito y sus Afro-Cubans" ("Amenizará el baile"; "Ecos de Broadway"; "Fabulous Machito Band"). One reviewer of the record "Adivinanza" interestingly pointed out that "the lyrics serv[ed] to introduce Graciela as a girl who causes the men a lot of hesitation before they dare answer her questions" ("Viva"). But, perhaps the most telling remarks came in 1955 when *La Prensa* reviewed one of the band's performances at the Palladium ballroom. The reviewer described Graciela as "the suggestive trigueña who sings songs and all kinds of melodies that she makes more attractive with her voice" ("Machito, Tito"). To describe Graciela as a "suggestive trigueña," a phrase that pointed to a racialized sexuality, was not without purpose. In the racial lexicon of Latin America and the Caribbean, the term *trigueña* references the color of wheat and is used to describe a woman of not-quite-white and not-quite-black color who also has dark blonde or light brown hair. This intermediate racial category is important, given that Graciela claimed a Black identity for herself. *La Prensa* targeted "an imagined community of pan-ethnic Spanish-speaking New Yorkers," so the phrasing renders Graciela more palatable to readers while still hinting at a hypersexuality that was often attributed to women of color (Abreu 2015, 127).

This was not unfamiliar terrain for Graciela. Her singing style often became linked to sexual expression. Graciela believed that "Sí, Sí, No, No" (a newer version of "Mi cerebro") became one of her signature pieces because she "added words and gestures that the audience loved," words and gestures that she claimed earned her the nickname "Graciela, la pintoresca" ("Graciela, the eccentric") (Pérez Gutierrez 2010, 152). Sexual playfulness and the use of double entendre was nothing new for Graciela. Alexandra T. Vazquez has shown that such behavior or posturing—a wink here, a purposeful misspoken word in English there—was typical of Graciela and other women performers: "Young women who perform publically require this fluency and facility with innuendo. You might even say that such skills are required of women (young and old) who leave the house generally speaking" (Vazquez 2013, 121). Yet, Graciela was at times reluctant to claim "Sí, Sí, No, No" as her signature piece. Vazquez proposes that this reluctance "perhaps came from the frustration felt from having her body and work treated as novelty" (ibid., 123–24). More broadly, Graciela's reluctance might have resulted, as Vazquez suggests, from a refusal to submit to categorization or characterization.

Arguably the most famous of the three women singers, Celia could not avoid contemporary reports that framed her career as one dependent on key collaborations with male performers and music executives. Reports cited Puente for creating space for Celia on the Latin music scene, noting he "gave Miss Cruz a musical home a decade ago" ("Celia Cruz"). Johnny Pacheco has also received credit for Celia's rising popularity in the mid-1970s. Latin music promoter and manager Ralph Mercado explained that it was when the pair began recording together that "her career really turned around" (Guillermoprieto 1983). And Fania co-founder Jerry Masucci's reported preference for Celia over La Lupe (and Graciela) solidified her position as the era's uncontested *salsera* ("Cuban Revolutions"; Salazar 2000; Troyano 2007).

La Lupe's move onto the music scene in New York City has commonly been attributed to her early partnership with Afro-Cuban percussionist and bandleader Mongo Santamaría. After La Lupe arrived in New York City in 1962, Mongo, as one writer phrased it, "came to her rescue and they recorded 'Mongo Introduces La Lupe'—her first 'salsa' venture" ("Cuban Revolutions"). The liner notes to the album clarify the relationship: "In this album, Mongo has had an opportunity to do something that always gives him the greatest satisfaction—to introduce new talent. This time it is La Lupe!" (quoted in Salazar 2000). This, of course, is an interesting role reversal given that the role of introduction has been typically assigned to white men. The partnership with Mongo dissolved over what seems to have been a disagreement over whether La Lupe, pregnant with her son, should travel with the band to perform in Puerto Rico (cf. Moreno-Velazquez 2000; Troyano 2007; Salazar 2000; González-Wippler 1984). The implications of this experience are too complex to unpack here, but two points must be noted for they transcend the confines of the music industry to reveal perceptions about Black motherhood, specifically, and working-class motherhood, generally: the apparent ease with which her male collaborators suggested she have an abortion and her understanding that she had to continue working, without any sort of maternity leave or formal childcare in place, or risk derailing her career.

La Lupe's musical partnerships with men have been both complicated and controversial. She recognized Puente's role in exposing her to wider audiences in the United States, but she hesitated to give him any more credit than that: "He had a lot to do with my growth in popularity. He did not create me. I have my own talent. But he was instrumental in my becoming famous here. The man had faith in me" (quoted in González-Wippler 1984). Her perspective skims over the ways in which race, gender, culture, and power shaped her relationship with Puente and his role in the rise and fall of her success and popularity. It all began, according to most reports, in 1965, when Puente heard La Lupe "singing at a New York City nightclub for Cuban exiles" and "persuaded her to make a record with him" (Zimmerman 1969; Gourse 1969). The result was "Que Te Pedí," a commercial and critical success for the pair. That the financial rewards of the arrangement fell mainly to Puente seemed to matter little to her: "I get 10 hits out of his 12 songs singing with Tito. He gets the money because they are under his name, but I don't care because now I am famous" (D. Moore 1971; Dove 1973). Whatever the payout, reports described the pairing of La Lupe and Puente as "the hottest on the Latin music scene" ("Cuban Revolutions").

But the partnership wouldn't last. The pair split in 1968, resulting in what came to be described as the "long-standing feud between the two artists to never appear together" ("Latin Fest"). Nevertheless, she was able to find other bands, including Machito's orchestra, to accompany her on stage and in the studio. She concluded that Puente's rejection and the sway he held over some bands and record companies failed to end her career and, instead, had the effect of confirming her independence and singular popularity: "But what he did was prove to the world that La Lupe could sing without him. He did not intend to do that, but that's what he did" (González-Wippler 1984).

"Well, There Aren't Really Many Female Salsa Singers . . ."

Competition, rivalry, and jealousy—all three characterize how Cuban singers, musicians, and performers have sometimes framed and remembered their relationships with their contemporaries in interviews, autobiographical writings, and casual conversations. Some admit that music industry insiders, often in collaboration with the popular press, invented or exaggerated these tensions to improve record or concert ticket sales. Performers have made countless remarks and offered numerous recollections, oftentimes without prodding from interviewers, that reflected on their interactions, collaborations, disagreements, and friendships with other musicians and entertainers. Popular press and oral history interviews suggest that Graciela, Celia, and La Lupe generally had less than positive things to say about one another. Given the stereotypical association of women with gossip and drama, the point here is not to repeat scandalous details and salacious rumors (although that does make for good storytelling) or to ignore that similar tensions developed among men (as was reportedly the case between competing "Mr. Babalús" Desi Arnaz and Miguelito Valdés). Nevertheless, the criticisms that each woman directed at her rivals reveal a great deal about the music business and the opportunities available to women performers.

Graciela and Celia had few kind words to offer one another. In an interview with Raul Fernández and René López, Graciela's only mention of Celia was more dismissive than critical, an afterthought really: she stated plainly that Celia had not been friendly to her but offered no other comment on the singer; her remark suggested neither outright resentment or jealousy, nor any trace of warmth or affection (Pérez 1998). We have seen, however, that Graciela did have moments of more direct critique such as when she asserted that Fania had offered Celia a contract only because she had previously refused to sign with the record company. To another interviewer, she revealed that part of her resentment toward Celia (and La Lupe) stemmed from what she believed was the mislabeling of specific Cuban musical styles as salsa, a common complaint made by many other Cuban musicians and Cuban music fans who also opposed the term. Graciela claimed that Celia and La Lupe sanctioned the use of the term "salsa" in the 1970s (although she admitted that it was Johnny Pacheco who first coined it): "Celia Cruz and La Lupe, who were with Fania, let them do that. Because if I had been with Fania, I would have told them, 'What salsa? You can play for me a mambo, a danzón, a son, but who said that salsa was music? It's a food thing.'" She noted that only she and Puente expressed objection (Merino 2006).

Differences in genre classification seem to have contributed to some of the tension between Graciela and Celia. Scholars, critics, fellow musicians, and fans have typically characterized Graciela as a singer of jazz. In many ways, Graciela belongs more to that lineage of "Afro" women jazz singers like Ella Fitzgerald and Billie Holiday, and, in fact, she deserves more credit than she has claimed and received—in both popular and academic circles—for her role in the development of Latin jazz. One exception is Alexandra T. Vazquez, who has argued that Graciela and Orquesta Anacaona's performances in Paris at the Chez Florence serve as significant moments of exchange between Cuban and Black American women (Vazquez 2013, 112). Celia, of course, is best known as a performer of salsa. Her take on Latin jazz was, at least on one occasion, less than positive, a perspective that likely shaped her view of Graciela and, more importantly, the apparent distance between the two performers. In 1980, when the Fania All Stars' album *Cross Over* lost out to Irakere's self-titled album for the Grammy Award for Best Latin Recording, Celia was reportedly upset not just because her album lost; she was most upset because the award went to what she considered a jazz and not a Latin album (Fernández, personal communication, 2015).

Another source of tension might be traced to comments made by other performers that support Graciela's contention that it was her step away from performing that opened opportunities up for Celia. In an interview conducted by David Carp on WNYC radio in 1993 with Black American jazz dancers Sugar Sullivan-Niles and Sonny Allen, Allen tells listeners: "But then you also, you know, you had Graciela, which was ooh, fantastic singer, you know. That, the best thing that ever happened to Celia Cruz is when Graciela decided not to sing no more, you know (laughs). I mean Celia should hear me say that (SSN laughs), I mean I love her, you know. But—when Graciela, when she had 'Sí Sí No No,' and at that time she was something else. But then Graciela came off the stage" (Sullivan-Niles and Allen 1993). There is the obvious suggestion that had Graciela not decided to take a step back from performing and recording, Celia would not have enjoyed the success she did. Perhaps it was an indirect comment on the fact that the music industry offered fewer opportunities for women, but, more likely, it seems Allen was suggesting that Graciela was the better performer. The latter perspective comes through in his description of Graciela's signature song "Sí, Sí, No, No," which he dubs "something else." Still, Celia was by this time a beloved icon who could not be criticized openly. Allen probably knew this and tempered his remark: "I mean I love [Celia] you know . . . And there's the greatest, I mean Celia Cruz is nothin' but actually Ella Fitzgerald in Latin music" (ibid.).

Graciela and La Lupe had no trouble positioning Celia as both a contemporary and rival. Celia, on the other hand, seemed to do her best to avoid uttering the name of either woman in press reports and interviews. She was the most famous of the three, so one might conclude that Graciela and La Lupe hoped to use Celia's celebrity to elevate their own significance, while Celia could easily disengage from the competition simply by not acknowledging it. Still, the move—which acts to both deflect and silence—is a curious one. When asked to name the salsa singer she liked most in a 1989 interview, Celia responded: "Well, there aren't really many female salsa singers, not long ago there was one . . . Linda Leida but she was killed by a jealous boyfriend . . . Apart from her, no, I don't know any . . . there aren't any" ("Cuban Revolutions"). Celia is not entirely wrong in her assessment that she had shared the stage with few other *salseras*. Still, that La Lupe failed to register on her radar, while Linda Leida, a little-known Afro-Cuban singer who performed and recorded with La Sonora Matancera in the late 1960s and 1970s, did is not without significance. Whether a strategic move to slight her competitors or not, Celia echoed news and industry reports that also cast aside the existence and contributions of other women performers on the salsa and broader Latin music scene ("Viva Latin!").

Celia drew comparisons to Black American jazz singers Ella Fitzgerald and Sarah Vaughan as well as the French cabaret singer Edith Piaf. One reporter noted that Celia's "range, virtuosity, and feeling make her Latin music's equivalent of Sarah Vaughan" (Palmer 1979). Mostly, Celia took the comparisons as compliments. One reporter noted, however, that Celia thought the differences ultimately outweighed the similarities, emphasizing that "they sang different genres of music and their lives and voices were also different" ("Cuban Revolutions"). In comparing women singers, critics often characterized their singing and performativity as a kind of sexual performance or sexual expression: "Whereas some female singers might croon a man's fantasy of what a woman should sound like—Donna Summer and Olivia Newton-John come to mind—Celia Cruz, like Edith Piaf before her and Aretha Franklin after, sings like what a woman knows she feels like. That stomping unrarefied womanly energy has propelled her career" (Guillermoprieto 1983). A reviewer of a concert at Madison Square Garden in 1975 singled out Celia for adding "a feminine touch to the all male show" (Jones 1975). Another reviewer noted that "she rips into the rhythmic exhortations of salsa tunes far more boisterously than most male singers" (Pareles 1983).

From the very start of her career, Celia worked to position herself as a talented vocalist and charismatic performer rather than as a sex object. Some argue that for her this was not so much a choice but rather the result of the fact that, even in her youth, she was not "conventionally beautiful," as well as the fact that she was closely chaperoned and guarded by her father and the members of La Sonora Matancera (Poey 2014; Negrón-Muntaner 2007). For the most part, though she danced onstage, she was always "a lady." Delia Poey explains, "If audiences expected Black female bodies on a stage to signify unbridled sexuality, Cruz's persona offered an alternative" (Poey 2014, 36). One report explained, "Not only is she a great singer, but also in personal matters she is one of the finest and most attentive people we have dealt with in the world of celebrity" (Valdés 1971). Celia was straight-laced, uninvolved in scandal, and she avoided songs that could be considered sexual or dirty; she had no equivalent of "Sí, Sí, No, No." That is not to say that her body failed to draw attention—her trademark fashion accessories included colorful wigs, flamboyant and sequined gowns, and platform heels. As Frances Negrón-Muntaner has argued, the wildness of her bright and elaborate wardrobe—a costume almost—had the effect of marking her as asexual, and, as she aged, helped her maintain an illusion of youthfulness (Negrón-Muntaner 2007). Given her marriage to Pedro Knight and that she was dubbed "madrina" (godmother) to the younger, up-and-coming Puerto Rican salsa performer, La India, Celia earned and claimed for herself a much more maternal and serious public persona.

La Lupe did not shy away from noting the musical influences of other women singers. She admitted that at a young age she listened to Olga Guillot and Celia Cruz and had dreams that she might be famous one day, too (Salazar 2000). Many observers hypothesized that La Lupe's onstage antics were caused by her association with santería, that she would become possessed by the saints and would enter a trance-like state during her musical performances. She admitted that she was formally initiated into the Afro-Cuban religious practice in 1969 for health reasons (Salazar 2000; "Cuban Revolutions"; Troyano 2007). Cuban music and musicians have long been associated with santería and other Afro-Cuban religious practices, including Abakuá and palo monte, and quite a few male performers incorporated, albeit usually in watered-down forms, drumming rituals or other performative elements from these spiritual practices into their musical performances for the consumption of mainstream audiences. Most notable in this regard are Miguelito Valdés and Desi Arnaz in their performances of "Babalú," an Afro-Cuban-inspired popular song written by Margarita Lecuona in the mid-1930s (R. Moore 1997, 137; Salazar 2002, 42; Abreu 2015, 2, 164).

For a woman to include aspects of Afro-Cuban religious practice in her performance, however, proved controversial. In a review of a 1969 performance at the Teatro Puerto Rico, a reporter observed that "an Afro-Cuban number" sent "one girl in the audience into a voodoo swoon and convulsions" (Zimmerman 1969). La Lupe used this negative association to her advantage when she connected Celia, who shunned such an association, to santería. La Lupe claimed: "Celia hasn't made saint, but she has necklaces . . . she doesn't want anyone to know she has these things. And nobody can blame her because people are always asking her about her beliefs and she wants to keep them a secret" (González-Wippler 1984). She then coyly added, as if with a wink, "Of course I didn't see her take the initiations. I'm only telling you what I've heard" (González-Wippler 1984; Aparicio 2002). La Lupe would have cause to feel aggrieved by Celia, for she and others have cited Fania's preference for Celia over her as the beginning of the end of her career (although, as we have seen, it was much more complicated than that). La Lupe was the darling of Tico Records, but when Fania bought the label in 1974, Masucci "chose to promote the more controlled, and conventional Celia Cruz, over her" ("Cuban Revolutions"). She charged that the lack of publicity ruined her chances of continuing to remain relevant and successful: "Because in this business, you must sell records if you want to stay alive musically" ("Cuban Revolutions"; cf. Troyano 2007; Salazar 2000; González-Wippler 1984).

La Lupe often drew comparisons to Eartha Kitt, Janis Joplin, and—like Celia—Edith Piaf. But unlike Celia, she embraced the comparison with Piaf, telling a reporter that the French singer and actress was the first professional singer she ever saw on television: "While Lupe didn't understand a word, she says she understood everything else—the style, the elan, the animated soul" (Gourse 1969). One reviewer hinted that comparisons with other women singers were unnecessary because La Lupe "easily makes most of today's gal singers pale by comparison" (Kirby 1969).

La Lupe's presence onstage led to very different reactions from observers and critics alike. A 1969 performance at Carnegie Hall serves as a case in point: "She kicked off her shoes as she sang, tugged at a long, tight skirt so she could hop around the stage, scratched her nose in the middle of a note, scratched her ear, scratched her forehead, beat her bosom, hoisted her skirt higher so she could kick, slapped her thighs, flung her long dark hair around" (Wilson 1969). At a performance at the swanky Chateau Madrid that same year, another reviewer noted: "Lupe's mystique is that she can put a little orgy into her songs. The audience watches her jump, cry out and generally unravel with the same fascinated attention they give Sinatra's swaying microphone. She makes the people feel, for a little while anyway, that the wild way is the only way" (Gourse 1969). Such behavior was common to La Lupe's performances throughout her career, prompting some to believe that she would become possessed by (evil) spirits and others to accuse her of being on drugs. She denied that she used drugs and attributed her behavior onstage to the fact that she was "free": "'But I do got class, believe me! I not pretty.' She nods seriously. 'Ho-kay, is true! But I come out—dress clean, hair nice, how you say, aesthetic. So nobody take off they shoes—they hypocrite. Maybe they new shoes—they hurt.' 'Feeling come from the foot. I think people like me because I do what they like to, but can't get free enough to do!'" (D. Moore 1971; Gourse 1969).

Fellow performers were generally less enthused about her raw expressiveness onstage, but La Lupe believed that her fans loved her more for it. She often referred to her fans simply as "my people," an audience she believed was made up mostly of Puerto Ricans, although one reviewer indicated a broader reach: "Her people, New York's 1.5 million Spanish-speaking residents, have bought more than a million of her records and have vaulted their empress beyond the enclave of Spanish Harlem to a wider American public" (Zimmerman 1969). But at times, La Lupe would eschew such mainstream appeal, insisting that she was "of the people." And, in an interesting way, reviewers noted that her performances functioned as an unveiling of sorts that endeared her to "thousands of Puerto Ricans, Cubans, Dominicans and other Latin Americans" who clamored to see her perform: "Systematically tearing away the accoutrements of stardom, she throws away her jewelry, lets down her hair, kicks off her shoes, rolls up her white suit-pants—until she once again becomes the peasant girl from Oriente Province in Cuba" (Zimmerman 1969).

Conclusion

In 1973, Graciela, Celia, and La Lupe faced a direct test to determine who really was "queen" of the Latin music scene. All three women had been nominated in the best female singer category at the Latin Awards Night, an awards ceremony sponsored by a New York City–based Latin music management company and held at the Cheetah nightclub. After weeks of collecting ballots at local retailers and Latin music hotspots, the winner was announced: Celia had bested Graciela and La Lupe to take the title ("Latin Award"; "Latin Scene"). At quick glance, the results are not entirely surprising or particularly meaningful given that this was an unscientific popularity contest of interest mostly to record executives and nightclub booking agents. But with more careful consideration, the contest and results confirm some of the central arguments made here: first, that all three Afro-Cuban women singers remained contemporaries (and rivals) into the 1970s; and, second, that these three Afro-Cuban performers both represented and resisted prescribed and traditional gender roles on the terrain of popular culture. Celia's win seems to suggest that her strategies for navigating and negotiating the racialized and gendered expectations of the Latin popular music scene offered the best odds for widespread popularity and commercial success. Still, the point here has not been to crown a "queen" but to (re-)claim space for multiple and simultaneous "queens." In this way, popular music studies can help make visible individuals, communities, and processes that are forgotten or thought to be unseen and unheard—in this case, the almost always complex and sometimes contradictory ways of thinking and doing of Graciela, La Lupe, and Celia—three performers with multiple and overlapping identities as Cuban women of color.

Notes

1. In subsequent references, I will refer to the three Afro-Cuban women performers under study by their first names because these were their stage names, the names by which most fans and contemporary observers (in print and other media) knew them.

References

Abreu, Christina D. 2015. *Rhythms of Race: Cuban Musicians and the Making of Latino New York City and Miami, 1940–1960*. Chapel Hill: University of North Carolina Press.

Advertisement. 1968. *El Diario-La Prensa*, November 4.

Advertisement. 1973. *El Diario-La Prensa*, August 19.

"Amenizará el baile del Festival de 'La Prensa' la Orq. De Machito." 1952. *La Prensa*, May 4.

Aparicio, Frances R. 1998. *Listening to Salsa: Gender, Latin Popular Music, and Puerto Rican Cultures*. Hanover, NH: University Press of New England.

———. 2002. "La Lupe, La India, and Celia: Toward a Feminist Genealogy of Salsa Music." In *Situating Salsa: Global Markets and Local Meanings in Latin Popular Music*, ed. Lise Waxer, 135–60. New York: Routledge.

———, and Wilson A. Valentin-Escobar. 2004. "Memorializing La Lupe and Lavoe: Singing Vulgarity, Transnationalism, and Gender." *CENTRO Journal* 16(2): 78–101.

"Arderá el MSG Con Festival Latino Esta Noche." 1973. *El Diario-La Prensa*, February 2.

Benson, Devyn Spence. 2016. *Antiracism in Cuba: The Unfinished Revolution*. Chapel Hill: University of North Carolina Press.

Billboard, April 29, 1950, 118.

"'Black Music' Set for Apollo Theatre Friday Night." 1973. *New York Amsterdam News*, April 14.

Boggs, Vernon W. 1992. *Salsiology: Afro-Cuban Music and the Evolution of Salsa in New York City*. New York: Excelsior Music Publishing Company.

Castro, Alicia. 2007. *Queens of Havana: The Amazing Adventures of Anacaona, Cuba's Legendary All-Girl Dance Band*. New York: Grove Press.

Cepeda, María Elena. 2010. *Musical ImagiNation: U.S.-Colombian Identity and the Latin Music Boom*. New York: New York University Press.

Conzo, Joe. 2010. Interview with author, March 20. Bronx, New York.

"Cuban Revolutions." 1989. *New Musical Express*, January 21.

Dove, Ian. 1973. "When La Lupe Sings, She Gets Involved." *New York Times*, February 4.

———. 1975. "Celia Cruz Marks 25 Years of Song." *New York Times*, September 22.

"Ecos de Broadway." *Ecos de Nueva York*, August 8, 1954.

"Fabulous Machito Band at Club Oasis Tonight." 1954. *Los Angeles Sentinel*, December 16.

Fernández, Raul A. 2006. *From Afro-Cuban Rhythms to Latin Jazz*. Berkeley: University of California Press.

———. 2015. Skype conversation with author. December 8.

Fiol-Matta, Licia. 2017. *The Great Woman Singer: Gender and Voice in Puerto Rican Music*. Durham, NC: Duke University Press.

Flores, Juan. 2016. *Salsa Rising: New York Latin Music of the Sixties Generation*. New York: Oxford University Press.

García, David F. 2010. "Contesting That Damned Mambo: Arsenio Rodríguez and the People of El Barrio and the Bronx in the 1950s." In *The Afro-Latin@ Reader: History and Culture in the United States*, eds. Miriam Jiménez Román and Juan Flores, 187–98. Durham, NC: Duke University Press.

García, María Cristina. 1997. *Havana USA: Cuban Exiles and Cuban Americans in South Florida, 1959–1994*. Berkeley: University of California Press.

González-Wippler, Migene. 1984. "La Lupe: The Queen of the Pack Is Back with a Vengeance." *Latin N.Y.*, March-April.

Gourse, Leslie. 1969. "Mira Lupe! Aiiiieeee!" *New York*, September 29.

Guillermoprieto, Alma. 1983. "Steam & Salsa!" *Washington Post*, January 9.

"Hispanic Rhythms." 1975. *Vogue*, November 1.

Jones, Joseph. 1975. "The Garden of Salsa Rocks." *New York Amsterdam News*, July 23.

Kirby, Fred. 1969. "La Lupe Gives Royal Act as the Latin Music Queen." *Billboard*, June 28.

"Latin Award Night in N.Y." 1973. *Billboard*, May 19.

"Latin Fest 3 in N.Y. June 2." 1973. *Billboard*, May 19.

"Latin Festival." 1973. *Variety*, June 13.

"Latin Scene." 1973. *Billboard*, June 2.

Leymarie, Isabelle. 2002. *Cuban Fire: The Story of Salsa and Latin Jazz*. New York: Continuum.

"Machito, Tito y D. Santos en el Palladium." 1955. *La Prensa*, October 14.

"Mario Bauzá's Legacy Lives On." 1993. *Richmond Afro-American*, August 21.

Merino, Juan Fernando. 2006. "Graciela pone picante a la salsa." *El Diario-La Prensa*, December 6.

Moore, Deedee. 1971. "She's Sex, Fire, Soul and Voodoo . . . La Lupe!" *Look*, April 20.

Moore, Robin D. 1997. *Nationalizing Blackness: Afrocubanismo and Artistic Revolution in Havana, 1920–1940*. Pittsburgh: University of Pittsburgh Press.

Moreno-Velazquez, Juan A. 2000. "La Lupe en Nueva York, un éxito extraordinario." *El Diario-La Prensa*, February 25.

Negrón-Muntaner, Frances. 2007. "Celia's Shoes." In *From Bananas to Buttocks: The Latina Body in Popular Film and Culture*, ed. Myra Mendible, 94–116. Austin: University of Texas Press.

Ortiz, Isabelle. 1979. "No Olvidará a Paris." *Canales*, July. Box 7, Folder 8, Carlos Ortiz Collection, Centro de Estudios Puertorriqueños.

Pacini Hernández, Deborah. 1995. *Bachata: A Social History of Dominican Popular Music*. Philadelphia: Temple University Press.

Palmer, Robert. 1979. "Garden Goes Latin with Salsa Festival." *New York Times*, August 31.

Paredez, Deborah. 2009. *Selenidad: Selena, Latinos, and the Performance of Memory*. Durham, NC: Duke University Press.

Pareles, Jon. 1983. "Salsa: Celia Cruz and Tito Puente." *New York Times*, November 3.

———. 1989. "Harlem on Her Mind." *New York Times*, October 20.

Pérez, Graciela. 1985. Interview with Max Salazar. May 10. David Carp Collection of Latin Jazz, Bronx County Historical Society, Bronx, New York.

———. 1998. Interview with Raul A. Fernández and René López. September 19. National Museum of American History.

Pérez Gutierrez, Graciela. 2010. "Eso Era Tremendo! An Afro-Cuban Musician Remembers." In *The Afro-Latin@ Reader: History and Culture in the United States*, eds. Juan Flores and Miriam Jiménez Román, 150–54. Durham, NC: Duke University Press.

Poey, Delia. 2005. "'¡La Lupe!': Performing Race, Gender, Nation, and Excess." *Women & Performance: A Journal of Feminist Theory* 15(2): 79–98.

———. 2014. *Cuban Women and Salsa: To the Beat of Their Own Drum*. New York: Palgrave Macmillan.

Rockwell, John. 1973. "Aficionados Hail Puente-Lupe Reunion." *New York Times*, June 4.

Salazar, Max. 2000. "Remembering La Lupe." *Latin Beat Magazine*, May.

———. 2002. *Mambo Kingdom: Latin Music in New York*. New York: Schirmer Trade Books.

Sullivan-Niles, Sugar, and Sonny Allen. 1993. David Carp interview on WNYC radio. September 14. David Carp Collection of Latin Jazz, Bronx County Historical Society.

"Teleprograma Con Estrellas Hispanas." 1969. *El Diario-La Prensa*, June 6.

"Tito Puente, La Lupe Will Headline Coming Garden Latin Music Festival." 1973. *New York Amsterdam News*, May 12.

Troyano, Ela, dir. 2007. *La Lupe: Queen of Latin Soul*. PBS: Independent Lens.

Valdés, Fabio. 1970. "A Quien Pueda Interesar." *El Diario-La Prensa*, March 27.

———. 1971. "Celia Cruz al Chateau Madrid." *El Diario-La Prensa*, September 28.

Varela, Jesse. 2005. "Graciela: First Lady of Latin Jazz." *Latin Beat Magazine*, September.

———. 2006. "Graciela: First Lady of Latin Jazz—Part III." *Latin Beat Magazine*, December/January.

Vazquez, Alexandra T. 2013. *Listening in Detail: Performances of Cuban Music*. Durham, NC: Duke University Press.

"Viva." 1954. *Melody Maker*, February 27.

"Viva Latin!" 1976. *Melody Maker*, February 21.

Waxer, Lise, ed. 2002. *Situating Salsa: Global Markets and Local Meanings in Latin Popular Music.* New York: Routledge.
Wilson, John S. 1969. "Carnegie Hall Jolted by La Lupe, Singer of Latin Soul Music." *New York Times*, June 16.
Zimmerman, Paul D. 1969. "Latin Bombshell." *Newsweek*, October 13.

Multimedia Playlist

CELIA CRUZ AND JOHNNY PACHECO, *Celia & Johnny*, 1974
GRACIELA WITH MACHITO Y SU ORQUESTA, *Esta Es Graciela*, 1963
LA LUPE, *La Lupe es la Reina*, 1969

CHAPTER 6

Challenging the Divide Between Elite and Mass Cultures

Opera Icon Beverly Sills

NANCY GUY

Passions in the opera world run hot and deep both on the stage and off. It is not uncommon for an operatic diva to elicit strong responses from aficionados. There rarely is a middle ground. Opposing fans take up verbal arms in the battle to defend their favorite divas. And, they typically couch denigrations of singers whom they do not favor in high-falutin prose embellished with specialist terminology such as fioritura, intonation, shades of metal, passaggio, etc. Factors beyond considerations of voice, musicality, and stage performance sometimes underlie artistic evaluations. These underpinnings may be foundational to critical judgments of artistic merit. With this essay, I look primarily to published reviews, blog posts, and fan statements to show how issues surrounding class shaped and continue to underlie the reception of the voice of American coloratura soprano Beverly Sills (1929–2007).

Sills rocketed to fame with a single performance when she took to the New York State Theater stage in Lincoln Center as Cleopatra in Handel's opera *Julius Caesar (Giulio Cesare)* on September 27, 1966 (Figure 6.1). Though she had been singing professionally for more than two decades, and had been a member of the New York City Opera since 1955, it all came together that night. *Newsweek* magazine reported, "The evening belonged to Beverly Sills. . . . Her sparkling coloratura voice negotiated every trill and tremolo with ease, clarity and melting beauty. Her every entrance sparked a stir of excitement in the audience as she built, aria by aria, her own pyramid of Cleopatra" (Saal 1966, 100). Opera houses around the world took note and the invitations began to pour in. Perhaps her greatest triumph in Europe was her debut at the famed Teatro alla Scala in Milan, Italy, in April 1969.

Figure 6.1. Beverly Sills as Cleopatra in Handel's opera *Giulio Cesare*. This role launched Sills into stardom when she performed it with her home opera company, the New York City Opera, in September 1966. Photo by Beth Berman. Used with permission.

Her performance as Pamira in Rossini's opera *The Siege of Corinth* (*L'assedio di Corinto*) was an unmitigated triumph, earning her both the affection of La Scala's audience, for whom opera can be a blood sport, as well as further acclaim back in the United States, including a *Newsweek* cover story. Until her retirement from singing in 1980 at the age of fifty, Sills was in constant demand in opera houses and concert halls. Summing up Sills's gifts following the artist's death in 2007, Katrine Ames observed, "At her peak in the 1960s and 1970s, she could float passages over a full orchestra; she could sing long runs in which each individual note was clear but which ran down a listener's back like melted chocolate. She had a trill that could wind a clock, and could color her voice from shimmering silver or almost transparent blue to dark red" (Ames 2007).

Sills was known for her down-to-earth demeanor. Born in Brooklyn, New York, to Jewish immigrant parents, she never dropped her Brooklyn accent, which she frequently peppered with Yiddishisms. She was forthright in a manner that could sometimes be grating to people invested in aristocratic, or even middle-class, sensibilities. Rather than hiding her modest background, she spoke freely of her times of financial struggle. Perhaps of greatest consequence to her career was the class-based tension between Sills and Sir Rudolph Bing, the General Director of the Metropolitan Opera from 1952–1970. While there may have been artistic or vocal factors contributing to Bing's intense dislike for Sills, there is no question that class tension (and perhaps a strong distaste for self-possessed women) played a role in his shunning of her. Her much-delayed Metropolitan Opera debut only occurred after Bing retired. The day after her debut on April 7, 1975, less than two months before her forty-seventh birthday, Peter Michelmore, writing for *The Herald* of Melbourne, Australia, opined that Bing simply didn't care for Sills: "For an opera star she seemed too happy-go-lucky, too unaware of her stature, and sometimes, when she described an opera plot in Brooklyn street slang, his hair would stand on end."

Bing's only mention of Sills in his 345-page *Memoirs*, published the year of his retirement, was a classist attack. Bing, who was born to a well-to-do Viennese family and became a naturalized British citizen, was rumored to prefer European over American singers. In discussing his opposition to the New York City Opera's move to Lincoln Center in 1965, Bing explained that he was initially concerned that the two companies would stage the same repertoire. However, he reported that over the years there had been only one programming conflict. The dispute centered on Beverly Sills. Sills aimed to perform Donizetti's three Tudor queen operas: *Anna Bolena*, *Maria Stuarda*, and *Roberto Devereux*. However, the Spanish soprano Montserrat Caballé also voiced an interest in undertaking the trilogy. Bing nastily commented, "We finally accepted the fact that Beverly Sills of the City Opera, having been born in Brooklyn, was entitled to priority in the portrayal of British royalty" (1972, 290). In fact, Sills did indeed take on all three queens beginning in 1970 with her portrayal of Queen Elizabeth I in *Roberto Devereux*, the role which she believed to represent her greatest artistic achievement. Recalling this history some forty years later, the Metropolitan Opera opined, "Beverly Sills confirmed her status as prima donna assoluta when she sang all three of Donizetti's Tudor queens . . . in a single season."[1] Sills also went on to record all three roles and remains one of only a handful of sopranos to do so.

Throughout most of the twentieth century, high-status individuals brandished cultural capital through their almost "exclusive involvement with classical music and 'high' cultural forms uncontaminated by mass culture" (Hubbs 2014, 24). Sills's appearances in popular mass media and her non-elite fandom elicited scorn from high-status individuals and those with upward aspirations. Her popularity beyond the hallowed halls of the opera house was, for some, reason enough to disparage Sills and especially her fans. The thinking went something like this: If average people appreciated her singing, it must be of low quality. Surely, the uninitiated could not appreciate great art. Following her rise to stardom in the mid-1960s, and even now as her artistic legacy continues to be debated, Sills has been targeted by gate-keeping elitists, such as Bing, in retribution for her down-to-earth, often cheery, sometimes imposing, and always Brooklynese manner. Unsurprisingly, these qualities were precisely what drew a broad range of people to her and her singing, many of whom might otherwise never have known opera.

Sills in the Mainstream Media

A brief look at how Sills became a familiar figure in the American media landscape is necessary. Sills was already a widely recognized figure in American popular culture when she made her Metropolitan Opera debut in April 1975. In the days following the event, the music critic for the *Los Angeles Times*, Martin Bernheimer, commented: "It was impossible, last week, to pick up any publication other than the telephone book and not read about Beverly Sills."[2] In fact, at the time, her image appeared on the cover of the San Diego phonebook (Figure 6.2).

The height of Sills's singing career, from the mid-1960s to 1980, came at what was the twilight for opera and the "high arts" in the American mass media. It was not uncommon in the 1960s and 1970s for opera stars to make guest appearances on talk shows, although none appeared as often as Sills.

Figure 6.2. Beverly Sills (center, wearing a drum) in San Diego Opera's production of Donizetti's *The Daughter of the Regiment* on the cover of the October 1974 San Diego telephone book.

Every major nationally televised talk show of her day invited her on. Her initial appearance came in June 1969 on *The Dick Cavett Show*. Six months later when Cavett moved his show to late night, the opening night lineup featured Beverly Sills, Woody Allen, and Robert Shaw. *Variety* magazine declared that the "opera star, perhaps Cavett's best 'discovery' as a talk show participant, brings great warmth, color, humor and sparkle to a show—along with her spectacular voice" (December 31, 1969).

Johnny Carson invited Sills to appear on *The Tonight Show* fifteen times beginning in 1971. Sills reported that Carson encouraged her to "Show 'em you look like everybody else, that you have kids, a life, that you have to diet" (Sills 1987, 202). He felt she would humanize opera. After being interviewed and chatting with the other guests, she typically sang two pieces: an abbreviated opera aria or art song, and a more popular piece such as a Jerome Kern or Victor Herbert number. Sills even guest hosted *The Tonight Show* twice, once in 1978 and again in 1979. She appeared on *The Mike Douglas Show* at least twelve times and co-hosted for a week in March 1971.[3] Merv Griffin invited her on to his program seven times. She was a featured guest on game shows such as *What's My Line?* In addition to the television appearances, *Newsweek* (April 12, 1969) and *Time Magazine* (November 22, 1971) both did cover stories on Sills; *Life Magazine* did a "Close-Up" piece titled "Unpretentious Prima Donna" (January 17, 1969). Other popular magazines, such as *Reader's Digest*, *Cosmopolitan* (August 1971), *Good Housekeeping* (June 1978), and *McCall's* (June 1977), among others, did Sills feature articles. These various appearances made hers a household name.

Through her appearances in mainstream print and television media, people in the United States who had little or no access to opera, either due to physical distance from performing arts centers or to socioeconomic barriers, gained exposure to it because of Sills. For some, after an introduction to the art through Sills, opera became a meaningful part of their lives. With my research, I have looked to evidence from the lives of Sills fans to dispel the misguided assumption, and often hostile charge, that opera appeals only to urban elite audiences.

Reaching Beyond the Opera House

Sills's fan base extended across socioeconomic borders. She retired from singing in 1980 and had spent the last quarter century of her life in administration, first as the General Director of the New York City Opera, then as the chair of the Lincoln Center board, and finally, as the chair of the Metropolitan Opera board. When she passed away in July 2007, nearly three decades after singing her last note in public, hundreds, if not thousands, of grieving fans posted on various internet sites recollections of their memories of Sills and of the role that she had played in their own lives. As I read through these heartfelt epitaphs (while nursing my own broken heart), I was struck time and again by the broad gamut of socioeconomic backgrounds of the people who reported on the impact she had made in their lives. One of the key sources for online epitaphs was the *Farewell Guestbook* posted on the top Sills website beverlysillsonline.com. Opened for remembrances within hours of her passing, when the site owners closed the *Guestbook* to new entries two and a half months later, it contained over 500 epitaphs. Another key site was the *New York Times City Room Blog*, which garnered just under 200 comments.[4] From these varied voices emerges evidence that Sills was highly successful in transcending class-bound definitions of culture. As one fan wrote, Sills "elevated opera from elitist to a shared experience, where one got to experience the possibility of the human voice as Olympian" (Hoffman 2007).

In his *Farewell Guestbook* entry, Tim Kee remembered watching Beverly Sills on television when he was young.[5] For Kee, who grew up and still lives in a small town in southern Illinois, Beverly Sills "WAS opera." Shortly before her death, he saw her guest appearance on *The View*. Seeing her again "brought back so many memories . . . She is that old friend who melted the years away." I wrote to him directly using the email address that originally accompanied his entry and asked him to further elaborate. He replied:

> We were definitely not "Opera" people. But Beverly was not typical. She was able to laugh at herself and have fun. One thinks of opera divas as high class. Beverly was able to appeal to everyone. . . I remember the shows that Beverly did with Carol Burnett. . . It was a rarity to see someone from the field of opera appear in slapstick comedic shows, but Beverly did. It was the fun of seeing someone from such a lofty place in society come down to the level of us, the common folk. THAT is what I was feeling when she passed. Beverly Sills made the opera accessible to everyone . . . It was for the "stuffed shirts" until she brought it into my family's blue collar household. . . . When she passed it was like losing a piece of my childhood that I really didn't realize was so important to me until it was taken away. (Email, July 28, 2009)

These sentiments were shared by Martha Campbell of Austin, Texas, in her *Farewell Guestbook* entry: "She will always be one of my heroes. As a girl growing up in the backwater, blue collar town of Beaumont, Texas, I was able to find a love [f]or Opera through her beautiful voice, and human warmth. I somehow felt I knew her, and I loved her."

Her earthiness was commented on in no less than thirteen *Farewell Guestbook* entries. Several contributors noted how Sills was responsible for their own appreciation of opera. Her approachability was key in drawing people to her and to her art as Julie Riddle of Woodland Hills, California, commented:

> Beverly Sills literally gave Opera to a generation of rock and roll babies! She did it through her willingness to be silly and charming with [*Sills and*] *Burnett at the Met*. She visited *Sesame Street* and the Muppets. She had the genius to run English translations for her audiences. . . . above all, she was the first Opera star to be, well, "one of US." Down to earth, and from the Heavens at the same time. . . For my 40-something generation, she was and always will be OPERA.

It is true that Sills made opera more approachable to the general public through her decision as General Director of the New York City Opera in 1983 to introduce simultaneous English translations that ran as supertitles on a video screen above the proscenium—an innovation that later became standard practice in opera houses around the world. The importance of Sills's many appearances on popular television shows, with her down-to-earth relatability, was further commented on by a contributor who self-identified as PMD from Philadelphia:

> I grew up watching Ms. Sills on the TV. She was one of the first opera stars to influence my love of the art. She brought this art form to people who either did not have the financial means to go to an opera house or would never think of going to an opera house in the first place. She made opera accessible to all not only because of her great artistry, but also because she was not what many people would stereotype as a "diva." She was the people's "diva." . . . human, funny, down to earth and made in America.

The Consequences of Being Popular

Sills suffered consequences for her approachability and for attracting admirers from varied backgrounds. Writings published after her passing suggest that her broad popularity and accessibility continue to threaten her standing as a legitimate bearer of the operatic tradition. The announcement by the New York Public Library for the Performing Arts in fall 2009, reporting that it had purchased Sills's personal scores at her estate sale, which was held in New York City on October 7, 2009, unwittingly hinted at this sentiment as it represented her scores as evidence that, despite her broad appeal, she was once a serious, dedicated opera singer:

In numerous interviews, talk shows, and autobiographies, Sills revealed herself as a cheerful and ebullient personality. But her scores reveal a different side of her. They show that she was a hard-working and dedicated performer. A number of her scores are marked (some in great detail), indicating her great commitment to singing with a striking attention to detail. (Kosovsky 2009)

Further evidence is found in Ira Siff's *Opera News* article "Pentimento," with its reference to the traces of an earlier painting hidden beneath layers of paint on a canvas. As Siff observed, Beverly Sills's vast accomplishments, including the administrative offices she held and her ubiquitous presence on television, "threaten[ed] to bury her greatest accomplishment, and the one that brought her all the others—her singing" (2007, 30). Siff is positive and sincere in his effort to peel back the layers of history, which obscured Sills's artistic legacy for some.

An obituary published in the British magazine *Opera* by music critic Peter G. Davis, a long-standing Sills adversary, was particularly noteworthy in its mean-spirited recounting of her popular appeal (2007). Davis's essay is largely a repetition of similarly worded attacks he peppered throughout his writings over more than three decades. In his essay "Beverly Sills—Media Heroine or Genuine Superstar?" published in the *New York Times*, Davis attributed Sills's fame among "people who have never set foot inside an opera house" to three elements: "Sills herself, through her talent and tenacity; her fans, by their loyalty and blind devotion; and the media, stimulated by a Johnny-come-lately eagerness to exploit a drama-laden success story regardless of the musical facts" (1975). Sills's fame both inside and outside of the opera house peeved Davis, who designated her a "self-absorbed media heroine" (1985, 79), a "calculating media darling" (1997, 496), and a "media creature named Supersills" (2000). Reflecting on Sills's career, Davis opined that it became difficult "to recall that once upon a time she was a great singer and a magical stage presence. She lost it all much too soon, in part because unwise repertory choices overtaxed her voice, but also because she decided that being a media heroine was more important than serving music as a singer" (1987, 94).

Davis also habitually demeaned her fans (1975, 1976, 1997, 2007) out of what seems to have been his frustration that "[e]ven as her vocal powers waned . . . Sills's fame and influential position in America continued undiminished" (1997, 496). In a brief review of Sills's recording of Bellini's *I Capuleti e i Montecchi*, which was recorded relatively late in her career, he takes a swipe at her fans: "Fans of this soprano have never overly concerned themselves with the current shredded state of her vocal equipment, and apparently remain contented with what's left: a shrewd dramatic presence and a keen musical sensibility" (1976). Davis's disparagement of fans was not reserved for Sills fans alone. In reviewing Renée Fleming's CD *Homage: The Age of the Diva*, he writes, "Sometimes Fleming does have a fresh idea, but too often it simply misfires—the almost comically extended climax of Tosca's prayer, for instance, or her mannered dissection of Leonora's first aria from *Il Trovatore*—though the voice is mostly gorgeous and the breath control astonishing, and that will be enough for the fans" (Davis 2006). That said, after Davis's death, his obituary, published in the *New York Times* on February 19, 2021, noted that he had regularly singled out Sills, along with the composer Philip Glass, as targets of his harshest criticisms (Risen 2021).

Postings to the opera blog Parterre Box surrounding the compact disc release in 2009 of Sills's 1973 recording of Bellini's opera *Norma* laid bare this long-standing and still operative bias against Sills fans, which, in this case, was clearly shaded with classist disparagement. Before sharing some of the details of the Parterre discussion, it is vital to contextualize *Norma*'s place in the world of opera devotion. It is fair to say that opera aficionados not infrequently fall into two camps—those that appreciate the singer-centered repertoire, such as bel canto works that allow for singer interpolation, and those that hold composer-centered opera in the highest regard (i.e., works in which singers are forbidden from adding ornamentation or cadenza of any type). For the latter camp, "masterpieces" are not for tampering. Wagner stands at the apex of the composer-centered world. His works demand singers with large, loud voices and tremendous physical stamina. In contrast, singers of bel canto works tend to have lighter voices and remarkable vocal agility. Before Maria Callas (1923–1977) launched the bel canto revival in the 1950s with her dramatic stage performances, these Italian operas dating from the early 1800s through roughly the 1850s were broadly viewed as insubstantial vehicles staged primarily to showcase songbird-like singers. The opera *Norma*, though a work from the bel canto repertoire (with its emphasis on smooth vocal production, flexibility, and light tone in the higher register), demands a similar degree of stamina from the title role soprano as does a Wagnerian work. The great Wagnerian soprano Lilli Lehmann (1884–1929) is said to have described the role of Norma as "more difficult than all three Brünnhildes of Wagner's *Ring* combined, a sentiment echoed 80 years later" by Maria Callas (Ardoin 1979). As Koestenbaum noted, "The role of Norma is surpassingly difficult. Sopranos assume Norma as divine mantle, maybe rashly, late in their careers" (1993, 213). The opera's most famous aria, "Casta Diva," is "the would-be Norma's test, an ascension into brightness which might melt her wings." Listeners "treat her prayer as itself another pretext for criticism and condemnation—another place where the diva might go wrong and justify our wrath" (ibid.).

Even the most ardent Sills lovers may concede that Sills's light coloratura soprano voice was perhaps not best suited to *Norma*. Robert Levine offered a well-balanced, though colorful, review of the CD release: Sills "offers some effortful singing and there's an unwelcome beat in her voice under stress, but she sings the role with her customary pathos and intelligence, and with spectacular fioratura (and some difficult embellishments to the vocal line), and frankly, few sopranos ever could sound as sad as Sills. Her voice is a bit small for the part, but compared to some of the hideous European sopranos singing the role today, she's Callas, Caballé, and herself rolled into one" (R. Levine n.d.).

Discussion on the Parterre Box blog of the upcoming CD release of Sills's *Norma* slipped into a thread posted on July 19, 2009, which centered on Renée Fleming's upcoming performance of Rossini's *Armida* at the Metropolitan Opera (La Cieca 2009a). It continued days later when the blog's hostess, La Cieca (a.k.a., James Jordan, a music critic in the New York area), posted their review of the CD (La Cieca 2009b). User **scifisci** ignited the uproar innocently enough when he aimed to poll users' opinions on the forthcoming CD, saying, "I am inclined to get it despite the inappropriateness of the role, simply because she sang many roles that were inappropriate for her very, very well i.e., the tudor queens" (July 20, 2009).[6] Following a few speculative comments, **Sanford** wrote in with the following: "Well, there are two ways to look at the Sills Norma. Either it doesn't stand comparison to Callas and the other greats who recorded it, or it stands head and shoulders above Trebs [Anna Netrebko, one of the world's current reigning sopranos] and other singers who have no business singing it. I prefer to hear the glass as half full" (July 20, 2009). The conversation took a dark turn when **marshiemarkII**, an unwavering Sills hater and soprano Hildegard Behrens's staunchest supporter, chimed in with a long and stingingly critical comment in which he declared Sills's *Norma* LP release "monstruous" and "possibly the worst record ever made, bar-none! That thin, wiry, shrill sound attempting Maria's, yes Maria Callas' greatest role, and with Caballe and Sutherland singing it contemporaneously!. One thing about Sills is she had balls, that much is certainly true, as she proved amply in her latter years" (July 21, 2009).

Further on in the discussion, which by this point had become quite heated, **marshiemarkII** turned his scorn toward Sills's defenders, taking up the "masterpiece" defense:

It is really astonishing how queens can be so irrational in defending their divas to the point of stooping to this tired "oh Norma is not that great shakes anyway" to justify her desecration of one of the summits, the top of Mount Everest of opera. What such an attitude ends up implying is that the singer you are defending really has NO artistic integrity, because otherwise why try to do it, if you do not really even believe in it?. The justification makes one really HATE the offender in question even more then. It was not just human frailty that caused the substandard performance, but rather a deliberate attempt to desecrate a masterpiece you hate, because you cannot really do justice to it in the first place. Norma's greatness as at the top of the bel canto dramatic repertoire is not open to question or discussion. IT SIMPLY IS. . . (July 22, 2009)

Into this raucous debate, **Graciella Scusi** hurled an undeniably classist slur at Sills's supporters: "I think the rather strong and passionate opinions here were triggered by a gaggle of *Beverly Sillsbillies*, some of whom very likely never heard her in her prime, making elevated and ludicrous comparisons" (July 22, 2009, emphasis added). **Graciella Scusi**'s slur was a clear reference to the 1960s sitcom *The Beverly Hillbillies*, "in which a family of dirt-poor Ozark mountaineers move to Beverly Hills after discovering an oil gusher on their land: sitting pretty in the world of perpetual sunshine, wealth, and glamour, they never lose their simple, trusting ways or their taste for moonshine and fresh-killed squirrel" (Hubbs 2014, 17). This newly coined term delighted **marshiemarkII**, who piped in with: "Bravissima Graciella, a true lady speaking some sense. I recall you trashed my diva once, but even then I liked you because of your well-informed opinions, this one is a classic" (July 22, 2009).

A few days later when a scuffle broke out over misspellings in La Cieca's review of the *Norma* CD, **marshiemarkII** came to the blog mistress's defense. **MarshiemarkII**'s comment is filled with classist scorn as he takes up the slur coined three days earlier by **Graciella Scusi**. "For such an impossibly pedantic twit, you might as well get your Italian right, Madame Cieca, as well as I, in an earlier post had it right, you are WRONG! . . . if you do not even know the italian words you are critcizing, then you really deserve oprobium for your pretentions above your station……Who gives a shit about an exclamation point!!!! *Typical SillsBilly!!!!!!!*" (July 25, 2009, emphasis added).

The Sacralization of Culture Problem

The contempt of Peter G. Davis, **marshiemarkII**, and others for Sills's popularity with listeners who might never have set foot in an opera house, if not for her, resonates with the ideals of the "sacralization of Culture," which began to take hold in mid-nineteenth-century America (and elsewhere). The result of the sacralization project was that average, non-elite citizens were eventually distanced from what we now term "classical" music, serious drama (such as Shakespeare), and other fine arts.[7] Turn of the century critic W. J. Henderson of the *New York Times* voiced the sacralization ideal well when he wrote that opera was "too important, too exalted an art form to present itself to an uninformed, eclectic audience, many of whom cared more for the performers than the art being performed" (quoted in L. Levine 1988, 103).[8]

Tied up with sacralization was the ascendency of the concept of the "work" of art—the notion that performers are mere servants to composers' intentions and their musical masterpieces. This idea resonates well with Davis's criticism that Sills failed in her role as a servant to music when she allowed herself to become a "media heroine" (1987, 94). In her study of opera in London between 1780 and 1880, Jennifer Hall-Witt traces how there was a significant shift over this period from opera being viewed as event-oriented to work-oriented. The event-oriented approach took the "singers as more important than the composer, seeing the arias as the most important feature of the opera" (Hall-Witt 2007, 44). Musicologist Martha Feldman points out that according to the traditional eighteenth-century view, "the very identity of an opera rested on performers and performative occasions," not on the composer's work, as later became the case (Feldman 1995, 470). Singers generally held the greatest power and commanded the largest salaries in opera's creative arena. Their singing, which included a good deal of improvisation, "could weave magic spells on distracted audiences, reflexively intertwining the arts of 'cantare' and 'incantare,' singing and enchanting" (ibid., 469). Reformists and critics sought to replace this dynamic, event-oriented perspective with a work-oriented view by diminishing the singers' creative input, which, in turn, bolstered the composers' authority. The idea was that performers and the audience must "revere the music, drama, and the composer's creative genius" (Hall-Witt 2007, 10). This ideology also took hold in the United States. For instance, Boston critic John Sullivan Dwight, who was active in the mid- to late 1800s, asserted that art should remain spiritual and pure, and ideally "never becomes secondary to the performer or to the audience" (quoted in L. Levine 1988, 120). Dwight went so far as to write "it would be better if the performer were invisible" (quoted in L. Levine 1988, 121).

Echoes of this attitude still ring today and were certainly in full force at the height of Sills's popularity. Part and parcel of this sentiment is an unmistakable element of fan bashing because fans are typically more invested in the performance than the work. That is, the fans of singers are inclined to take the work as a vehicle for the performance, not as an unchanging monument. Dance critic Alan M. Kriegsman's review of Sills's *Lucia* performance from the Wolf Trap Opera Company in 1971 provides an example of how fans are subject to ridicule due to their taking an event-oriented rather than a work-oriented attitude. He found the evening's performance of *Lucia di Lammermoor* unremarkable, certainly not "memorable"; but he noted that his "was not at all the sentiment of the overflow crowd, which found cause for unbridled jubilation. They's come to hear Beverly Sills do her stuff, and they lapped it up, though from the way the show stopped at her entrance, one had the feeling the fans were so primed for cheers it didn't matter much how Sills sang" (*Washington Post*, July 23, 1971). Kriegsman's use of the word "They's" smacks of a classist attack with the implication being, of course, that Sills fans are uneducated: unversed in proper English.

This recalls for me the time when I was invited to join a panel titled "Thinking through Performance: Operatic Production since 1960" at the 2011 annual meeting of the American Musicological Society. I was the sole ethnomusicologist on the panel, where my singer-centered ethnographic approach to Sills's performance turned out to be most unwelcome. My presentation was a detailed reconstruction of aspects of Sills's debut of Donizetti's *Anna Bolena*, one of the many operas for which we have no video record of her performance in the role. My goal was to understand what she did and to know how her audience reacted. My focus was entirely on her performance and its real-time reception. I used her annotated personal score, photographs, a pirated recording of the performance, which included the sounds of her audience's reaction, including verbal comments, and interviews with audience members who still recalled her characterization of Bolena as my guides. As soon as I finished my presentation, Philip Gossett (1941–2017), the musicological authority on bel canto source materials, rushed to be the first to pose a question. Gossett's primary aim was to lodge a searing criticism of Sills. He said, "What *you* need to understand is that Beverly Sills would destroy any opera to gain applause." With this, he put the work above its performance and denigrated the performer/audience relationship. I later understood that Gossett and Sills had tangled in the past, or at least that is what he claimed. With her long gone, he was still settling scores, in this case, by belittling her rapport with her audience.

The musicological literature on opera is not kind to fans, who are often more invested in performance than in the details of "the work." Historical musicologists have, on the whole, either ignored or denigrated opera fans and the relationships that form between performers and their listeners, either on stage or off. It is well known, for example, that gay men number significantly among opera's most fervent enthusiasts.[9] Carolyn Abbate's description of the "cults" surrounding famous singers as comprising "fans who may worship wardrobes as passionately as they do musical virtuosity" (2001, 50) is not only dismissive, but also carries a fairly unveiled homophobic tone. Abbate's self-conscious distancing from fandom, performance, and the work of individual singers fundamentally impacts her work. In her book *In Search of Opera*, she largely avoids discussion of specific singers or performances, even while admitting that their absence "may well seem a great irony, even a fatal defect" (ibid., xii). Following in the late nineteenth-century tradition, she keeps her focus on composers and their works rather than performance.

The tensions between Gossett and Sills stemmed from around the time of her Metropolitan Opera debut. Gossett gave a lecture at the New York Public Library in which he critiqued the edition of Rossini's *L'assedio di Corinto* (*The Siege of Corinth*), the vehicle for her debut. Conductor Thomas Schippers had put together a highly idiosyncratic performing edition that drew on three different Rossini operas: *Maometto II* (premiered in Naples in 1820), *Le Siège de Corinthe* (Rossini's earliest French opera, written in 1826), and *L'assedio di Corinto* (an Italian translation of *Le Siège de Corinthe*) (Gossett 2006, 119–20). Schippers drew most of his materials from the florid Naples work and about 20 percent from the more austere French opera (ibid.). The "ludicrous result," to borrow Gossett's words, was a score and libretto that were inconsistent in style and enormous in size (ibid., 121). With this performing edition, Schippers had sought to strike a balance between honoring the composer's intentions and creating a vehicle that allowed singers interpretive freedom. For Gossett, the Schippers's edition was generated following the principle that "an opera is an entertainment and can be freely manipulated as long as the result is a good show" (ibid., 122). From his comment on my presentation, it was clear that he strongly disapproved of this approach. Gossett reports in his book *Divas and Scholars* that for his "pains" in critiquing the work during his New York Public Library lecture, he "earned this barb from Sills: 'I think that some so-called musicologists are like men who talk constantly of sex and never do anything about it'" (2006, 121). Gossett cited, wittingly or not, the exact wording of Sills's "barb" as it was reported by historian Gary Wills in an article Wills published on May 1, 1975, in the *New York Review of Books*. However, according to Wills, Sills made this comment in reference to Peter G. Davis (who had also harshly criticized the Schippers's edition). One can only speculate as to why three decades later Gossett would claim that he was the target of Sills's scorn.

Conclusion

In an adept yet concise overview of Sills's singing career written for *The New Yorker* on the occasion of her Farewell Gala in 1980, music critic Andrew Porter cautioned that in evaluating her legacy, Sills's future biographer "must weigh the role of the modern 'media,'" with its ability "to inflate the popular reputation of, say, a Pavarotti out of all proportion to his artistry." Porter went on to say that he did not believe that the publicity, such as the *Newsweek* and *Time* covers, "harmed Sills's artistry. She is too scrupulous a musician." He suggested that her prevalence in the media might "account for a carping note found in many of her reviews: a corrective to unthinking, 'unhearing' popular adulation" (Porter 1980, 179).

Through her crossing of the highbrow/popular cultural divide, Sills inspired listeners who might never have had the chance or inclination to explore new worlds of artistic appreciation and musical engagement. As the sacralization of Culture ideal—a legacy of the nineteenth century—still holds currency, Sills's broad stardom continues to make her the target of elitist scorn.

Notes

Portions of this chapter are taken from *The Magic of Beverly Sills* (Guy 2015). Copyright 2015 by the Board of Trustees of the University of Illinois. Used with permission of the University of Illinois Press.

1. https://www.metopera.org/user-information/nightly-met-opera-streams/articles/queen-for-a-season/. Accessed May 16, 2022.

2. The quote appeared on a press release from Edgar Vincent-Cynthia Robbins Associates, Public Relations Personal Representation.

3. Many thanks are due to Roy C. Dicks, owner of the Beverlysillsonline.com site, for combing through various sources in establishing this figure.

4. Sills's admirers shared their thoughts on other social media sites, including in YouTube comments and in the comment sections for articles reporting her death. For example, fifty-one statements were posted in the comment section for an MSNBC story titled "Opera Legend Beverly Sills Has Died at 78: Brooklyn-Born Diva was Global Icon of Can-do American Culture." http://boards.msn.com/MSNBCboards/thread.aspx?boardid=78. Accessed July 12, 2009.

5. I have retained the names of contributors to the *Farewell Guestbook* and *New York Times City Room Blog* for three reasons. First, at the time of writing, both are still available online. Contributors' identities are, therefore, easily available if a reader chooses to crosscheck. Second, I believe that the epitaph writers should be recognized for their thoughtful contributions. Third, these contributors posted their epitaphs in a public forum. As Joseph B. Walther argued, "It is important to recognize that

any person who uses publicly available communication systems on the Internet must be aware that these systems are, at their foundation and by definition, mechanisms for the storage, transmission, and retrieval of comments (2002, 207, emphasis in the original). Therefore, retrieving epitaphs from these sources is no different from using "newspapers stories, broadcasts, the Congressional Record, or other archival data, for research" (ibid., 206–7). I apply this perspective to my extensive quoting of posts made to the Parterre.com blog.

6. I have chosen not to correct the spellings or punctuations of the original posts, nor have I signaled errors by adding [*sic*].

7. For a vivid description of the ways in which opera was woven into the lives of a broad segment of the population in early and mid-nineteenth century America, see L. Levine 1988, especially pages 85–146.

8. Katherine K. Preston, in her work on opera in late nineteenth-century America, finds that itinerant troupes performing opera in English translation attracted large audiences in much of the country (especially beyond the East Coast where the shadow of "aristocratic" institutions such as the Metropolitan Opera loomed large). Through their touring, opera continued to have a place on the American popular stage well after foreign-language opera ascended to elite status in the 1870s and 1880s (Preston 2003, 350).

9. Perry Brass, in his insightful yet tragic blog post "Did AIDS Kill New York City Opera?," speculates that the AIDS epidemic, which ripped through New York City's gay community in the 1980s, essentially eliminated a good number of devoted opera supporters and left the New York City Opera without a potentially substantial donor base. Not insignificantly, the person on whom Brass focuses in his essay, Richard Gold, was enamored with Beverly Sills; Sills attended Gold's funeral, as she did for many associates and colleagues who died of AIDS (Brass 2016).

References

Abbate, Carolyn. 2001. *In Search of Opera*. Princeton, NJ: Princeton University Press.
Ames, Katrine. 2007. "Remembering Beverly Sills." *Newsweek*, July 2. https://www.newsweek.com/remembering-beverly-sills-104479.
Ardoin, John. 1979. "Why They All Want to Sing 'Norma.'" *New York Times*, March 11.
Bing, Rudolph. 1972. *5000 Nights at the Opera: The Memoirs of Sir Rudolph Bing*. Garden City, NY: Doubleday.
Brass, Perry. 2016. "Did AIDS Kill New York City Opera?" *HuffPost: The Blog*, September 30. https://www.huffpost.com/entry/did-aids-kill-new-york-city-opera_b_4003493. Accessed October 13, 2022.
Davis, Peter G. 1975. "Beverly Sills: Media Heroine or Genuine Superstar?" *New York Times*, October 12.
———. 1976. "Recordings Review." *New York Times*, June 20.
———. 1985. "Prime Time." *New York Magazine*, April 1, 79–80.
———. 1987. "Settling Old Scores." *New York Magazine*, June 1, 93–94.

———. 1997. *The American Opera Singer*. New York, NY: Bantam Doubleday.
———. 2000. "Drama Queen." *New York Magazine*, September 25.
———. 2006. "Diva Emergency." *New York Magazine*, November 6. https://nymag.com/arts/classicaldance/classical/reviews/23483/. Accessed October 19, 2022.
———. 2007. "Obituaries: Beverly Sills." *Opera* (September): 1064–66.
Feldman, Martha. 1995. "Magic Mirrors and the Seria Stage: Thoughts toward a Ritual View." *Journal of the American Musicological Society* 48(3): 423–84.
Gossett, Philip. 2006. *Divas and Scholars: Performing Italian Opera*. Chicago: University of Chicago Press.
Guy, Nancy. 2015. *The Magic of Beverly Sills*. Urbana: University of Illinois Press.
Hall-Witt, Jennifer. 2007. *Fashionable Acts: Opera and Elite Culture in London, 1780–1880*. Durham: University of New Hampshire Press.
Hoffman, Henry. 2007. "Remembering Beverly Sills." *City Room Blog*, *New York Times*, July 3. http://cityroom.blogs.nytimes.com/2007/07/03/remembering-beverly-sills/.
Hubbs, Nadine. 2014. *Rednecks, Queers, and Country Music*. Berkeley: University of California Press.
Koestenbaum, Wayne. 1993. *The Queen's Throat: Opera, Homosexuality, and the Mystery of Desire*. New York: Poseidon Press.
Kosovsky, Bob. 2009. "The Scores of Beverly Sills Come to the Music Division." *Music Division* (blog), New York Public Library, October 27. https://www.nypl.org/blog/2009/10/27/scores-beverly-sills-come-music-division.
La Cieca [James Jorden]. 2009a. "Island Magic." Parterre.com (blog), July 19. https://parterre.com/2009/07/19/island-magic/. First accessed July 24, 2009. Last accessed September 25, 2020.
———. 2009b. "Norma, Is That You?" Parterre.com (blog), July 24. https://parterre.com/2009/07/24/norma-is-that-you/. First accessed July 24, 2009. Last accessed September 25, 2020.
Levine, Lawrence W. 1988. *Highbrow/Lowbrow: The Emergence of Cultural Hierarchy in America*. Cambridge, MA: Harvard University Press.
Levine, Robert. n.d. "Bellini: Norma/Sills, Verrett." www.classicstoday.com. https://www.classicstoday.com/review/review-15010/. Accessed March 22, 2021.
Porter, Andrew. 1980. "Musical Events: Beverly!" *New Yorker*, November 10, 177–85.
Preston, Katherine K. 2003. "Between the Cracks: The Performance of English-Language Opera in the Late Nineteenth-Century America." *American Music* 21(3): 349–74.
Risen, Clay. 2021. "Peter G. Davis, Music Critic of Wide Knowledge and Wit, Dies at 84." *New York Times*, February 19.
Saal, Hubert. 1966. "Going for Baroque." *Newsweek*, October 10, 100.
Siff, Ira. 2007. "Pentimento." *Opera News*, October, 30–33.
Sills, Beverly, with Lawrence Linderman. 1987. *Beverly: An Autobiography*. New York: Bantam Books.

Walther, Joseph B. 2002. "Research Ethics in Internet-enabled Research: Human Subjects Issues and Methodological Myopia." *Ethics and Information Technology* 4: 205–16.

Wills, Garry. 1975. "Gorgeous Sills." *The New York Review of Books*, May 1.

Multimedia Playlist

Beverly Sills: Made in America. Deutsche Grammophon. 1 videodisc (84 min.). 2006.

Beverly Sills: The Great Recordings. Deutsche Grammophon (B00002469-02). 2 compact discs, compilation released in 2004.

Guy, Nancy. 2015. *The Magic of Beverly Sills*. Urbana: University of Illinois Press.

Manon. Full-length opera by Massenet. Deutsche Grammophon (B00002470-02). Sills as Manon in one of her signature roles. 3 compact discs. Originally released on ABC records in 1972.

Signature Arias:
"Willow Song" from Moore's opera *Ballad of Baby Doe*
"Se pietà di me non senti" from Handel's opera *Julius Caesar* (*Giulio Cesare*)
"Da tempeste il legno infranto" from Handel's opera *Julius Caesar* (Giulio Cesare)

La Traviata. Video Artists International. VAI DVD 4207. Sills as Violetta. 1 videodisc (135 min.). Full-length opera originally recorded in 1976, released on DVD in 2001.

PART III

Multiplicities of Representations

Introduction
Ruth Hellier

Throughout my childhood, growing up in Britain in the 1960s and '70s, singing and listening to singing were woven into my everyday life. I reveled in experiencing multiple vocal styles, playing with vocalities and being aware of the opportunities and constraints of how and what to sing. As a professional creative artist, singer, actor, teacher, and researcher since 1983, I have explored numerous performative possibilities of voices and bodies. I am particularly interested in structures of power, diversity, equity, and inclusion, engaging performance studies and feminist studies approaches. With my performance research in Mexico in the 1990s, my listening and performing were opened to other vocal worlds. These were expanded further in 2008 through my collaborations with a wonderful singer from California in the United States: Ixya Herrera. Aware of the opportunities that singing offers to generate multiplicities of representations, Ixya designs her vocal and embodied styles to create emotional connections with many audiences (Hellier 2013a).

Singing, singers, and songs are not singular and fixed, but always in processes of transformation, with seemingly endless opportunities to be re-created and re-imagined. Singing offers so many possibilities as a composite performance complex. A singing voice and all elements of performativity are immensely adaptable. Vocal style, repertoire, language, embodied choreographies, costumes, and accompanying musical formations are all open for decision-making. A singer can therefore perform multiplicities of representations. An individual singer is able to stand in for and connect with a collective. A singer can be a representative of and for groups and communities of peoples, be they nations, races, genders, ages, or linguistic groups. One singer can represent an ideological or political perspective and create connections of patriotism, of ethnic allegiances, and of allyship.

Significantly, a singer can re-create their singing performance for different listeners and different audiences in different contexts. A singer can adapt to shifting configurations of history, of borders, of politics, of language, of gender, and of memory, altering their singing performance choices to connect with other listeners. So, an individual singer can transform even as intricate political histories alter different forms of allegiances, inclusion, and exclusion. They are performing through multivocality, using their singing voice to engage their multiplicity in relation to age, genre, language, religion, and location (Hellier 2013b). So, multivocality indicates multiplicity and complexity, crossings and inter-connections. I introduced the idea of multivocality in my volume on *Women Singers in Global Contexts* to foreground notions of intersectionality, individuality, and multiplicity. In other words, each singer is a multiplicity of identities, actions, feelings, and vocalities (ibid.). Each singer embodies multiple performative identities.

So, making decisions about how to sing, what to sing, where to sing (and more) is a multifaceted and ongoing process. These choices are not innate or spontaneous but the result of a deep awareness of specific listeners and audiences. A singer and their collaborators create performances by being fully aware of the constraints and opportunities available to them in any specific context. They have the power to control each performative element within evolving power dynamics. They can play with, against, and through stereotypes, shaping and crafting the ways in which they represent ideas of identity, including nation, ethnicity, gender, and race. And they seek to generate emotional engagement, for "We listen to and absorb music, not just intellectually, but corporeally" (Brown and Edell 2016, 56).

The idea of a singer performing multiplicities of representations connects with the idea of the positionality of listening. In other words, listening to singing is always situated and specific—in a specific place, political context, or historic moment, for example. Listening positionality is both personal and collective. And, significantly, listening is guided by positionality as an intersection (Robinson 2020, 37–38). In other words, a listener listens with their own multiple identities which are layered and complex.

Cases of multiplicities of representations through singing and song are threaded through the three chapters that follow. The authors discuss individual singers whose careers and performances have encompassed multiplicities of representations. Carol Silverman portrays the life of pioneering Macedonian Romani singer Esma Redžepova (1944–2016), whose career spanned over sixty years. She performed in an immensely complex and everchanging area of Europe, dealing with histories of exclusion, transcontinental connections and lineages. Esma deliberately made decisions to embrace multiplicities of representations by performing varied repertoires, languages, and choreographies. The Taiwanese singer Teresa Teng (1953–1995) is the focus of Michael K. Bourdaghs's narrative. Although not from Japan, Teng was able to have immense value as a symbol for specific Japanese audiences by re-inventing her singing personae in Japan. Carol A. Muller describes experiences of five Black South African women singers between 1950 and the present, with careers during and after apartheid, in South Africa and New York. Each singer engages with multiple languages and genres, demonstrating opportunities for singing in changing political contexts and with new technologies.

What is evident from these chapters is that singers do not generate a single history, but rather create unfolding narratives for multiple listeners that are complex and often contradictory. Attending to multiplicities of representations avoids the danger of a single story, as Nigerian novelist and poet Chimamanda Ngozi Adichie has described (2009). A song is never simply a song but always an entanglement of changing multiplicities.

References

Adichie, Chimamanda Ngozi. 2009. "The Danger of a Single Story." Global TED talk, October 7. www.youtube.com/watch?v=D9Ihs24Izeg.

Brown, Lyn Mikel, and Dana Edell, with Montgomery Jones, Georgia Luckhurst, and Joneka Percentie. 2016. "'I Love Beyoncé, but I Struggle with Beyoncé': Girl Activists Talk Music and Feminism." In *Voicing Girlhood in Popular Music: Performance, Authority, Authenticity*, eds. Jacqueline C. Warwick and Allison Adrian, 56–74. London and New York: Routledge.

Hellier, Ruth. 2013a. "Ixya Herrera: Gracefully Nurturing 'Mexico' with Song in the U.S.A." In *Women Singers in Global Contexts: Music, Biography, Identity*, ed. Ruth Hellier, 92–111. Urbana: University of Illinois Press.

———. 2013b. "Vocal Herstories: Resonances of Singing, Individuals, and Authors." In *Women Singers in Global Contexts: Music, Biography, Identity*, ed. Ruth Hellier, 1–37. Urbana: University of Illinois Press.

Robinson, Dylan. 2020. *Hungry Listening: Resonant Theory for Indigenous Sound Studies*. Minneapolis: University of Minnesota Press.

CHAPTER 7

Artful Politics of the Voice

"Queen of Romani Music"
Esma Redžepova

CAROL SILVERMAN

One of National Public Radio's 50 Great Voices, Esma Redžepova (1944–2016) is perhaps the most famous Romani singer in the world. She toured internationally for over fifty years, gave more than 10,000 concerts (many for humanitarian causes), received numerous prizes, and recorded hundreds of albums.[1] The legacy of this Macedonian Romani superstar vocalist is intertwined with issues of gender, ethnicity, race, and representation, and my chapter is accordingly informed by an interdisciplinary theoretical framework encompassing performance studies, emotion/affect studies, gender and sexuality studies, and critical Romani studies.[2] Esma's extraordinary success is due to several factors: First, her non-Romani mentor/husband helped her to create a new niche on concert stages. Second, she resisted gender norms dictating that Muslim Romani women should not sing professionally. Third, although her image drew on stereotypes of Romani women as exotic, emotional, and sexual, she was able to recast those stereotypes in a respectable light. Finally, she succeeded in bridging the musical worlds of Roma and non-Roma to attract a transnational Balkan audience. Her songs helped to reconfigure Yugoslav multiculturalist heritage to include Roma, yet Roma continue to occupy a racialized subaltern position in relation to the state. Four years after her death, North Macedonia has neglected her legacy.

I first met Esma Redžepova and her husband, Stevo Teodosievski, on a 1996 tour to New York City and hosted them in my parents' home in the Bronx. I was a guest in Esma's home many times for several weeks, helped arrange four of her tours to the US (1996, 1997, 2004, and 2016), accompanied her on several tours, and conducted many interviews and informal conversations with her, her husband, and her band members. I also facilitated and translated for Esma at many of her singing workshops in the United States. I am a professional Balkan singer who has learned from Esma and many other Balkan and Romani teachers. Since Esma's death, I have continued relationships with several branches of her family in North Macedonia and Germany and with many of her fostered children who are now professional musicians. This chapter draws on some aspects of my earlier work on Romani musicians in the Balkans and the diaspora (Silverman 2003, 2011, 2012, 2019), two biographies (Teodosievski and Redžepova 1984 and Katin 2015), and news media sources.

Professional music has been an important medium of exchange between Roma and non-Roma for centuries, and the musical marketplace has been the site where emotions and images are exchanged. The association of women's voices with authenticity, emotion, and sexuality provides symbolic capital for the marketplace. Esma used her voice, body, and stagings to strategically craft her signature style. Below, I examine the gendered and racialized politics of Romani representation, and then analyze Esma's life history, repertoire choices and sound aesthetics, use of her body via dance and costume, and involvement in politics.

"Gypsy" as "Other"

Linguistic evidence shows that Roma are a diasporic ethnic group that migrated from northwest India to the Balkans by the fourteenth century. Initial curiosity about Roma by Europeans quickly gave way to discrimination, a legacy that has continued until today. Roma were viewed as intruders, probably because of their dark skin, non-European physical features, foreign customs, and association with magic (Petrova 2003). Stereotypes about Roma abound, encompassing the romantic (musical, sexual, artistic) along with the criminal (dangerous). Roma are racialized in these stereotypes, often referred to as "blacks," with connotations of being dirty, untrustworthy, and thieving. Roma inspired fear and were expelled from many European territories. Bounties were paid for their capture and repressive measures included confiscation of property and children, forced labor, branding, and so on. In Romania, Roma were slaves from the fourteenth to the nineteenth centuries. Perhaps the most tragic period in Romani history was the Holocaust, when over 500,000 Roma were murdered.

The communist regimes in Eastern Europe defined Roma as a social problem. They were targeted for integration into the planned economy, forced to give up their traditional occupations, and assigned to the lowest skilled and lowest paid state jobs. Today, European Roma face inferior and segregated housing and education, poor health conditions, and shorter life expectancy. Discrimination is widespread in employment and the legal system, and even educated people routinely express disdain for "Gypsies." Hate speech and racial profiling are common in the media. Perhaps most troubling are the hundreds of incidents of physical violence against Roma perpetrated by ordinary citizens and also by the police.[3] In response to discrimination, a human rights movement has mobilized since 1989 via a strong network of activists and NGOs.

Balkan Roma have been professional musicians for centuries, playing for peasants and urbanites of many classes and ethnicities in cafes and family celebrations, but excluded from elite concert stages. Their professional niche, primarily male and instrumental, required knowledge of the musical repertoire of co-territorial peoples. Roma became multi-musical as well as multi-lingual and developed an openness to innovation. There is neither one worldwide nor one pan-European Romani music. Rather, Roma constitute a rich mosaic of groups that distinguish among themselves musically. Yet their artistry in music does not erase their rejection; they are revered as musicians and reviled as people (Silverman 2012).

The positive yet dangerous coding of Romani otherness hinges on their romanticization by non-Roma as free souls, their association with the arts, especially music, and their proximity to nature and sexuality. As Paloma Gay y Blasco has written: "Gypsies/Roma occupy a central place in the collective imagination of the West. They are objects of both revulsion and fascination and have, through the centuries, been pictured, narrated and 'known' *ad nauseam*" (2008, 297). Using Edward Said's concept, we can claim that Roma are "orientalized."[4] Ken Lee extends Said's argument: "Whilst Orientalism is the discursive construction of the exotic Other *outside* Europe, Gypsylorism is the construction of the exotic Other *within* Europe—Romanies are the Orientals within" (2000, 132). Katie Trumpener emphasizes the association of Roma with an ahistorical, timeless nostalgia: "Nomadic and illiterate, they wander down an endless road, without a social contract or country to bind them, carrying their home with them, crossing borders at will" (1992, 853). At the same time, they are reviled as unreformable liars and rejected from civilization. This contrast expresses the "ideology of Gypsy alterity—feared as deviance, idealized as autonomy" (ibid., 854). Roma, then, serve as one of Europe's quintessential others.

Esma's Early Years

Esma was born in 1943 in Skopje, North Macedonia, to a poor Muslim family. Her father was a disabled bootblack. She remembers experiencing discrimination at a young age: a doctor whose house she cleaned wrongly accused her of stealing; in school, she was sometimes taunted with the slur "Gypsy" (Katin 2015, 103, 101). Esma sang and danced in school productions and in 1957 she won an amateur competition called "The Microphone Is Yours." She feared her parents' wrath for singing in public and hid the prize money in her clothing, but they found out when neighbors congratulated them. Esma explained, "According to our tradition it was a shame to sing publicly" (Interview, May 20, 1996). In fact, Esma's sister had already sullied the family's reputation by refusing an arranged marriage and becoming a singer. Esma also resisted her parents' desire to marry her off in her teens.

As a result of the competition, Esma was brought to the attention of Stevo Teodosievski (1934–1997), an Eastern Orthodox ethnic Macedonian accordionist and folk music arranger who later became her mentor and husband. He was struck by her potential and remarked, "You have some talent, but you really will have to work" (Interview, May 20, 1996). Stevo wanted to take her on as a pupil and train her but Esma's parents refused. Stevo managed to convince them that he would make her into an elite artist for the concert stage, not a cafe singer, if they would postpone marriage arrangements. "When Stevo promised [my father] faithfully that he would help me to become a good and famous singer—not a singer in any old nightclub—when my father had reassured himself that Stevo's intentions were honest, that he would look after me, he finally agreed" (Teodosievski and Redžepova 1984, 95). A few days later, she started to tour.

The stigma of singing in public and traveling with an older man undermined Esma's morality, and her parents faced many challenges. More than once, her father was berated, and he forbade her to return to Stevo, but she defied him. The couple eventually married in 1968. In that era, inter-ethnic marriages were virtually unknown, and thousands came to gawk at their wedding. Meanwhile, they constantly traveled. Esma's first tour was to Bulgaria, then Paris, Australia, and the United States in 1970, in addition to many local tours.

Situating Emotion

Esma's vocal style is characterized by her rich timbre, technical ability in ornamentation, and the sheer power of her voice; but above all, she is known for the emotional quality of her voice, to the point that she even cries while singing. The association of Roma with emotion is historic. In fact, David Malvinni (2004) represented the centrality of emotion in Romani music with an equation: I (improvisation) + V (virtuosity) = E (emotion). Mattijs Van de Port, who observed bars where Roma performed for Serbian patrons, claimed that the "Gypsy" musician unlocks the soul: "For the Serbs, Gypsies also embody a combination that Julia Kristeva (following Freud's discussion of the uncanny) has called 'the disturbingly strange,' the 'otherness' of our 'ourness,' which we do not know how to handle. In other words, Gypsies represent what we are although we are not allowed to be it" (Van de Port 1998, 153–4). He found that through Romani music, Serbian patrons mined emotional states via long and cathartic mimetic enactments. More than just a "safety valve" for pent up emotions, the Gypsy bar gives rein to the emotional imagination (ibid., 205).

Emotions, despite appearing to be innate, universal, and essential, are embedded in specific cultural contexts that are often tied to inequality (Abu-Lughod and Lutz 1990). The anthropologist Michelle Rosaldo points out that "emotions are not things but processes that are best understood with reference to cultural scenarios and associations they evoke" (1984, 141–3). Similarly, Sara Ahmed (2004) argues that emotions are cultural practices, not psychological states. Furthermore, emotions give value through bodies, and emotions have political implications as well: they create "others" by marginalizing some bodies (ibid.). Lila Abu-Lughod and Catherine Lutz claim that "emotional discourses can serve . . . for the relatively powerless as a loci of resistance and idioms of rebellion . . . or even as a means of establishing complementarity with status superiors" (1990, 14–15). For Roma, music has been one of the positively coded arenas in a long history of exclusion. Indeed, Roma have carved out a traditional performance niche from their historical association with emotion.

In Balkan communities, performances are evaluated by patrons for their affective impact. Alexander Markovic notes that "music is closely associated with celebratory culture . . . because music is believed to be inherently emotional. Good musicians are appreciated for their ability to act as catalysts for celebrants' emotional expression through their musical services" (2017, 164). Moreover, many authors have claimed that Romani musicians are particularly recognized as masters of finding a way to reach patrons to transmute their emotions, divine their requests, and furthermore to access their souls (Van de Port 1998, 182). Over and over again in Eastern Europe, we hear of the virtuosic performances of Roma moving people to tears, of the seemingly endless variations in melody, and of the capturing of emotion in music. Proverbs attest that "a wedding without a Gypsy isn't worth anything" (Bulgarian) and "give a Hungarian a glass of water and a Gypsy fiddler and he will become completely drunk" (Hungarian). Musicians delicately refine how to produce these affective experiences that seem "natural" but are actually highly coordinated. Moreover, Romani music performance provides a useful case to examine the "affective turn in ethnomusicology," which, according to Ana Hofman, is related to sensory (emotion) and embodiment more than discourse. "Affect is seen as a potential, a bodily capacity. . . . It is embodied in the automatic reaction manifested in the skin, on the surface of the body and in the heartbeat, but it is still something that goes beyond the body" (Hofman 2015, 36). The embodied and gendered nature of affect is a resource Esma extensively mined.

Gender, Embodiment, Sexuality, Voice

Due to the pioneering work of feminist music scholars, gender has become a primary analytic in understanding musical performance (Hellier 2013; Dunn and Jones 1994; Magowan and Wrazen 2013). In unpacking the intersectional dimensions of Romani performers, we can see that the association of Romani women with unbridled sexuality and emotion has a long history. The "Gypsy seductress" is an iconic figure in literature, folklore, and visual culture (e.g., Carmen and Esmeralda). Domnica Radulescu points out that Gypsy women in the Middle Ages were both feared and admired as entertainers (palm readers, dancers, musicians). Their supposed sexual freedom caused them to be labeled as witches at the same time that their freedom was admired (Radulescu 2008, 195).

Romani women iconically fulfill the fantasies of non-Roma as wild creatures given to their emotions. Romani women stereotypically embody seduction, while men embody violence. Note that sexual prowess is commonly attributed to marginal people of color, often to control and criminalize them (Hancock 2008). Note also that marginalized ethnic groups have little control over how they are depicted. Moreover, Romani performers may strategically embrace stereotypes (re: Gayatri Chakravorty Spivak's concept of "strategic essentialism") to monopolize various musical niches (cf. Spivak 1996, 214; Eide 2016). Labels such as "exotic," "passionate," "genetically talented," and "soulful," for example, are not only found in marketers' advertisements but also defended by some Romani performers such as Esma. Yet she cleverly re-made these stereotypes, thus producing new subjectivities.

The gendered profile of Romani women is located in both the female body and the female voice. As Leslie Dunn and Nancy Jones point out, feminists use voice, as in "giving voice," to refer to empowerment as well as to the "literal audible voice" that has often been silenced (1994, 1). Furthermore, the voice is often associated with subjectivity, emotions, privacy, authenticity, and vulnerability, which in turn are often gendered as female (Hellier 2013, 5). Along with the voice, the female body is an affective tool. "Emotional efficacy resides in the way in which sounds and movements are cognitively and affectively integrated" (Magowan and Wrazen 2013, 4). For Esma, the double association of women and Roma with sexuality was powerful raw material that needed to be reframed.

In contrast to the stereotype, the display of female sexuality among Balkan Roma is actually very regulated. Within Romani communities, female professional singing and dancing are associated with sexuality because the voice and body are displayed for men for remuneration. Historically, this ideology existed among all ethnicities and religions in the Balkans, but today it is strongest among Muslims and Roma (Silverman 2003). Thus, there are very few female professional Romani vocalists. One way to circumvent public disapproval is to marry a musician; one's husband (or father or brother) then serves as the protector of his wife's honor. Indeed, Esma followed this path by marrying Stevo Teodosievski, her mentor.

Breaking Barriers, Pioneering a Niche

Under the banner *Esma—Ansambl Teodosievski* (Esma, Teodosievski's Ensemble), the couple achieved instantaneous success with daring innovations. Esma was the first Balkan Romani musician—male or female—to achieve commercial success in the elite non-Romani world; she was the first openly identified Romani performer to sing for non-Roma in the Romani language while wearing Romani attire and dancing in Romani style; she was the first female Romani artist to record in Yugoslavia; and she was the first Macedonian woman—Romani or non-Romani—to perform on television.

Stevo's strategy was not to allow Esma to perform at cafes and weddings, but only at concerts and for radio and television recordings. In effect, Stevo created a new category of Romani female elite concert artist that didn't have the stigma of a cafe/wedding singer. Singing in the Romani language displayed Esma's pride in her heritage: "It was kind of a shame to sing in Romani in my time; many singers hid the fact that they were Romani. When I came out singing my own songs in Romani, many came out after me" (Interview, July 15, 1997). Describing the prejudicial attitude of Yugoslav music production, Esma remembered that "many singers passed [as other ethnic groups] because there was an embargo on Romani singers. There was discrimination against them as performers. I risked a great deal when I said I was Romani and I want to sing in my own language. . . . I opened the way for Roma, . . . to admit that they are Roma, and not to be ashamed they are Roma" (Interview, May 29, 1997).

Esma and Stevo endured the racism of Macedonian producers. Stevo was repeatedly told: "Take . . . other singers—why a Gypsy?" His colleagues said cruelly, "Stevo, why have you brought this Gypsy to disgrace us?" (Teodosievski and Redžepova 1984, 95). Producers deliberately denied young Esma opportunities. Stevo recalled, "They chased me out of Macedonia because of Esma. . . . They said, 'Why do you play that Romani music? Let it go—you are not Romani'" (Interview, May 20, 1996). The taunts became so stifling that in 1960, Stevo and Esma decided to move to Belgrade, the capital of Yugoslavia, where they would have more opportunities. Esma said, "People . . . were talking too much about us in Skopje, and we had to get out of that environment" (Interview, May 20, 1996). Exclusion was so virulent that Esma's songs were not played on Macedonian radio and television for twenty-five years; Esma bitterly recalled, "Two or three persons had closed the doors of Radio Skopje for us" (Katin 2015, 257). Meanwhile, Esma emerged as a star—she sang for Yugoslav President Tito and visiting heads of state, and Tito took her on diplomatic trips.

Style and Image

Stevo created a specific niche for Esma that emphasized her Romani ethnicity, but also tapped into Yugoslav multiculturalism. The Romani niche resonated with historic tropes of the eternal iconic "Gypsy" entertainer. For example, a 1972 RTV Belgrade review stated that perhaps her songs were "sung by one of her dark-skinned forebears along the reaches of the Indus or the holy river Ganges and carried through the centuries all over this planet, as their eternal heritage of which they are so proud" (quoted in Teodosievski and Redžepova 1984, 141). Another review states, "This music reveals the Gypsy philosophy, the simple philosophy and wisdom close to all colors and tongues" (ibid., 143). And Esma's phrase "I live for singing" was proof that Roma are born only to perform. Stevo and Esma cultivated these stereotypes as long as they were positive, but they also strategized around these limitations.

Reviews during Esma's early years focus on her Romani heritage in stark gendered, racialized, and bodily terms. From sound and gender studies, we affirm that sounds are embodied and music is heard and seen through bodies. Indeed, visual difference has long been used to "other" groups. Critics repeatedly described Esma as dark-skinned, hot-blooded, happy-go-lucky, and genetically talented. Racializing press quotes from the 1960s–1970s include: "She is a Gypsy girl, hot blooded, happy as a bird! For her money means a new hat, a ticket for the movies, a new dress, nothing more" (Teodosievski and Redžepova 1984, 138); "Esma has a lovely dark complexion, it would be a wonderful advertisement for suntan creams and lotion; it has the shade of well-baked bread. She has large, almond shaped eyes, the color of shiny coal, slightly prominent cheekbones and shiny pearly teeth" (ibid., 141).

Rather than rejecting these characterizations, Esma and Stevo crafted a trademark image and staging that made them respectable, for example, through costuming. Esma never wore immodest outfits that revealed skin. Rather, she appeared in *dimije* (wide pantaloons), which linked her to Roma, to other Muslims in the Balkans, and to tradition. Esma further innovated with modern-style headpieces. Esma also cultivated ties to India in the early 1970s when Roma in Macedonia were beginning to develop a sense of their history. Esma and Stevo made their first (uninvited) trip to India in 1969, followed by two invited trips. In 1976, the ensemble drove from Skopje to India by car; and they were crowned "King and Queen of Romani Music" at the First World Festival of Romani Songs and Music.

Stevo and Esma consciously widened their Romani image by tying the ensemble to pan-Yugoslav multiculturalism. The emblematic phrase of Tito's Yugoslavia was "brotherhood and unity" (*bratsvo i edinstvo*) and the ensemble embodied it via repertoire and costuming; for example, for a 1980 album cover (Figure 7.1), Esma dressed in the colors of the Yugoslav flag. Esma performed folk songs from all six Yugoslav republics, dressed in the folk costume of each, and also in various European costumes plus modern styles (Figure 7.2). She further broadened her repertoire with songs of neighboring Balkan countries, and later songs in German, Hebrew, Russian, and Hindi. She toured to countries with significant Yugoslav migrant populations, such as Australia, Austria, Canada, and the United States, and thus became a transnational star. Her appeal to all Yugoslav ethnicities spanned several generations and many continents. On her 2016 US tour, audience members from multiple ethnicities stood in line for hours to bow before her and kiss her hands. Fans from ten to eighty years old rented buses and drove from many hours away to see and hear her live. They called her a "living icon," and she evoked for them strong nostalgia for a multicultural, peaceful Yugoslavia.

In the 1960s, Esma and Stevo refined a performance trademark whereby all the musicians stood up, giving them unprecedented freedom of movement. Typically, they swayed in rhythm, evoking the backup singers in western pop groups of the 1960s. And most daring, Esma danced the characteristic Romani solo *čoček*—an improvised dance usually performed by women that

Figure 7.1. Esma–Ansambl Teodosievski, 1980; Jugoton LSY 61475.

utilizes hand movements, contractions of the abdomen and pelvis, shoulder shakes, movement of isolated body parts, such as hips and head, and small footwork patterns.[5]

Because solo female dance is often interpreted as sexualized, its dynamics are carefully monitored in Romani communities. Although women want to show off their prized skills, they need to delicately negotiate the propriety of the display, such as where and for whom they perform. Some displays are crass and transgressive, such as those performed in bars, whereas others are appropriate, such as those performed for one's family. As mentioned

Figure 7.2. Odžačar, Odžačar, Esma–Ansambl Teodosievski, 1970; Jugoton SY 1690.

earlier, performing *čoček* professionally for strange men would be viewed negatively, and the same is true for singing. But Esma bravely took ownership of this characteristic dance genre and presented it to the larger public as a Romani symbol. She modified the movements to be subtle and playful rather than sexual, and thus made it respectable and part of her version of Romani "authenticity."

Stevo and Esma also emphasized respectability by creating a wholesome family image for Ansambl Teodosievski, with a maturing Esma as a maternal symbol. Stevo established a school where he trained forty-seven mostly Ro-

Figure 7.3. Esma Redzepova–Ansambl Teodosievski, 1970; Jugoton U MC 85.

mani boys, the majority of whom were from disadvantaged homes.[6] All of the members of the ensemble came from Stevo's school. They all received lodging, meals, and clothing free of charge, and their music instruction launched their careers. Esma was their adopted mother and vocal coach. She never had children of her own, but these children still call her "mama." Stevo was a strict teacher; neither Esma nor Stevo believed in talent, but rather in hard work.

Reflecting their "family," Esma's songs became staged performances with the whole group in movement (Figure 7.3). The youngest boys played the *tarabuka* (goblet drum), which had never before been played on a concert stage, as they joyfully danced with Esma. Often, they (and sometimes Esma) were barefoot, evoking both humble poverty and domesticity. Not only did the young boys provide charismatic dramatic interest, but their participation also created a wholesome family image, defusing the sexuality of a Romani woman performing. These scenarios also created intimacy with the audience—a safe window into the "authentic" Romani world.

A 1965 Austrian TV show in which Esma appeared illustrates another innovation of her ensemble: one that bridged the divide not only between East and West but also between tradition and modernity via music, language, and costuming. In the first part of the show, staged in a "village," Esma wears a Romani costume and dances čoček (Redžepova 1965a). By contrast, in the second part of the show, she wears a western cocktail dress and high heels, has short bobbed hair, and peeks through a curtain with a mod art design. To "Romano Horo" (a Romani dance, sung in Romani), she dances the twist, the most popular dance in the West at the time (Redžepova 1965b). The rhythm of the song is pseudo-Latin with a pseudo-clave (wooden sticks) and cowbell rhythmic pattern. The show ends with "Makedo," a pop song entirely in German, where she encourages Germans to try Macedonian dances and songs.

The traditional part of the show includes Esma's most famous song, "Čhaje Šukarije" ("Beautiful Girl"), which has been covered by hundreds of singers, often without attribution (Redžepova 1965a); Esma calls it "her identification card." Esma wrote the melody in Phrygian mode and the lyrics when she was nine years old, and Stevo composed the arrangement. The rhythm is a čoček (2/4) and the lyrics in Romani are about love:

> Čhajorije šukarije, ma phir urde pala mande, čhaje,
> Haljan pekljan man, mo vogi ljiljan, čhaje šukarije
> Irin dikh man, čhaje…
>
> Beautiful girl, don't walk here after me, girl!
> You ate me up and burned me, you took my heart, beautiful girl
> Turn, look at me, girl!

Esma's voice is focused and emotional, featuring delicate ornamentation, yelps and glottals, and a wide range of dynamics. The male instrumentalists engage in a question/answer dialogue with her and harmonize in the chorus, reminiscent of the "doo-wop" style. The young drummer catches our attention, the musicians sway, and Esma dances in Romani style, but demurely, with neither hip nor pelvic movements.

Jennifer Stoever's work has pointed out that although "difference" is usually highlighted visually, it is also heard (2016). Writing about the "sonic color line" with regard to Black American music, she claims, "Listening operates as an organ of racial discernment, categorization, and resistance in the shadow of vision's alleged cultural dominance" (4). This is highly relevant for Roma, who are excluded from dominant visual and auditory categories and are expected to have "marked" bodies and voices. Stoever explains:

> The sonic color line describes the process of racializing sound—how and why certain bodies are expected to produce ... particular sounds ... Through the listening ear's surveillance, discipline, and interpretation, certain associations between race and sound come to seem normal, natural, and "right." (2016, 7)

Thus, there is collusion between the producers of sound (Roma) and listeners (non-Roma) to craft voices that sound "Gypsy." Hierarchical power relations are embedded in this process of auditory profiling (Stoever 2016, 20). Esma took the emotional, passionate historical formula of the "Gypsy singer" as raw material and reworked it. She neither dismantled the sonic color line nor the racialized listening practices associated with it; rather, she elevated them to respectability and debuted them on elite stages, thereby widening the horizons for herself and those Roma who followed her.

Emotion is Esma's trademark affect, expressed in both her voice and her stagings. Her voice showcased a range of emotions evoked in song texts—joy, sadness, bitterness, anger, jealousy—often using cries, yelps, and glottals; and her hand gestures referred to narrative themes. Similar to professional female Ottoman entertainers and to generations of male musicians, she masterfully played to audience sentiment. A 1972 Radio/TV review remarked upon her "unusual voice, now whispering, now almost shrieking, then begging, imploring, full of promise, challenge" (Teodosievski and Redžepova 1984, 139). Stevo trained Esma in vocal technique, and for two years she practiced at least four hours a day. In an interview, she illustrated the difference between the raw material she brought to Stevo and how he refined her vocal style (NPR 2010). She developed a rhythmic vibrato, crafted a technique of repeated metered melodic ornaments (turns and mordents), and she added her affective flair that, all together, became her vocal signature.

"Hajri Ma Te Dikhe, Daje" ("May You Not See, Mother") nicely illustrates Esma's iconic emotional style; in this song, Esma enacts the lament of a young girl being married off to an older man. In a 2001 video, her face is totally obscured by a black veil and she virtually cries while she sings (Redžepova 2001). The sobs become part of the unmetered melody as musicians bow their heads in sympathy; at the end of the song, the veil is removed and the emotion shifts. The Romani lyrics are quite poetic:

> Hajri ma te dikhe, daje, so dindžan man tuda
> Ko gavutne Roma, daje, but buti kerena, hari maro hana.
> Me terni daje, dade mori, me da rovava
> Ko brazde sovava daje mori, hari maro hav.

> May you not see, mother, what you did to me
> You married me to (poor) peasants, who work too much
>   and eat very little.
> I'm young, dear mother, father, I'm crying
> I sleep in the garden furrow and eat very little.

Not only did Esma's vocal style emphasize emotion, but also most of her song lyrics are about emotions—sadness and joy, primarily due to love, either fulfilled or unrequited; they tap into recognizable themes.

Esma and Stevo were also pioneers in producing music videos. Their films appeared just when television was debuting, and they correctly predicted that visuals would capture the public. Stoever asks how the sonic color line has been shaped by the rise of new audio and visual technologies (2016, 7). I note that Esma developed her "Balkan Gypsy" voice in tandem with emerging technologies such as records, radio, and television. These media brought music into your home, creating a domestic intimacy with "exotics," the safety of home mitigating the danger of "others." Racial danger was also mitigated by collaborations with well-known non-Roma performers, displayed on screens. Throughout her career, Esma sang duets and collaborated with many non-Romani musicians both to broaden her audiences and to bring Roma into mainstream media.

Humanitarianism, Politics, and Legacy

Esma is well known for her humanitarian activities. Over the decades, she sponsored over two thousand benefit concerts for orphanages, hospitals, disabled people, and victims of natural disasters. Her motto was: "If I have two of something, I will always give away one." She also was an honorary president of the Red Cross and won several awards from UNICEF. She had a special interest in women's issues, and in 1995, the Macedonian Association of Romani Women incorporated her name in its title. In 2010, she took part in a United Nations conference on women as part of the Macedonian delegation. Esma embraced a broad humanitarian stance rather than a particular Romani activist stance, and her public statements repeatedly stressed pacificism and cross-cultural understanding: "We are born naked and we die naked and we don't carry anything with us to the next world. So fighting doesn't make sense. The greatest barrier to all people is war" (Interview, July 15, 1997). She similarly stated, "There are no national barriers for me" (Katin 2015, 89), and she opined, "I would like the world to function based on equality and tolerance, eliminating borders" (ibid., 244).

Esma was very vocal about her patriotism for Yugoslavia and Macedonia. This ideology positioned her as an ally of the nation/state rather than an oppositional minority activist. Esma saw herself as an "Ambassador of Macedonia" more than for Roma, and some Romani activists objected to this. She had dresses made of the Macedonian flag, and, in interviews and song compositions, proclaimed her loyalty to the nation. Her biographer noted that "she is a lover of her country, and she speaks about it with journalists, politicians, ... and audiences" (Katin 2015, 15). Many of her video clips featured imagery that appealed to nationalist pride.

Despite experiencing anti-Romani racism as a child and in her career, Esma neither spoke out against it, nor composed songs about it, nor targeted her generosity toward Roma specifically. When a journalist asked her, "Do any of your songs address prejudice against Roma?" she answered: "No, my songs are about Roma tradition and culture, not the way others see us. When it comes to criticism, I refuse to receive it" (Katin 2015, 246). In fact, she did not believe discrimination existed in Macedonia. She repeatedly emphasized the positive aspects and often argued with activists, such as her cousin Šani Rifati. It wasn't until 2002 that she was involved in a benefit specifically for Roma. Esma claimed that Roma could become whatever they wanted in Macedonia. This stance is contradicted by reliable documentation of structural discrimination and human rights abuses against Roma in employment, education, health care, media, the legal system, and physical abuse by police. A cursory glance at the European Roma Rights Centre website under North Macedonia lists dozens of cases over several decades of anti-Romani violence, evictions, prison deaths, school segregation, and other forms of discrimination.[7]

Esma stressed Macedonian patriotism in the realm of politics and Romani music in the realm of cultural pride. For example, Esma and Stevo organized the first Romani music festival in Macedonia, Šutkafest, in 1993 with little attention to discrimination. Furthermore, when Rifati introduced concerts during her 2002 American tour with lectures on Romani history and discrimination, Esma objected, claiming it would alienate the audience. When Rifati asked her to open her concerts with a Romani rather than a Macedonian song, Esma refused. Sometimes, Esma included the Romani anthem in her concerts, but she recorded it in Serbian, not Romani (Redžepova 2011). In general, Esma resisted artistic advice from activists, arguing that they were not performers. She defended the artistic, entertainment, and commercial value of music as cultural display.

Esma became directly involved in party politics after Macedonian independence in 1991, and in the 2000s, she endorsed the ruling VMRO-DPMNE party, performing at its many events in her flag dress. She visibly supported its controversial plan "Skopje 2014," a massive construction project involving nationalist monuments and the display of ancient Macedonian heritage. In 2005, she was elected a member of the Skopje City Council, aligned with VMRO-DPMNE, and served for several terms.

When Esma and Stevo left Belgrade in 1989 to return to Skopje, due to the looming Yugoslav war, they started work on a humanitarian and documentation project entitled the Home of Humanity and Museum of Music. This ambitious project included the construction of a clinic for underserved people, a recording studio, a performance space, and a museum and archive of music documenting their career. The economic crisis of the war years, in addition to Stevo's death in 1997, slowed work on this project. In 2010, the city of Skopje granted Esma rights over the land for the museum/home where she lived (Katin 2015, 267). Esma briefly considered retiring after her husband's death in 1997, but instead continued her career with renewed energy together with her now-grown "children." She toured regularly, including in the US in 1997 and 2016, sought new international collaborations, and continued building the museum's collections.

Unfortunately, since Esma's death in 2016, her estate has been mired in a legal battle. A complicated lawsuit in progress contests Esma's assets and song rights, and the museum's future appears bleak. The house itself is mired in controversy, although it seems clear Esma left it to the city of Skopje. Tragically, the house has been repeatedly vandalized, but family members have preserved many museum objects. A recent headline captures the tragedy: "The Furniture Is Torn Apart, the Aluminum from the Windows Is Sold for Small Change, and the Thieves Defecate Inside—New Theft in the House of Queen Esma" (Milenkovska 2020). Esma was a very social person and hosted a steady stream of visitors related to music and her humanitarian work. Her home was not only beautiful and spacious but also a destination. Another tragedy is how Esma's legacy is being ignored by the government—neither her birthday nor the anniversary of her death are commemorated. Her fans and children, however, regularly reminisce about her on social media. In October 2020, the accordionist Simeon Atanasov, one of her adopted "children" and arranger of several hit songs, started a campaign to lobby the government to create the museum.

Conclusion

In surveying Esma's extraordinary career, we can appreciate the innovations she made, considering the challenges she faced. Under the tutelage of her non-Romani mentor, she created an unprecedented niche for Romani music and dance that opened the path for many artists. Moreover, she promoted female vocal arts by capturing the power of emotion while refashioning sexuality into respectability for the elite concert and recording stage. Images and voices of Romani women rely on listeners' historical racialized tropes and stereotypes. Although they are rarely in charge of the institutions that shape their performances, some Romani women have managed to demonstrate their agency, exert control over specific realms of artistry, and carve out new domains of performance.

Esma resisted the exclusionary practices of producers with her pioneering display of Romani language, dance, music, and costume, but she eschewed an activist agenda in favor of Macedonian patriotism and universal humanism. She acquiesced to the demands of the commercial establishment by endorsing positive Romani stereotypes, yet she simultaneously redefined those stereotypes. She engaged in selective resistance, based on strategic decisions about what she could actually accomplish and how resistance would affect her career. Indeed, resistance is often paired with accommodation.

Esma's multiple performative identities—Romani, Macedonian, Yugoslav, European, Muslim, female, motherly, philanthropic, and her "rags to riches" life trajectory—all point to her complex subjectivity and wide appeal. As Katherine Meizel suggests in this volume, when singers perform across cultural styles, genres, spaces, and temporalities, they perform "not only *in multiple vocalities*, but more importantly they are *performing multivocality* in the negotiation of self" (Meizel, this volume). Artists of color such as Esma "use multiple ways of singing to create otherwise-denied spaces where their self-narrations can sound" (Meizel 2020, 6).

As NPR claimed: "Some singers are one-hit wonders; others make a few albums and then fade away. And then there are those who stay popular for generations. Esma Redžepova is one of those" (2010). Today, three generations of fans still sing along with her hits. Esma is a living legend for many Macedonians, as well as for other Balkan peoples and many Roma around the world. And yet her legacy remains ignored by the country she loved.

Notes

1. Her prizes include "Queen of Romani Music" in India (1976), European Primadonna (1995), Millennium Singer in Russia (2000), Mother Teresa Award in Macedonia (2012), Order of Merit of Macedonia (2010), and National Artist of the Republic of Macedonia (2013), in addition to many Yugoslav prizes. Esma was also nominated for the Nobel Peace Prize in 2002 and 2006.

2. Note that I use Macedonia to refer both to the Republic of Macedonia during the Yugoslavia period and to the post-1991 independent country. In 2019, the name changed to North Macedonia.

3. In 2016, the Fundamental Rights Agency reported that: "Some 80% of Roma surveyed live below their country's at-risk-of-poverty threshold; every third Roma lives in housing without tap water; every third Roma child goes to bed hungry at least once a month; and 50% of Roma between the ages of six and 24 do not attend school" (FRA 2016, 3). For details of recent abuses in Macedonia, see reports such as FRA 2018, those from the European Roma Rights Centre (www.errc.org), and those listed in the link in footnote 7.

4. Edward Said's (1978) concept of "orientalism" refers to how the West constructs the East as backward, irrational, violent, that is, essentially inferior. This was used to justify colonialism.

5. Note that *ćoček* can also refer to the musical genre used for this dance, in 2/4, 7/8, and 9/8. The dance is clearly an heir to the dances of Ottoman female professional dancers, but in Romani communities its subtlety and restraint distinguish it from contemporary belly dancing. See Silverman 2003, 2008, 2012.

6. During the last few years of her life, Esma trained a Romani young woman, Eleonora Musafovska, to be her protégé.

7. See http://www.errc.org/search?country=124&theme=&area=&keyword=&search_submit=.

References

Abu-Lughod, Lila, and Catherine Lutz. 1990. "Introduction: Emotion, Discourse, and the Politics of Everyday Life." In *Language and the Politics of Emotion*, eds. Catherine Lutz and Lila Abu-Lughod, 1–45. Cambridge, UK: Cambridge University Press.

Ahmed, Sara. 2004. *The Cultural Politics of Emotion*. New York: Routledge.

Dunn, Leslie C., and Nancy A. Jones, eds. 1994. *Embodied Voices: Representing Female Vocality in Western Culture*. Cambridge, UK: Cambridge University Press.

Eide, Elisabeth. 2016. "Strategic Essentialism." In *The Wiley Blackwell Encyclopedia of Gender and Sexuality Studies*, ed. Nancy A. Naples, 1–2. Chichester, West Sussex, UK: Wiley Blackwell. https://doi.org/10.1002/9781118663219.wbegss554.

European Roma Rights Centre. 2020. "Police Brutality in North Macedonia." Facebook, October 21. https://www.facebook.com/EuropeanRomaRightsCentre/photos/a.367490363319026/3403957413005624.

FRA (European Union Agency for Fundamental Rights). 2016. "Second European Union Minorities and Discrimination Survey: Roma—Selected Findings." November 28. https://fra.europa.eu/en/publication/2016/second-european-union-minorities-and-discrimination-survey-roma-selected-findings.

———. 2018. "A Persisting Concern: Anti-Gypsyism as a Barrier to Roma Inclusion." April 6. https://fra.europa.eu/en/publication/2018/persisting-concern-anti-gypsyism-barrier-roma-inclusion.

Gay y Blasco, Paloma. 2008. "Picturing 'Gypsies': Interdisciplinary Approaches to Roma Representation." *Third Text* 22(3): 297.

Hancock, Ian. 2008. "The 'Gypsy' Stereotype and the Sexualization of Romani Women." In *"Gypsies" in European Literature and Culture*, eds. Valentina Glajar and Domnica Radulescu, 181–91. New York: Palgrave.

Hasdeu, Iulia. 2008. "Imagining the Gypsy Woman: Representations of Roma in Romanian Museum." *Third Text* 22(3): 347–57.

Hellier, Ruth. 2013. "Vocal Herstories: Resonances of Singing, Individuals, and Authors." In *Women Singers in Global Contexts: Music, Biography, Identity*, ed. Ruth Hellier, 1–37. Urbana: University of Illinois Press.

Hofman, Ana. 2015. "The Affective Turn in Ethnomusicology." *Muzikologija* 18: 35–55.

Katin, Slave Nikolovski. 2015. *Esma Redžepova-Teodosievka*. Skopje: Makedonska Iskra.

Lee, Ken. 2000. "Orientalism and Gypsylorism." *Social Analysis* 44(2): 129–56.

Magowan, Fiona, and Louise Wrazen, eds. 2013. *Performing Gender, Place, and Emotion in Music: Global Perspectives*. Rochester, NY: University of Rochester Press.

Malvinni, David. 2004. *The Gypsy Caravan: From Real Roma to Imaginary Gypsies in Western Music and Film*. New York: Routledge.

Markovic, Alexander. 2017. "Gypsy Fingers Are Unique! Identity Politics and Musical Performance among Romani Musicians in Vranje, Serbia." PhD Dissertation, University of Illinois at Chicago.

Meizel, Katherine. 2020. *Multivocality: Singing on the Borders of Identity*. New York: Oxford University Press.

Milenkovska, Vesna. 2020. "Mebelot Razparcen, Aluminiumot od Prozorcite se Prodava za Sitna Para, a Kradcite Vrsat Nuzda Vnatre—Nova Krazba vo Domot na Kralicata Esma" (The Furniture Is Torn Apart, the Aluminum from the Windows Is Sold for Small Change, and the Thieves Defecate Inside—New Theft in the House of Queen Esma). http://mms.mk, July 20. https://mms.mk/155080/.

NPR (National Public Radio). 2010. "Esma Redzepova: Queen of the Gypsies." April 5. https://www.npr.org/transcripts/125580636.

Petrova, Dimitrina. 2003. "The Roma: Between a Myth and the Future." *Social Research* 70(1): 111–61.

Radulescu, Domnica. 2008. "Performing the Female 'Gypsy': Commedia dell'arte's 'Tricks' for Finding Freedom." In *"Gypsies" in European Literature and Culture*, eds. Valentina Glajar and Domnica Radulescu, 193–215. New York: Palgrave.

Redžepova, Esma. 1965a. "Esma Redžepova—Čaje Šukarije" [Čhaje Šukarije]. www.youtube.com. https://www.youtube.com/watch?v=UcEJzOHH1mw&list=RDUcEJzOHH1mw&start_radio=1&t=35.

———. 1965b. "Esma Redzepova: Romano Horo." www.youtube.com. https://www.youtube.com/watch?v=fP9FYpp6p6s.

———. 2001. "Esma Redzepova—Hajri ma te dike daje—Skopje Concert (very rare)" [Hajri Ma Te Dikhe, Daje]. www.youtube.com. https://www.youtube.com/watch?v=2eYuF9lG09g.

———. 2011. "Esma Redzepova—Dzelem dzelem." www.youtube.com. https://www.youtube.com/watch?v=nyBv3qFxquA&list=RDnyBv3qFxquA&start_radio=1.

Rosaldo, Michelle. 1984. "Toward an Anthropology of Self and Feeling." In *Culture Theory: Essays on Mind, Self, and Emotion*, eds. Richard A. Shweder and Robert A. LeVine, 137–57. Cambridge, UK: Cambridge University Press.

Said, Edward W. 1978. *Orientalism*. New York: Vintage Books.

Silverman, Carol. 2003. "The Gender of the Profession: Music, Dance, and Reputation among Balkan Muslim Rom Women." In *Music and Gender: Perspectives from the Mediterranean*, ed. Tullia Magrini, 119–45. Chicago: University of Chicago Press.

———. 2008. "Transnational Chochek: The Politics and Poetics of Balkan Romani Dance." In *Balkan Dance: Essays on Characteristics, Performing, and Teaching*, ed. Anthony Shay, 37–68. Jefferson, NC: McFarland Press.

———. 2011. "Music, Emotion, and the 'Other': Balkan Roma and the Negotiation of Exoticism." In *Interpreting Emotions in Russia and Eastern Europe*, eds. Mark Steinberg and Valeria Sobol, 224–47. DeKalb, IL: Northern Illinois University Press.

———. 2012. *Romani Routes: Cultural Politics and Balkan Music in Diaspora*. New York: Oxford University Press.

———. 2019. "Esma Redžepova." RomArchive. https://www.romarchive.eu/en/music/balkan/esma-redzepova/.

Spivak, Gayatri Chakravorty. 1996. "Subaltern Studies: Deconstructing Historiography." In *The Spivak Reader*, eds. Donna Landry and Gerald MacLean, 203–237. London: Routledge.

Stoever, Jennifer Lynn. 2016. *The Sonic Color Line: Race and the Cultural Practices of Listening*. New York: New York University Press.

Teodosievski, Stevo, and Esma Redžepova. 1984. *On the Wings of Song*. Kočani: Dom Kulture Beli Mugri.

Trumpener, Katie. 1992. "The Time of the Gypsies: A 'People Without History' in the Narratives of the West." *Critical Inquiry* 18: 843–84.

Van de Port, Mattijs. 1998. *Gypsies, Wars, and Other Instances of the Wild: Civilisation and Its Discontents in a Serbian Town*. Amsterdam: Amsterdam University Press.

Multimedia Playlist

There are hundreds of videos of Esma's songs on YouTube. Some of her famous songs are:
"Abre Kako Dilineja" ("Hey, Crazy Uncle")
"Cekaj Života" ("Wait, Life")
"Čhaje Šukarije" ("Beautiful Girl")
"Džarem Džarem" ("I Traveled")

"Hajri Ma Te Dikhe, Daje" ("May You Not See, Mother")
"Ibraim" ("Ibrahim")
"Ker Ta Mange, Daje" ("Make Me, Mother")
"Nakhtareja Mo Ilo Phangljan" ("He Closed My Heart with a Key")
"Romano Horo" ("Romani Dance")
"Svadba Makedonska" ("Macedonian Wedding")
"Zošto Si Me Majko Rodila" ("Mother, Why Did You Give Birth to Me")

CHAPTER 8

Teresa Teng

Embodying Asia's Cold Wars

MICHAEL K. BOURDAGHS

> When I performed in the past, I was always a little nervous. I would just stand there and sing the words, but I didn't dare to really let go with my emotions or gestures. It was only after coming to Japan that I learned what performing really means. I learned how to free myself and how to express my emotions to the utmost. Only this can truly be called singing.
> —Teresa Teng (Ku 1995, 9)

In February 1979, Japanese media exploded with a breaking celebrity scandal: Teresa Teng (1953–1995) had been arrested in Tokyo. The Taiwanese singer had entered Japan illegally, using a fake Indonesian passport purchased on the black market in Hong Kong. Initially admitted without incident, she was arrested a few days later after the Indonesian embassy reported to Japanese authorities about a previous episode two weeks earlier in Taipei, when Teng attempted to enter Taiwan using the same forged document. Held in custody by Japanese immigration officials for a week, the singer was finally expelled from Japan, banned from returning for one year. On her way out of the country, she held a tearful press conference at Tokyo's Narita International Airport, apologizing to her Japanese fans for the trouble she had caused.

The scandal was reported widely outside of Japan, too. Teng by 1979 was already a transnational superstar across East and Southeast Asia, and Chinese-language media in Taiwan, Hong Kong, Singapore, Malaysia, and elsewhere reported her arrest. In the Chinese-speaking world, however, the singer was known as Deng Lijun (鄧麗君), a stage name that the young Deng Liyun (鄧麗筠, her birth name) adopted in the mid-1960s at the beginning of her career in Taiwan. Upon entering the Japanese market in the mid-1970s, she became Teresa Teng (テレサ・テン), written in the Japanese katakana syllabary used primarily for foreign loan words. Teresa Teng was also the name she used in English-speaking markets such as Hong Kong, as well as markets such as Indonesia that used the Roman alphabet.

That pseudonym—chosen by Teng's Japanese record label over the objections of her parents (Hirano 2015, 92–95)—echoed with Cold War tensions. It was an emphatically English-sounding name coined for a performer who arrived in Tokyo as an established superstar in colonial (Hong Kong) and formerly colonial (Taiwan, Malaysia, Singapore, Indonesia) Southeast Asia. It existed in parallel with her other stage name, Deng Lijun, which primarily circulated along an alternate network that by the 1980s eventually reached—and became an existential threat to—the People's Republic of China. Teng's multiple names provide an entryway into mapping the tensions of Cold War East Asia. Teresa Teng's music circulated across multiple circuits of transnational popular culture during the Cold War and its aftermath. As they traveled, her songs carried with them problematic memories of vanished linkages that latched onto different local histories and musical genres, generating an array of conflicting desires and anxieties. As we will see below, she ironically became famous for singing in the *enka* genre, often identified closely with the culture of a specifically Japanese national identity.

Here, using both Teng's recordings and popular press coverage from the time of her career, as well as more recent biographies and scholarly studies, I will trace the singer's career through two different networks, both of which were haunted by fraught relations to vanished historical pasts. First, I will briefly map the travels of Deng Lijun across the Cold War Sinosphere—the global network of speakers of Sinitic languages that existed in often fraught relationships with the putative "homeland" of the People's Republic of China. Second, I will trace a tangled network that connected Teresa Teng to the Japanese empire that dissolved with Japan's defeat at the end of 1945 but remained a source of acknowledged and unacknowledged popular emotions in the decades that followed.

Between the Two Chinas of the Cold War

The 1979 passport scandal was ironic for many reasons, not least because of Teng's squeaky clean image. For starters, the singer was born in Taiwan in 1953, just eight years after residents of that island lost their status as subjects of the Japanese empire. Japan acquired Taiwan as its first overseas colony in 1895; had colonial rule not ended in 1945, a Taiwanese would not have needed a passport to travel to Tokyo in the first place, because they would already have been a subject of the Empire of Japan. Teng was actually the daughter of mainlanders who fled to Taiwan only after the 1949 Chinese Revolution, when the former Japanese colony became the home in exile for the ferociously anti-communist Chinese Nationalist government, transforming the Straits of Taiwan into one of the tensest flashpoints during the Cold War era. Moreover, Teng's Taiwanese Republic of China (ROC) passport no longer worked to gain automatic entry to Japan in 1979 because seven years earlier, Tokyo had switched diplomatic recognition from Taipei to Beijing, in retaliation for which the ROC government imposed special restrictions on travel to Japan. Teng acquired the fake travel document in an attempt to sidestep these complications and facilitate the constant travels across the region that her transnational career required.

The 1979 scandal, hence, was a byproduct of several tectonic shifts that underwrote Cold War geopolitics in East Asia. These include the 1945 collapse of one regional hegemonic power (the Empire of Japan); the subsequent scramble for territory and influence in the region that produced multiple partitions and civil wars in former Japanese colonies and Japanese-held territories (Taiwan, Korea, Vietnam, Okinawa, and Indonesia, among others); the 1949 Chinese Revolution and the subsequent establishment of the rival anti-communist ROC government-in-exile in Taiwan that still claimed to be the legitimate government of China; and the dramatic maneuvers of the early 1970s when Tokyo, following Washington's lead, sought to isolate the USSR by establishing diplomatic ties with the People's Republic of China (PRC), thereby isolating the ROC government on Taiwan.

Teng's 1979 arrest was one instance of the multiple ways the singer throughout her career became a projection of often ambiguous Cold War geopolitical imaginaries, of conflicting ideological mappings of the global order. As an illegal immigrant and pathological foreign invader, as a "traditional" East Asian female who simultaneously modeled the new role of a modern woman, as a high-status brand commodity whose transregional success signaled the attainment of new rungs on a capitalist trajectory of development, Teng embodied the Cold War in multiple, often contradictory ways (Chow 2007, 105–20). A substantial body of previous scholarship explores Teng's role in the Cold War in relation to global Chinese communities. For listeners in the PRC, Taiwan, Hong Kong, and elsewhere, Teng's embodied performance seemed to re-member the body of a transnational community shattered by Cold War rivalries: she became "an emblem of the cultural unity of greater China—mainland China, Taiwan, and ethnic Chinese communities worldwide—even as its political divisions refused to heal" (Gordon 2012, 26).

In relation to China's Cold War, Teng carried out a two-sided performance. She enacted both the Cold War divide and its subsumption into a new unity. She was an anti-communist voice performing morale-boosting shows for the troops as the ROC's "sweetheart of the military," greeting defectors from the PRC as heroes. She broadcast ideological messages across the Taiwan Straits during the shortwave radio propaganda wars of the 1970s and via the massive loudspeaker complex the ROC pointed at the mainland from the contested island of Quemoy (Cheng 2020a; Cheng 2013). Yet she was also the figure who in the PRC during the 1980s, in part by appealing to nostalgia for "Yellow Music," the banned popular music of pre-revolutionary 1930s and '40s Shanghai (Jones 2001), bridged the gap between anti-communist and communist China. Her songs flooded into the PRC via pirated cassette tapes, enacting a kind of virtual unity among the multiple Chinas (Cheng and Athanasopoulos 2015; Lin 2017). In Andrew Jones's analysis, she managed to bring the portable transistor-based circuit of Taiwanese and Hong Kong popular music and infiltrate the similarly transistor-based but stationary circuit of public loudspeakers and official radio pronouncements that predominated in the PRC. In doing so, Teng introduced a "modulation" in the local PRC sound environment by evoking "new sounds, new ways of listening, and new affective interiorities," triggered in large part by the signature timbre of Teng's singing voice (Jones 2020, 172).

Her popularity in the PRC led first to a crackdown in the mid-1980s as the government declared her music a source of bourgeois spiritual corruption. The ban gradually subsequently eased up—until, that is, Teng became a vocal supporter of the 1989 Tiananmen Square democracy movements and her airy pop ballads acquired an unexpected new life as political anthems among the students who gathered in the Square to demand political reforms. The June 1989 violent suppression of the movement in many ways marked the turning point in Teng's career in the Sinophone world, as she retreated from the limelight and moved to Paris. Another turning point came following the singer's unexpected death in 1995. Her Cold War history as a fierce anti-communist propagandist in the 1960s and '70s and as the voice of the Tiananmen Square democracy movement would largely be expunged from her image in the PRC: a newly depoliticized version of the singer was resurrected so that by 2008 she could become the heroine of *Love U! Teresa*, a musical staged in Beijing in which she was "marketed by and to China as the best template for promoting the One China Policy" (Cheng and Athanasopoulos 2015, 59). Teng has posthumously been transformed into a pop culture heroine of the PRC, a country in which Teng herself never once set foot. Within the post-Cold War Sinophone circuit, Teng persists as a site for projection of various anxieties and desires, as a simultaneously enticing and threatening object that requires constant and careful management.

Japan, Taiwan, and the Bandung Movement

Teng's position across the Cold War Sinosphere is fairly well known. Let me turn now to Teng's performance in another, less studied circuit: that of Japan's Cold War. If, taking a cue from Teng's claim in the epigraph to this chapter that "It was only after coming to Japan that I learned what performing really means," what modes of performance did she engage in for her fan base in Asia's richest country? And what meanings and values were attached to her music as it circulated through Cold War Japan?

Most existing scholarship on Japan's Cold War culture focuses on the American-Japan relation, for good reason: Japan was essentially a client state of the United States through the Cold War period, a member in good standing of the First World of liberal capitalist democracies. But here I want to think in particular of yet another version of Cold War Japan: the Japan that sent an official delegation to the 1955 Bandung Conference of Asian and African Nations and that liked to imagine itself an ally of the decolonizing nations of Asia and Africa and of the nonaligned movement. A Japan, that is, that claimed at least honorary membership in the Third World. This version of Cold War Japan helps us understand the appeal in the 1970s and '80s of a figure like Teresa Teng.

Japan's participation in Bandung was in many ways incoherent. As a former empire rather than colony, Japan in a sense had no business participating in the conference. As one historian has put it memorably, Japan at Bandung was a cat attending a mice convention (Ampiah 1995). If anything, Japan's former colonies of Korea and Taiwan should have attended the 1955 conference, but both were blocked by Cold War geopolitics from sending delegations—Korea because the officially nonaligned conference hesitated to choose between the rival North and South Korean governments, Taiwan because the PRC, one of the main sponsors of the conference, claimed it as a renegade province. The notion of a Bandung Japan was, that is, a contradiction: it represented simultaneously both a break from and a continuation of Japan's history of imperialism.

Following the collapse of the empire in 1945, Japan's position within Cold War East Asia became, in sum, a question of considerable ambiguity. On the one hand, the matter of Japan's imperial violence against its neighbors, its attempt to subsume the entire region under its own rule, became an inconvenient memory. The pre-1945 image of Japan as a multiethnic empire was repressed from popular memory, replaced by a new myth of Japan as a homogeneous, monoethnic society with its own cultural traditions that distinguished it from the rest of Asia (Oguma 2002). The post-1945 memories of the war shifted the focus away from the violence Japan had inflicted on its Asian neighbors and toward instead a victim narrative that stressed the suffering of the Japanese people at the hands of the American military (Igarashi 2000). Ironically, this new image was in part promoted by Japan's new ally, the United States, which for Cold War strategic reasons needed to generate a new vision of Japan as an anti-communist democratic model of "modernization" grounded in its distinct national cultural traditions (Harootunian 1993).

But Japan's repressed ties with Asia remained a tantalizing presence, a kind of ghostly echo of the past that was both threatening and appealing. As I've already noted, Japan's former colony of Taiwan—Teresa Teng's birthplace—was prevented from participating in the Bandung Conference. Through the 1950s and '60s, the ambiguities of Japan's involvement with Bandung were mirrored in its relations with the ROC. As Leo Ching notes, due to the "abrupt dissolution of the Japanese Empire by an external mandate instead of through prolonged struggle," neither Taiwan nor Japan underwent a process of decolonization/deimperialism, a failure that "prevented both Japan and Taiwan from addressing and confronting their particular colonial relationship and the overall Japanese colonial legacy" (Ching 2001, 20–21). This incomplete decolonization was further "exacerbated by the postwar Cold War system under American hegemony in the region" (Ching 2019, 21). Taiwan was "liberated" from Japanese colonialism in 1945, only to be reoccupied in 1949 by the toppled Nationalist government fleeing the mainland. The ROC adopted anti-Japanese cultural policies, yet its anti-communist ideology and authoritarian developmentalism were deeply rooted in Japanese colonial policies. Continuity with the imperial past was disavowed, and yet "the irrepressible traces of colonial practices, in both their sedimentation and permutation . . . continue to disrupt the symbolic order of a putatively 'post'-colonial, 'post'-war Japan" and Taiwan (Ching 2001, 5).

These Cold War currents swirled around the figure of Teresa Teng as she transformed herself into a superstar in Japan. As a glamorous transnational celebrity, she occupied a tenuous position, as placeholder for Japan's disavowed but desirable connection to East Asia. As a performer from a former colony who sang and performed in Japanese, Teng became an ambiguous figure, the object simultaneously of desire and suspicion, praise and condemnation. Teng's massively popular hit songs in Cold War Japan solicited real pleasure by summoning nostalgic memories of what was believed to have been lost—as well as attractive possibilities for a better future in which Japan was reunited with the rest of Asia. But at the same time, they also generated troubling reminders of loss, triggering psychic pains and paranoid delusions. Traveling across the phantom circuit of the lost Japanese empire, she became, that is, a kind of fetish: a magical object that was eminently desirable because it seemed to offer what the self was missing, but that was at the same time eminently loathsome because it served as a reminder of the painful loss. In the ambivalences that haunted her performances in Japan, Teng became a projection of the desires and fears of a Japanese mass audience trying to negotiate its way through the minefields of Cold War conflicts.

Situating Teresa Teng in Japanese Popular Music History

Teng's bungled attempt to enter Japan on a fake Indonesian passport inadvertently touched on one of the key relations of Japan's Cold War. The Indonesia archipelago (then a colony of the Netherlands known as the Dutch East Indies) was under Japanese occupation from 1942–1945; after armed struggle, the Republic of Indonesia won independence in 1949 and would go on to become a leader of the decolonizing and nonalignment movement—including its role as host to the Bandung Conference. Japan maintained a special relation with postcolonial Indonesia throughout the Cold War, including making the country the largest single recipient of Japanese overseas aid across the period (Miyagi 2017).

Teresa Teng also knew Indonesia well. From early in her career she enjoyed a large fan base there among the local ethnically Chinese community, and by issuing a substantial body of self-covers of her own Chinese and Japanese hit songs in Indonesian-language re-recordings, she worked actively to broaden her audience in the archipelago. Her Indonesian connections would in turn contribute to her popularity elsewhere. One of her best-known Mandopop numbers, "Sweet as Honey" (Mandarin: "Tian mi mi"; Japanese title: "Suiito," 1979; lyrics by Zhuang Nu), is an adaptation of "Dayung sampan," an Indonesian/Malayan folk song that Teng had previously recorded in an Indonesian-language version.

Teng was already well known in Indonesia and much of Southeast Asia when Japan Polydor Records signed the budding regional superstar to a record deal in 1973. A child musical prodigy, Teng released her first album in Taiwan in 1968 at the age of fourteen, quickly also becoming a star in the new rising medium of television there (Jones 2020). She moved quickly to expand her fan base into neighboring regions, with concert appearances and record releases in Singapore, Indonesia, and in particular Hong Kong, which from 1971 became her home base (Cheng 2020b). Executives from Japan Polydor met with her there to persuade her to challenge the largest popular music market in Asia, and as a result in late 1973 Teng moved to Tokyo, where Watanabe Productions—since the late 1950s a dominant force in the Japanese entertainment business—took charge of grooming the singer for her debut in what was already the world's second largest economy.

Early Japanese press coverage declared her the "second Agnes Chan" (the Hong Kong–native Chan, also signed to Watanabe Productions, had her first Japanese hit in 1972) and focused on Teng's cute image and her newcomer status: she still spoke little Japanese and as the native of a tropical island was excited by her first sight of snow ("Nerai wa Agunesu Chan nidaime?" 1974; "Akogare no yuki to hatsutaimen" 1975). In an early interview, Teng was asked how long she planned to stay in Japan. "Well, I don't really know," she responded, "I suppose it will depend on what the future results of my career are. But I want to stay in Japan for a long, long time!" ("Shinjinshō wa gatchiri itadaki…pisu: Daizadankai" 1975).

Polydor had high expectations for Teng in Japan. Her 1974 debut single, "Maybe Tonight, Maybe Tomorrow?" ("Konya kashira, ashita kashira"), featured lyrics by Yamagami Michio and music by Tsutsumi Kyōhei, both established hitmakers. The musical style of the record and the message of its lyrics positioned Teng as peer to such teen idol singers as The Candies. She sings in an almost flirtatious, bright and playful style. The featured instrument in the orchestral arrangement is an electric guitar played with a country-music style twang, and the bouncy mid-tempo number features syncopation and pronounced rhythmic variations. It is an expertly groomed instance of 1970s pop fluff. But the debut single unexpectedly flopped, reaching only #75 in the Japanese hit charts (Nakamura 1991, 480). Clearly, the number did not answer to whatever it was the mass Japanese audience might want from the newly imported singer.

Japan Polydor shifted directions for Teng's second Japanese single and stumbled onto the magic formula. "Airport" ("Kūkō," lyrics by Yamagami, music by Inomata Kōshō) became an enormous hit and won for Teng several awards, including New Artist of the Year honors at the Japan Record Awards. A minor-key composition, "Airport" fooled my ears into thinking it used the *yonanuki* pentatonic scale characteristic of the *enka* genre, but Noriko Manabe has pointed out that it actually employs a heptatonic scale, even as it signals the *enka* style (personal communication, March 23, 2022). Although the name *enka* has been in use since the late nineteenth century, the form identified today as *enka* emerged only in the 1960s, when it was defined through contrast with newly dominant youth-oriented genres such as rock and folk. Although hybrid in style, *enka* is often celebrated as the most "Japanese" of popular music genres, and despite its rather recent coinage, mythic histories of the form often connect it to the hoary past. Although the genre has flexible parameters, common elements include a minor-key melody built on a *yonanuki* scale (a pentatonic scale without the fourth and seventh degrees of a natural minor scale), over-the-top emotional expression in both lyrics and singing style (which often features melisma and strong vibrato), references to rural locations in the lyrics, plus a performance style marked by restrained bodily movement and formal costume, whether kimono or eveningwear (Yano 2002; Wajima 2018).

"Airport" followed *enka* generic conventions in both composition and lyrics, which depict heartbreak, albeit with a modern update: instead of the conventional *enka* landscape of a provincial port town, the song takes for its setting an airport. The speaker is a woman parting from her (presumably married) lover, telling him to go back to "that woman," while she herself will somehow carry on. In a tour de force performance, Teng's voice unfolds across a wide, almost violent emotional register, ranging from soft whispers to explosive melodramatic crescendos. In typical *enka* style, Teng employs vibrato and melisma to highlight the emotional peaks of the song, while at other moments her voice quivers, seemingly on the verge of breaking with emotion. The orchestral arrangement foregrounds a dialogue between an assertively brassy trumpet and a sadder, softer saxophone that parallels the emotional tension of the lyrics.

Teng would follow her success with "Airport" with several other hits in the *enka* style. Between 1974 and 1981, she released ten more singles on the Polydor Japan label. All were re-released elsewhere in Chinese-language re-recordings, circulating across the Sinosphere network and becoming part of Teng's standard repertoire across the region. None were mega-hits in Japan: 1977's "Where Is My Hometown?" ("Furusato wa doko desu ka") was the most successful, reaching #42 on the Oricon charts. But the subgenre *enka*, aimed at an older and less affluent audience, wasn't usually expected to top the pop charts, which in Japan as elsewhere have since the 1960s been dominated by youth-oriented genres.

With these singles, by the late 1970s, Teng had established herself as a solid, if not spectacular, presence within an established corner of the Japanese music industry—but also one characterized by a somewhat exotic image that harkened back to memories of the Japanese empire. The press attributed the popularity of her 1976 single, "Nighttime Ferry Boat" ("Yoru no Feriibōto"), for example, to the publicity poster image of the singer, in which she appeared for the first time in Japan wearing a *cheongsam* "China dress," complete with a revealing leg slit. "When I wear a China dress in Taiwan, nobody bats an eye, so I wonder why it causes such a fuss here," she was quoted, perhaps ingenuously, as saying ("Ijō ninki, Teresa Ten no Chaina-fuku" 1976). She would wear a *cheongsam* on stage for her first full one-woman concert in Japan in 1977, as well (Itō 1977). Her 1980 single "You" ("Nii [Anata]") likewise blended Chinese and Japanese elements: the title is the second-person pronoun a woman would use to address her male lover, given in both Mandarin and Japanese.

The 1979 passport incident brought this stage of Teng's Japan career to a halt. After her one-year ban on re-entering the country expired, she made a few brief visits to Japan, but during the early 1980s the singer focused on building her career in the Sinophone world, including her first inroads into the PRC market via clandestine imports and pirated cassette tapes. It was not until 1984 that she returned to the Japanese market in full force. Now signed to the Taurus Record label, she released "Atonement" ("Tsugunai") in 1984—and broke into the top ten on the Oricon chart for the first time in her career. With music by Miki Takashi and lyrics by Araki Hitohisa, both veteran songwriters, "Atonement" launched the second, more successful, phase of Teng's career in Japan. In a 1984 interview, Teng was asked what had changed in her approach to the Japanese market. "Before, I was trying to make myself a part of Japan. But this time, I've come to Japan as a foreigner, as a representative of Southeast Asia" ("Teresa Ten: Ima Ajia ni Kagayaite" 1984). In the promotional build-up for the single, her record label stressed this aspect, publicizing the fact that Teng had in recent years become an underground hit even in the PRC despite campaigns by the Beijing government to denounce her music as degenerate ("Teresa Ten-san Chūgoku de fukkatsu" 1985; Hirano 2015, 231).

"Atonement" won both the Japan Cable Award and the All Japan Cable Broadcasting Award: it was the most requested song for the cable broadcasting service that supplied numbers on request to subscribers, particularly prevalent in small bars and clubs. Teng would win both prizes again the following year with "Lover" ("Aijin," another Araki/Miki composition) and yet again in 1986 with "Leaving It Up to the Flow of Time" ("Toki no nagare ni mi o makasete," also Araki/Miki). The latter also took home a Gold Prize at the 1986 Japan Record Awards. Teng was now indisputably a superstar in Japan. This string of hits established synchronicity between Japanese hit charts and those elsewhere in East Asia, where Teng re-recorded most of the same numbers in Mandarin. In a sense, Teng was realizing the dream of Bandung Japan, enacting a harmonious reunion between the former imperial power and its ex-colonies across the region.

There is some disagreement among critics about how to characterize Teng's style in this second phase of her Japan career. Some stress the ways "Atonement" and her other 1980s singles depart from the *enka* genre: Teng, they aver, was reintroduced to Japan as an international superstar singing in a transnational pop style. Misaka Hiroshi—the Taurus Records producer in charge of the Singapore recording session for "Atonement" as well as her subsequent hits on the label—would recall that in planning Teng's comeback in Japan, he deliberately avoided her earlier *enka*-laden image. In that effort, he turned to the "New Music" genre, a hybrid pop style that combined elements of folk and rock and had dominated Japanese pop charts since the mid-1970s. Misaka reports that Teng herself eagerly latched onto this concept and even asked if singer-songwriter Nakajima Miyuki, a New Music superstar, could compose a piece for her (Hirano 2015, 121–35).

Likewise, influential music critic Nakamura Tōyō, while noting some *kayōkyoku* (the broader category of Japanese-style popular music that includes *enka*) elements in Teng's 1980s recordings, celebrates "Atonement" and her subsequent hits for allowing the singer to finally give voice to her hard-won Chinese identity, freeing her from the obligation to artificially mimic the Japanese *enka* genre. Nakamura situates these Japanese comeback numbers as the natural conclusion to the arc Teng's career followed in the late 1970s and early 1980s, when she recorded covers of classic 1930s and '40s Shanghai pop songs such as "When Will You Return?" ("Heri jun zailai") and then the celebrated 1983 concept album *Light Exquisite Feeling* (*Dandan youqing*), a collection of pop ballads composed around lyrics drawn from Tang and Song dynasty poetry. With "Atonement," Nakamura argues, Teng was liberated from the Japanese *enka* genre and finally allowed to perform the role of a Chinese singer in Japan (Nakamura 1991, 473–500).

Clearly, "Atonement" is not a 1960s style *enka* song in the manner of, for example, Misora Hibari's classic 1966 recording, "Mournful Sake" ("Kanashii sake"). Compared to her 1970s Japanese singles, Teng uses less melisma and vibrato in her vocal performance, the backing orchestra is largely replaced by electronic synthesizers in the manner of much 1980s pop, and the arrangement features backing vocals characteristic of New Music and 1980s City Pop. But the song, like Teng's subsequent 1980s singles, also includes many elements characteristic of *enka*. Another break-up song, "Atonement" features a melancholic woman involved in a romantic break-up—in this case, an imminent divorce. Offering words of advice for her soon-to-be ex-husband, she anticipates the loneliness about to descend in her own life. Teng's singing style follows the graceful bel canto conventions of mainstream pop, and the song, while in D minor, uses appoggiatura and other tactics to produce a cleaner, brighter sound than is usually found in *enka*. But the orchestration and structure of the piece signal *enka* in other ways. In "Tsugunai," for example, foregrounded instrumental embellishments come from a mandolin (somewhat reminiscent of Nino Rota's theme music for *The Godfather*) that echoes the Spanish guitar ornamentations common to conventional *enka*. Andrew Jones hears echoes of Portuguese fado singer Carlos do Campos's 1977 recording of "Fado do Campo Grande" in the number, as well (personal communication, March 13, 2021).

It seems appropriate to think of "Atonement" and Teng's subsequent Japanese singles as belonging to a 1980s subgenre we might call neo-*enka*. A 1986 survey of recent *enka* singles in the *Yomiuri* newspaper, for example, described Teng's "Leaving It Up to the Flow of Time" as "a mellow song in a folk-inflected *enka* style that we haven't heard before; she seems to be aiming at an image change" ("Kongetsu no enka kara" 1986). Likewise, in his history of *kayōkyoku*, Kō Mamoru identifies the same song as pioneering a new hybrid form that combined traditional *enka* with a new "adult-oriented pop" style (Kō 2011, 201–4). And while Teng's mid-1980s singles in some ways deviated from the traditional *enka* formula, that gesture put her very much in sync with other *enka* singers from the same period who sought to renovate the style by incorporating elements borrowed from contemporary pop genres. These include, for example, a number of 1980s singles recorded by the "Queen of Enka," Misora Hibari (1937–1989), who also turned to such New Music and City Pop composers as Okabayashi Nobuyasu and Sakamoto Ryūichi in an effort to freshen up her sound. We could also mention Sakamoto Fuyumi's experiments in renewing the genre, such as her 1991 collaboration with rockers Hosono Haruomi and Imawano Kiyoshirō under the moniker H.I.S. or her 1996 reggae-inflected single, "Fireflies Paper Lantern" ("Hotaru no chōchin").

In other words, the question whether Teng's 1980 Japanese singles belong to the *enka* genre depends on which elements you wish to stress. More important for my purposes is to note that this question of how to situate Teng in the history of Japanese musical genres is very much a Cold War question, related to the suppressed memories of the Japanese empire. The most obvious parallel to Teng in Japanese popular music history was Yamaguchi Yoshiko, the wartime idol who claimed to be Chinese and achieved region-wide popularity under the stage name Li Xianglan (Japanese: Ri Kōran). In fact, in Japan Yamaguchi was the singer most famously associated with the Yellow Music standard number "When Will You Return?," which Teng revived in the late 1970s. But Yamaguchi is not the figure typically used to explain Teng's place in Japanese music history—she is instead associated with the singer celebrated as the Queen of Enka. Teng, that is, is celebrated as "the second Misora Hibari" or "the Misora Hibari of Taiwan" (for example, "Teresa Ten fuhō nyūkoku" 1979). Many Japanese-language accounts, for example, repeat the well-known story of how by the age of seven or eight Teng in Taiwan had already learned how to sing *enka* diva Hibari's 1952 hit "Apple Oiwake" ("Ringo oiwake") (Nakamura 1991, 476; Hirano 2015, 70–2; Watanabe 1996, 182–206).

The question whether Teng's 1980s singles belong to the *enka* genre takes on importance because *enka* was a key mode through which Cold War Japan negotiated its problematic relations with the rest of Asia, as well as its anxieties as a junior, less-than-equal partner under US leadership in the region. As I have argued elsewhere, *enka* provided a venue for both repressing and expressing the memory of the Japanese empire, for celebrating what distinguished Japan from its neighbors in Asia while disavowing what linked them—and vice versa (Bourdaghs 2012, 49–84). Often identified as the most purely "Japanese" of pop music genres, as the musical "soul of Japan," *enka* is on the one hand a product of the post-1945 ideology that redefined Japan as a peace-loving, homogeneous, single-ethnic nation, disavowing its pre-1945 status as a multiethnic empire. Yet with its roots in continental Asian folk and popular musics (including the "continental ballads" of the 1930s and '40s sung by such figures as Yamaguchi Yoshiko/Ri Kōran), *enka* also expressed Japan's connectedness with its neighbors in the region. It functioned simultaneously, that is, as a reminder of continuity with the history of Japan's empire and as a marker of discontinuity with that past. *Enka* signaled both the absence of the empire, including Taiwan and Korea, and their phantom presence as an object of desire in the Cold War present of the 1960s, '70s, and '80s.

In the case of Misora Hibari, this ambivalence emerged largely in the form of rumors. Throughout her long career, the Queen of Enka, supposedly the most Japanese of singers, was dogged by a whisper campaign that she was not "really" Japanese at all, but rather ethnically Korean. In this manner, the phantom presence of the empire could still be enjoyed (and simultaneously loathed) at one remove. What could only exist as a rumor for Misora Hibari became more explicit with Teng. As we have already seen, recordings from her earlier, clearly *enka*, phase such as "You"—not to mention "Hong Kong Nights" ("Hon Kon no yoru," 1977) or "Taipei Nights" ("Taipei no yoru," 1980)—openly signaled the continental traces that lingered in *enka* both in the orientalist ornamentations of their arrangements and their lyrical content. Her 1980s neo-*enka* recordings likewise continued the flirtation of expressing the desired yet disavowed links with the continent.

In many ways, Teng performed the Cold War dream of a Bandung Japan, reconnecting the archipelago to its regional neighbors in peaceful harmony. She played an important role as what Ha Miu Yin Serina calls a "cultural intermediary," introducing contemporary Japanese hit songs to Sinophone audiences in Hong Kong, Taiwan, Singapore, and elsewhere via her Mandarin and Cantonese cover versions, while at the same time introducing her Mandopop repertoire to Japanese audiences (Ha 2016). A 1984 article in the left-of-center *Asahi Journal* trumpeted Teng's comeback as an opportunity to rethink Japan's place in the transnational popular music market. "We have been too focused on the United States and not enough on Asia," the author declares, but

> it seems that an interest is emerging in seeing the current situation of Japan's music as a part of Asia (and not as an isolated island outpost of the West).
>
> For example, I have a feeling that we will soon see research that will take up *enka*, the "music closest to Japanese people's sensibility" from a folklore studies standpoint in the context of the *kayōkyoku* of Japan, Korea, Taiwan, and Hong Kong—taking up their interrelatedness, the subtle distinctions in their lyricism, the similarities and differences in their melodies and singing styles. (Maeda 1984)

As a kind of popular culture fetish, Teng seemed to offer Japanese listeners a replacement for what had been lost in 1945, for what 1955's Bandung Conference had tantalizingly offered. As such, multiple, often contradictory, desires could be projected onto her. On the one hand, Teng presented the fantasy of a subservient, female East Asia, eager to please her Japanese audiences by learning their language (and apologizing tearfully when she caused trouble), an unstable combination of the cheerful and cute girl from next door and a source of exotic romance and erotic fantasy. On the other hand, she offered the possibility of a reunited China that was both modern and traditional, a spiritual ally for Japan. For those on the political left, in particular, she offered the dream of a Japan that was not a client state of the United States, but rather an ally of its nonaligned and decolonizing neighbors in Asia. For those on the right, she offered the dream of Japan as leader in an East Asian version of modernity or postmodernity.

Within the ghostly circuit of the Japanese empire, Teng generated the pleasure of a phantasmic restoration of wholeness to a supposedly shattered Japan as regional superpower, but at the same time served as a troubling reminder of the empire's missing limbs, as a kind of threat to wholeness. As a result, her performance became a screen for projecting another set of Cold

War fantasies—these in a more paranoid, painful mode. She was the foreigner who entered Japan under false pretenses—and perhaps a disease-bearing foreigner at that. At the time of her shocking 1995 death from an asthma attack at the age of forty-two, it was widely rumored in the Japanese tabloid press that the real cause of death was AIDS or perhaps a drug overdose. That she had a French boyfriend and died in Thailand, widely reported at the time in Japan as a regional center of the AIDS epidemic, seemingly added credence to the rumor. A few years later, another set of rumors arose and circulated widely in the Japanese tabloid press: perhaps Teng had been a spy all along, they speculated (Arita 1995 and 1998). Today, she remains an object of fascination in both Japan and China, a quarter century after her death, still the object of television specials, holographic resurrections, staged musicals, and CD reissues, and as her music and image are recirculated, she continues to embody the tensions, fantasies, and anxieties of Cold War histories that can and can't be acknowledged.

Note

I am grateful to acknowledge support for research on this article provided by a 2019 travel grant from the Northeast Asia Council of the Association for Asian Studies.

References

"Akogare no yuki to hatsutaimen." 1975. *Shūkan Heibon* 17(6): unnumbered pictorial section.

Ampiah, Kweku. 1995. "Japan at the Bandung Conference: The Cat Goes to the Mice's Convention." *Japan Forum* 7(1): 15–24.

Arita Yoshifu. 1995. "Teresa Ten wa supai datta ka: tatakau utahime no shinwa kanketsu hen." *Ōru Yomimono* 50(9): 220–30.

———. 1998. "Teresa Ten ansatsu supai eizu-setsu wa mattaku dema desu." *Bungei Shunjū* 76(12): 366–67.

Bourdaghs, Michael K. 2012. *Sayonara Amerika, Sayonara Nippon: A Geopolitical Prehistory of J-Pop*. New York: Columbia University Press.

Cheng, Chen-Ching. 2013. "The Free Voice of China: Pirate Radio Broadcasts of Teresa Teng from Taiwan and Hong Kong during the Cold War Period in Asia." In *The Soundtrack of Conflict: The Role of Music in Radio Broadcasting in Wartime and in Conflict Situations*, eds. M. J. Grant and Férdia J. Stone-Davis, 131–42. Hildesheim, Germany: Georg Olms Verlag.

———. 2020a. "'The Eternal Sweetheart for the Nation': A Political Epitaph for Teresa Teng's Musical Journey in Taiwan." In *Made in Taiwan: Studies in Popular Music*, eds. Eva Tsai, Tung-hung Ho, and Miaoju Jian, 201–10. New York: Routledge.

---. 2020b. "Love Songs from an Island with Blurred Boundaries: Teresa Teng's Anchoring and Wandering in Hong Kong." In *Made in Hong Kong: Studies in Popular Music*, eds. Anthony Fung and Alice Chik, 107–14. New York: Routledge.

Cheng, Chen-Ching, and George Athanasopoulos. 2015. "Music as Protest in Cold-War Asia: Teresa Teng (Deng Lijun), the Enlightenment for Democracy in the 1980s and a Case of Collective Nostalgia for an Era that Never Existed." *Lied und populäre Kultur/Song and Popular Culture* 60: 41–60.

Ching, Leo T. S. 2001. *Becoming "Japanese": Colonial Taiwan and the Politics of Identity Formation*. Berkeley: University of California Press.

---. 2019. *Anti-Japan: The Politics of Sentiment in Postcolonial East Asia*. Durham, NC: Duke University Press.

Chow, Rey. 2007. *Sentimental Fabulations, Contemporary Chinese Films: Attachment in the Age of Global Visibility*. New York: Columbia University Press.

Gordon, David B. 2012. "Prodigy of Taiwan, Diva of Asia: Teresa Teng." *Education About Asia* 17(1): 26–29.

Ha Miu Yin Serina. 2016. "The Role of Cultural Intermediaries in the Spread of Japanese Pop Music to Hong Kong in 1980s." PhD Dissertation, University of Hong Kong.

Harootunian, H. D. 1993. "America's Japan/Japan's Japan." In *Japan in the World*, eds. Masao Miyoshi and H. D. Harootunian, 196–221. Durham, NC: Duke University Press.

Hirano Kumiko. 2015. *Teresa Ten ga mita yume*. Tokyo: Chikuma Shobō.

Igarashi, Yoshikuni. 2000. *Bodies of Memory: Narratives of War in Postwar Japanese Culture, 1945–1970*. Princeton, NJ: Princeton University Press.

"Ijō ninki, Teresa Ten no Chaina-fuku." 1976. *Shūkan Heibun* 18(40): 119.

Itō Tsuyoshi. 1977. "Jitsuryoku o shimeshita fāsuto konsāto: Teresa Ten." *Shūkan Heibon* 19(19): 176.

Jones, Andrew F. 2001. *Yellow Music: Media Culture and Colonial Modernity in the Chinese Jazz Age*. Durham, NC: Duke University Press.

---. 2020. *Circuit Listening: Chinese Popular Music in the Global 1960s*. Minneapolis: University of Minnesota Press.

Kō Mamoru. 2011. *Kayōkyoku: jidai o irodotta utatachi*. Tokyo: Iwanami Shoten.

"Kongetsu no enka kara: zenpan ni rikisaku wo sorou." 1986. *Yomiuri Shinbun* evening edition, February 28, p. 11.

Ku, Lin-hsiu. 1995. "Teresa Teng Forever," trans. Phil Newell. *Sinorama Magazine* 20(7): 1–18.

Lin, Pei-yin. 2017. "How China Is Changed by Deng Lijun and Her Songs." In *Taiwan's Impact on China: Why Soft Power Matters More than Economic or Political Inputs*, ed. Steve Tsang, 179–202. Cham, Switzerland: Palgrave Macmillan.

Maeda Yoshitake. 1984. "Ajia ongaku saihyōka e no michi o hiraita Teresa Ten." *Asaji Jānaru* 26(14): 83.

Miyagi, Taizo. 2017. *Japan's Quest for Stability in Southeast Asia*. London: Routledge.

Nakamura Tōyō. 1991. *Chikyū ga mawaru oto*. Tokyo: Chikuma Shobō.

"Nerai wa Agunesu Chan nidaime? Teresa Ten." 1974. *Sandē Mainichi* 53(12): unnumbered pictorial section.

Oguma, Eiji. 2002. *A Genealogy of "Japanese" Self-Images*, trans. David Agnew. Tokyo: Trans Pacific Press.

"Shinjinshō wa gatchiri itadaki…pisu: Daizadankai." 1975. *Heibon* 30(6): 145–48.

"Teresa Ten fuhō nyūkoku." 1979. *Mainichi Shinbun*, February 19, p. 14.

"Teresa Ten: Ima Ajia ni Kagayaite." 1984. *Mainichi Shinbun* evening edition, March 2, p. 4.

"Teresa Ten-san Chūgoku de fukkatsu." 1985. *Yomiuri Shinbun* evening edition, January 7, p. 2.

Wajima Yusuke. 2018. *Creating Enka: "The Soul of Japan" in the Postwar Era*, trans. Kato David Hopkins. Nara, Japan: Public Bath Press.

Watanabe Yasushi. 1996. *Teresa Ten no shinjitsu: Higeki no utahime, kokkyō o koeta ai*. Tokyo: Tokuma Shoten.

Yano, Christine R. 2002. *Tears of Longing: Nostalgia and the Nation in Japanese Popular Song*. Cambridge, MA: Harvard University Asia Center.

Multimedia Playlist

AGNES CHAN, "Poppy Flower" ("Hinageshi no hana"), 1972
SAKAMOTO FUYUMI, "Fireflies Paper Lantern" ("Hotaru no chōchin"), 1996
MISORA HIBARI, "Apple Oiwake" ("Ringo oiwake"), 1952
———, "Mournful Sake" ("Kanashii sake"), 1966
TERESA TENG, "Airport" ("Kūkō"), 1974
———, "Atonement" ("Tsugunai"), 1984
———, "Leaving It Up to the Flow of Time" ("Toki no nagare ni mi o makasete"), 1986
———, "Maybe Tonight, Maybe Tomorrow?" ("Konya kashira, ashita kashira"), 1974
ZHOU XUAN, "When Will You Return?" ("Heri jun zailai"), 1937
YAMAGUCHI YOSHIKO, "When Will You Return?" ("Heri jun zailai"), 1952

CHAPTER 9

Women, Political Voice, and the South African Diaspora, 1959–2020

CAROL A. MULLER

The voice of mine has taken me to great heights.
(Miriam Makeba, in Makeba with Mwamuka 2004, 246)

> *My gut feeling is that jazz came out of being ripped away from your continent, and your culture being taken away from you.*
> (Sathima Bea Benjamin, in Muller and Benjamin 2011, 167 and 236)

Uhadi is the name chosen because it references the musical bow as the root of our music.
(Sibongile Khumalo, in Muller and Khumalo 2018)

> *I really see my path in South African jazz as a hybrid: it's like jumping on a train and you have no idea where it is going to.*
> (Melanie Scholtz, in National Arts Festival 2009)

The stage is a place I own, it can be a proxy for home.
(Thandiswa Mazwai, in Nelson Mandela University 2020)

There are many pathways to understanding the power of song in the contemporary world. Sometimes, we simply say that power is demonstrated by "popular" musicians who convey universally meaningful messages in music and words that are in English, accessible or formulaic, and sell many copies. Most "popular" musicians were born in Europe, the United States, or Canada—what we call the "Global North"—and, more recently, Latin America. "Cosmopolitan" is how we can think about other musicians who come from places outside of the metropolitan centers of twentieth-century musical production like London, New York, and Los Angeles, who sing opera, folk, or play in a European-style orchestra—these musicians originate elsewhere in the world but have been educated in "western" schools and universities, and sing/play in a universally familiar musical style. A third category of "transnational" singers encompasses those who come from one place and sing for communities of people who were born in that place but who have moved elsewhere—their music works as a vehicle of sentimental connection to unify consumers across national boundaries. There is also a category called "world" musician, which similarly indicates a singer from elsewhere, but who uses the sounds of home, of "culture"/ethnicity/deep tradition and language in a way that is unfamiliar but palatable to the mainstream consumer.

In this chapter, we are going to think about the power of song as sung by those we will identify as "diasporic." By diaspora we mean those who for a variety of reasons have scattered beyond the countries in which they were born—the reasons for diaspora may be religious, gendered, or ethnic/racial persecution. In this chapter, I use the term "diasporic" to talk about South African singers because these singers left their home country, South Africa, often because they were provided an opportunity to sing in the new country when it became impossible to function as singers in their home countries. There was also an ideological identification with the racial struggles and triumphs of those in the new country, the United States, that resonated with political struggles back home. Then, in the early 1990s, with the move away from white minority "apartheid" rule in South Africa, those musicians were able to return home. But, as discussed in this chapter, that return was not easy because for many women musicians there continues to be a feeling of unease due to high levels of gender-based violence all over post-apartheid South Africa. In a strange way, it is still musical performance, either as newly created or invoking the voices of past political struggle, that continues to be the imagined space of home and belonging for these singers.

This chapter provides a South African case study that expands the conventional ways of thinking about a specifically "African" diaspora from those Africans who were sold into slavery (1616–1865), to include Africans who have lived under colonial control in Africa and in the twentieth and early twenty-first centuries left and sometimes returned to Africa, for largely political, educational, and economic reasons, but who still feel a kind of cultural and perhaps gendered displacement, an unbelonging, after they return. These are the feelings generated by being in diaspora.

Until quite recently, scholars mostly thought about the music of "the African diaspora" as a music that came with Africans sold into slavery who arrived in the ports of the southern United States—field hollers, spirituals, and, following Reconstruction (1865–77) and Black migration beyond the South, ragtime, jazz, the music of the civil rights struggle, hip-hop, and so on. This tendency began to change with the publications of British- and Caribbean-born scholars, including Paul Gilroy's *The Black Atlantic: Modernity and Double Consciousness* (1993) and various works by Stuart Hall, the Jamaican-born British cultural theorist. The "Black Atlantic" is a conceptual space for thinking about the continuous exchanges across the Atlantic Ocean that have formed a larger Black diasporic cultural identity—an identity that is always a hybrid form and not solely located in the United States. This concept opened a space for ongoing narratives of African-originating music and musicians in dialogue with those who traveled to and from the Caribbean, South America, the United States, and the United Kingdom—a "new" African diaspora of the twentieth and twenty-first centuries. It is in the context of this "new" African diaspora that we tell the story of the South African women singers that appear in this chapter. I have already explored this through the life of jazz singer Sathima Bea Benjamin (1936–2013) in a book coauthored with her called *Musical Echoes: South African Women Thinking in Jazz* (Muller and Benjamin 2011). In this chapter, we expand that thinking to a larger group of women, and to include the issue of returning home and creating new forms of home and belonging in music that draw on contemporary South African heritage and culture.

The first part of this chapter begins with thinking about two women singers—Miriam Makeba (1932–2008) and Sathima Bea Benjamin—who left South Africa in the mid-twentieth century in search of professional opportunities that were increasingly foreclosed at home because they were women of color who often performed for interracial audiences. When they left South Africa, they did not believe that they would be gone for more than a couple of years. What turned their stories from professional opportunity to new forms of diaspora was political activism abroad: led by singer Miriam Makeba, who was brought to the United States by musician and activist Harry Belafonte, these women increasingly used their voices to educate the Global North about what it meant to live Black and "coloured" under apartheid. Through their performances and speeches, they called for the international community to put an end to the racist regime in South Africa: the regime often responded by banning them in South Africa and taking away their passports. In 1990, however, the apartheid government ended, a new constitution was written, democratic elections were held, and the first Black State President, Nelson Mandela, was voted into power in 1994. This meant that, unlike Africans who were sold into slavery in the Americas and never returned to Africa, South Africans in diaspora and exile could return to their home country.

Returning home to South Africa after decades away has presented significant challenges to women in its newly democratic but not always equal society, a society that had been colonized and controlled by European and British ideas, patriarchy, and culture for four hundred years. Because of that history of colonization, the country and most of its people had lived in a condition of displaced identity—all things African were deemed "uncivilized" and forbidden by the European minority. The challenges, then, for South African women in the 1990s, both those who had returned and those who had stayed in the country, were to figure out ways to decolonize contemporary South Africa, to create a more hybrid nation state—one that was both modern and that fostered a better feeling of an "African" way of being in the world, specifically for women singers. In this chapter, we can think through those contemporary challenges as we briefly discuss the music of three singers: opera/jazz singer Sibongile Khumalo (1957–2021), opera-trained jazz singer Melanie Scholtz (b. 1979), and multi-genre singer King Tha/Thandiswa Mazwai (b. 1976). These singers began to create a specifically South African home by honoring the African ancestors in their music; narrating the stories of their own African cultural and political heroes and histories; engaging the HIV/AIDS epidemic; and fighting for gender equity and sexual freedom, access to affordable and African-centered education, and against gender-based violence. For these women, the challenge in the 1990s was to create a newly envisioned, more equitable space of belonging—a more clearly defined contemporary South African "home." In this sense, the feeling of cultural displacement, dispersal, and "diaspora" is addressed by looking locally at the great diversity of African languages, music, and culture inside South Africa, but also more broadly on the African continent as a whole. The desire of the singers is to heal the wounds of separation that diaspora engenders through physical and cultural displacement by performing sounds of the deep past and the contemporary moment, woven together into something distinctly South African in sound, language, experience, and identity.

A South African Diaspora of Women Musicians (1959–1990)

In August 1959, South African singer Miriam Makeba somehow boarded an airplane out of South Africa to attend the Venice Film Festival. *Come Back, Africa* was a pseudo-ethnographic/fictional film secretly created in South

Africa by the independent American filmmaker Lionel Rogosin about Black urban life and music-making under apartheid in late 1950s South Africa. Two popular songs sung by Makeba were featured at the end of the film, a performance that would turn Makeba into a star in Europe and the United States. The film won the Critics Award in Venice. By screening the film in the United States before the Venice Film Festival, Rogosin had secured Makeba an appearance on the Los Angeles-based Steve Allen television show, and a substantial run at New York City's Village Vanguard. Waiting in London for her US visa, Makeba was performing at the BBC at the same time as the Jamaican-born American citizen singer-songwriter, actor, and activist, Harry Belafonte. Belafonte saw the film, and gave Makeba his contact information. Makeba contacted Belafonte as she left for the United States, and from 1959 through 1968, Belafonte actively promoted Makeba's performing and recording career in the United States and elsewhere. Makeba's *Come Back, Africa* film appearance infuriated the apartheid government in South Africa, and they withdrew her passport in 1960, an action that was personally very hard for Makeba—she had left her child Bongi with her mother, fully expecting to return home. Makeba's banning by the apartheid regime constituted a punitive action that only made her more of a hero in the minds of many Black South Africans.

In 1962, Makeba sang for President John F. Kennedy's birthday celebration, and in 1963 and 1964, she testified to the United Nations Committee on Apartheid. In 1967, Makeba and Belafonte won a Grammy for their recording *An Evening with Belafonte/Makeba*, and her song "Pata Pata" went to number five on the charts and was translated into many languages. Makeba had a fallout with Belafonte after she married Stokely Carmichael/Kwame Toure, the leader of SNCC (the Student Nonviolent Coordinating Committee) and the "Honorary Prime Minister" of the Black Panthers, in 1968. In response to her marriage to Stokely Carmichael, the American entertainment world turned against Makeba, canceling record deals and concert events. In response, the president of the newly independent Republic of Guinea gave Makeba an honorary passport and invited her and her husband to live in his country. As a result, Makeba would come to be known as "Mama Africa," the voice of a growing number of independent African nations who gave her honorary passports and invited her to sing at their celebrations. She later had a brief stint in Belgium until 1990, when Mandela was released from prison and invited her to return home to a country transitioning out of apartheid and into a democratic dispensation.

In February 1962, the South African singer Sathima Bea Benjamin joined her pianist/composer/musical partner, Dollar Brand (who would become

Abdullah Ibrahim after converting to Islam in 1968), to travel to Europe in the hopes of finding a more productive space to play and sing jazz. A year later, they recorded with American jazz pianist, bandleader, and composer Duke Ellington and Billy Strayhorn in the Barclay Studios in Paris. At the time, Ellington was also an A&R man for Frank Sinatra's Reprise Records label. Although Sinatra did not consider Benjamin's voice sufficiently marketable, with Ellington's support, the careers of the three musicians in the Dollar Brand Trio (Dollar Brand on piano, Johnny Gertze on bass, and drummer Makhaya Ntshoko) were launched with an album bearing Ellington's name as producer. While Benjamin and Brand/Ibrahim remained in Switzerland, visiting other parts of Europe and settling in London for a while, they traveled to perform with Ellington at the Newport Jazz Festival in 1965. Ellington secured their visas, and ultimately green cards and US citizenship. After Benjamin, Ibrahim, and their two children came to live permanently in New York following the 1976 Soweto Uprising, Benjamin would go on to create her own record label, Ekapa (Xhosa for "at or from the Cape"), and begin to record her own voice through that label. Her 1982 album, *Dedications*, was nominated for a Grammy Award, quite an achievement for a small, relatively unknown record label.

Two women, two different stories, and two distinct voices emerged in this new South African diaspora. How do we generalize the contours of this moment/movement? I have been thinking about diaspora since 1989, when I began a two-decades-long dialogue with South African–born, and for many years, New York–based jazz singer Sathima Bea Benjamin. With the musical echo as its core metaphor, Benjamin's story of arriving in New York from apartheid South Africa first in the 1960s and more long-term in 1977, required an expansion of ideas about the African diaspora set in motion by the slave trade to the United States. While South Africans were not part of that mostly West African slave trade, they had been subject to four hundred years of colonial occupation (1652–1990) and the apartheid regime (1948–1990) that ran parallel to the Civil Rights movement (1954–1968) in the United States. As Benjamin commented to me more than once, this was why South Africans were attracted to American jazz—because jazz was originally made by those who were ripped away from their continent, Africa. South Africans had their country taken away from them through colonialism, segregation, and apartheid, and they resonated with the dispossession, suffering, and freedom in the sounds of Black American jazz. With the arrival of South African musicians and the changes in US immigration policies introduced by President Lyndon B. Johnson in the 1960s, it was clear there was a new kind of South African diasporic consciousness forming in the United States and South Africans needed to find a way to articulate its contours.

The South African musical diaspora evoked in Makeba's and Benjamin's music and biographies highlights four diasporic moments that give us insight into the new diasporic experiences of South African women performers who went into musical and political exile between 1959 and 1990. Although not fleshed out in any detail, the stories of both women are characterized as follows:

(1) Predeparture
Before leaving South Africa, they learned to sing, dance, and act in school and church choirs, passionately listening to and copying American and British popular music and films. Being a woman in public performance was frowned upon, they were often the only women among male performers, and it was often dangerous. They both had some recording opportunities before departure.

(2) Departure and Arrival
They left, stepping into the unknown, primarily as performers, not political advocates. Accompanied or invited by male performers, they traveled first to Europe and then on to the United States. Makeba settled in the United States almost immediately with the help of Lionel Rogosin, Max Gordon of the Village Vanguard, and the management and strategic purpose of Harry Belafonte. Benjamin traveled all over for fifteen years, until Duke Ellington helped her and her partner Abdullah Ibrahim with immigration papers that enabled them to settle in the United States.

(3) A New Diasporic Aesthetic
This new sense of identity was generated by greater activism in support of the anti-apartheid movement abroad that impacted their compositions, performances, and recording contents. This happened quickly for Makeba, who arrived in New York City just after the Sharpeville Massacre (1960), in which three of her family were killed. She testified before the United Nations several times, with the first in July 1963. Her activist voice became stronger throughout the 1960s, until she married Stokely Carmichael in 1968. Then, she moved back to Africa. This meant that her impact on the United States lessened as Benjamin's voice became more prominent from the mid-1970s through 1990, although Makeba became known as "Mama Africa," representing the Republic of Guinea all over. The live and recorded performances of both women began to reflect this shift.

(4) Return
Neither of the singers was invited to perform at President Nelson Mandela's inauguration in May 1994. Benjamin went as Abdullah Ibrahim's wife, and Miriam Makeba wasn't invited at all (although Belafonte was there). For these women, returning to South Africa

created some ambivalence—home was not as welcoming as they had hoped. And for other women who stayed at home under apartheid, South Africa was often a dangerous place characterized by police, army, and gender-based violence, as we will see further on in the discussion of the contemporary singer Thandiswa Mazwai.

Both Makeba and Benjamin were mothers while living in diaspora. Both created song performances around what was arguably the turning point in the anti-apartheid struggle in South Africa, mass mediated globally—the June 16, 1976, uprising of school children in the township of Soweto in Johannesburg. The children were protesting the government forcing them to be taught at school in Afrikaans and not either English or their mother tongue—Zulu, Xhosa, Tswana, and so forth (there are eleven official languages in South Africa). Both women used songs to memorialize that moment in South African political history, two of which are discussed below. Although we will not focus on it here, the culminating production commemorating the Soweto Uprising was the musical theater piece *Sarafina!*, written and produced by Mbongeni Ngema, first performed in South Africa (1987), then at Lincoln Center (1988–9), then Broadway, and finally adapted into a Hollywood feature film starring Whoopi Goldberg and Miriam Makeba in 1992 (Roodt 1992).[1] In the middle of this performance run was the 1990 release of Mandela and other political prisoners from prison. This started the transition from apartheid to Black majority, democratic rule with the installation of South Africa's first Black president, Nelson Rolihlahla Mandela. What was prophesied in the musical theater performance *Sarafina!* was realized in person in February 1990—Nelson Mandela was free to walk the streets of Soweto after twenty-seven years of political imprisonment, and those in self-imposed and government-mandated political exile could return home. Two songs that memorialize Soweto as the turning point of the anti-apartheid struggle are discussed below and currently easiest to locate on Youtube:

(1) Makeba: "Soweto Blues" (Makeba 2015), written by Hugh Masekela. Here, we see Miriam Makeba's introduction with the backup band and clips of the song with her interview commentary, detailing the sadness of June 16, the joy associated with Mandela's release, and the deep disappointment associated with returning to a country not yet ready for her voice.

(2) Benjamin: "Children of Soweto" (Benjamin 2013) is Benjamin's own composition, an anthem-styled song recorded as part of what she called her Liberation Suite (shadowing Abbey Lincoln and Max Roach's 1960 Freedom Now Suite). Benjamin recorded the Suite on her 1986 album, *Memories and Dreams* (Ekapa). The suite includes

three of her originals: "Africa"—the quintessential voice of diasporic longing; "Children of Soweto"; and "Nations in Me—New Nation a Comin'," a song written after she attended the 1975 independence celebrations of the former Portuguese colony Mozambique. Benjamin traveled to represent the South African delegation in exile and was struck by the full spectrum of racial diversity in Mozambique, an observation that made her reflect on the diversity of her own racial heritage.

While travel abroad offered real opportunities, including the capacity to record their voices with others to varying degrees, both Makeba and Benjamin also lived with significant loss. Stripped of their passports and the capacity to return to South Africa, they were ever on the move in search of work and personal safety. Their children suffered from the rootlessness and displacement of diaspora and exile, often with serious consequences for their emotional and physical health. At times, both were victims of domestic violence or partner infidelities. In one way or another, they both invoked narratives of ancestral presence, through dreams, visions, and other spiritual experiences. They used their music as a vehicle for personal, collective, cultural, and emotional healing, often with a narrative of the sangoma, or traditional healer, tied to their well-being and song performances.

Perhaps the most important characteristic of diasporic experience for these women is the transformation of voice, as both sound and political position. Overall, I suggest that we think about the South African diaspora as causing both women to reconstitute their singing less as entertainment as it had been in South Africa, and more as representing the voices of political struggle at home. This may not have been their intention when they left South Africa, but it was what they were thrust into and what came to be expected of them as women of color from South Africa performing in the United States—in many ways because of the parallel civil rights struggles of Black Americans. While they could not vote in South Africa, their voices came to stand in for the repression and silencing of all Black voices by the apartheid regime while they lived and performed abroad. And they did so always from their perspectives as mothers—both of their own children and, as we hear in the two examples discussed above, identifying powerfully with the mothers of South African children lost, wounded, or killed in the struggle against the apartheid regime.

Returning Home: A New Kind of Diaspora

In the 1990s, South Africans began to go home to a country gradually and not always peacefully transformed from a colonial/apartheid regime to an ideally non-racial democratic dispensation. Both Makeba and Benjamin would return to South Africa as the country made this transition, although it soon became clear that issues of gender equity had not been addressed in the political struggle or its negotiated settlements. Despite their work as political voices of the anti-apartheid struggle abroad, only Benjamin attended Nelson Mandela's presidential inauguration, and she was only invited as partner to her musician husband, Abdullah Ibrahim, who was invited to perform. Miriam Makeba was completely excluded. After her return, Makeba engaged in the battle against HIV/AIDS in South Africa, supporting rural women and girls living at the edges of the epidemic. Benjamin carried the private burden of caring for an adult son suffering from mental illness, a condition that seemed to be the result of his being born into the uncertainties that political exile, domestic violence, and diaspora imposed.

The imagined possibilities of returning home set in motion a new stage of contemporary South African diasporic consciousness, one shaped by the contradictory realities of a newly liberated nation. While government power was turned over, political negotiations did not adequately address land redistribution or sufficient economic restructuring and rebuilding. There was also the global HIV/AIDS epidemic with its center in the province of KwaZulu Natal. The promise of freedom, the capacity for empowerment, and the gradual growth of a meaningful Black middle class would take a full generation to begin to come into being for some. Righting the wrongs of the past has included telling local histories even if in borrowed forms, including *Winnie Mandela: The Opera*, *Princess Constance Dinizulu Magogo*, and *uShaka*, all three renderings of South African history as operatic narrative with South African singers.

To capture some of this moment of return and rooting in South African history and culture, let us take a brief look at two women who both identified first as opera and then as jazz singers—Sibongile Khumalo and Melanie Scholtz—both university-educated recipients of the Standard Bank Young Artist Award for contributions to South African jazz. Both women viewed the voice as a vehicle for personal truth-telling, for experimenting with personal freedom, and for honoring the heroes and sounds of South Africa's apartheid past. For Khumalo, jazz was a space for remembering the era of 1950s township jazz optimism, and for Scholtz, it was a means of paying tribute to previous generations of freedom fighters, poets, artists, and musicians who used words, sound, and images as their weapons in the struggle.

Sibongile Khumalo was born in Soweto in 1957, and lived her life in that space, for many years surrounded by her father, the Professor of Music Khabi Mngoma. Khumalo's operatic voice narrated a story of the orally transmitted deep Zulu past, carried by the sound of one of Africa's oldest instruments, the Zulu/Xhosa musical bow known as the *uhadi*. That ancient bow and Khumalo's operatic voice conveyed the story of Zulu history as transmitted in the early twentieth century by the Zulu royal historian, Princess Magogo, with a score by South African composer Mzilikazi Khumalo. That operatic narrative was staged at Chicago's Ravinia Music Festival in 2004. Broadcast by National Public Radio, *Princess Magogo* was the first Zulu language opera performed by South Africans in the United States.[2] In 2006, Sibongile Khumalo returned to Chicago with Mzilikazi Khumalo's second Zulu opera, *uShaka*. While the South African playwright Welcome Msomi's *uMabatha*—an adaptation of Shakespeare's *Macbeth* into early nineteenth-century tribal Zulu culture—had staged a form of Zulu song, dance, and language in New York City in the 1970s using the voices of township choirs, Sibongile Khumalo's goal was to present the richness and beauty of Zulu history and culture through the technically powerful and rich tones of the operatic voice.

Several years later, Khumalo returned to the United States as a jazz singer to perform with Lincoln Center Jazz.[3] She called her jazz ensemble "Uhadi," the name of the traditional Zulu/Xhosa musical bow used in the Magogo opera. For Khumalo, the bow articulated the roots of South African music, and its single string could be metaphorically stretched to accommodate the racial diversity of the Uhadi musicians, allowing for flexibility, new combinations, and improvisation between five musicians whose mother tongues were all different. With the global optimism of South Africa's transition to a democratic "rainbow nation" at that time, the American centers of elite cultural production—Ravinia and Lincoln Center—were reconstituted as sites for the narration of southern African history through their musical performances. This was no longer South Africans longing to be like their American counterparts, but rather wishing to tell specifically South African stories to American audiences. They had listened to America, and now they wished for Americans to hear from them.

The Cape Town-born, post-apartheid, opera-trained jazz singer Melanie Scholtz came to live permanently in New York City as a singer, composer, pianist, and collage artist, after having worked a few years as a studio musician in the Czech Republic. Fiercely independent, she produced five albums of her own work, including a project, *Freedom's Child*, where she collaborated with and paid tribute to the anti-apartheid activist and poet James Matthews. She is what is known as a "born free"—someone born at the end of apartheid—and although she didn't experience its terror, she strives to honor those who did. The poet James Matthews was one of the radical voices of the post-apartheid era, whose work Scholtz recalled studying as required reading for English literature in school. Quite serendipitously, she was thinking of working with a poet when she happened upon Matthews sitting on a park bench in the center of Cape Town. They decided to collaborate. The results can be seen in "Freedom's Child," where her voice pays tribute to her political ancestors, those who fought for political transformation and freedom (see Expresso Show 2013).

Diaspora in the Recent and COVID-19 Moment

South Africa is now three decades into the new political dispensation and many of the country's younger musicians have little or no memory of the harshness of apartheid rule. The diasporic longing that characterized what we called the South African diaspora has started to shift, for many, away from the United States, now redirected toward South Africa's newfound position on the African continent. Following in the footsteps of "Mama Africa" Miriam Makeba, South African musicians have traveled to many parts of Africa, and many African musicians have also performed in South Africa. There are the Kora Music Awards, the All Africa Music Awards, and numerous pathways of electronic and virtual collaboration and partnership across the continent.

For many, however, South Africa's fledgling democracy is increasingly experienced as a space of uncertainty, contingency, growing inequality, despair, and perhaps even unbelonging. Although there has been a gradual growth of a meaningful Black middle class, locally called the "black diamonds," South Africa is now the country with the highest level of income inequality in the world. Overcoming the traumatic experiences of the latter years of township life with the inevitable loss of family—mothers, fathers, uncles, and siblings—to political violence has been underacknowledged but remains an urgent public health challenge. In addition, the freedom to express oneself through the full spectrum of gendered identities has often been met with violence. Although violence against women has a long history in apartheid/colonial South Africa, gender-based violence targeting lesbian/gay and "nonconforming" gender identities has increased exponentially. There is ongoing pressure not only to address the wrongs of apartheid but to dig deeper into the centuries of European colonization in the region, as expressed in both the #rhodesmustfall and #feesmustfall student movements of 2016. As a result, the broader focus has shifted from political empowerment—the right to vote and to fair representation—to the urgent need for affordable African-centered education through which Africans produce and transmit their own history, culture, and languages, and tell the true stories of European colonization, in addition to rapid job creation and individual healing.

It is in this context that we take a look at the final singer, Thandiswa Mazwai, known as King Tha, the radical, multi-genre, deep-thinking storyteller, healer, and lesbian womanist/feminist. Born in the Eastern Cape in 1976—the year of the Soweto Uprising—she grew up with her journalist and activist parents on the streets of Soweto. She recalls that in her parents' home, books were all around her, and so she read the writings of Pan-Africanists Frantz Fanon, Steve Biko, Chinua Achebe, and others. Thandiswa Mazwai studied at the University of the Witwatersrand in Johannesburg and is now a member of the emergent Black upper middle class "black diamonds."

One of the founding members of the post-apartheid electronic genre kwaito, King Tha was the lead singer for the group Bongo Maffin, and continually experiments with new formations, both as a soloist and with all-women groups, always honoring and remembering the heroes, male and female, of the anti-apartheid struggle at home and abroad. Her more recent womanist-focused performances have caused women to throw their bras onstage as King Tha performs; she clearly conveys a powerful message for Black women's empowerment in South Africa. She has traveled throughout the African continent and across the Global North, and occasionally performs in Radio City Music Hall, the Apollo, and for the Afropunk and jazz communities in New York City. In 2017, she performed two original songs at a Southern African TED event.

> You can watch the performance here:
> https://www.youtube.com/watch?v=-guHd9Zrbn4
>
> King Tha sings two original songs: "Iyeza" ("Medicine"), which she explains is for our madness and rage, and "Zabalaza" ("Rebel"), a song she dedicates to the university students in South Africa who in 2016 insisted on the decolonization of university campuses in South Africa via two movements: #feesmustfall and #rhodesmustfall. She adds that there was also a new vigor given by these students to the feminist movement: patriarchy must fall. King Tha integrates her performances into the larger history of political struggle, particularly of the anti-apartheid movement of the 1970s and 1980s, arguing that the struggle for freedom is not over. She sings "Aluta Continua" (Portuguese for "the struggle continues"), the old slogan of the anti-apartheid struggle, over and over as she ends this performance with her voice raised in the high registers—signaling the sounds of traditional healing and spirituality—as she descends to finish her anthem for women's strength and freedom.

I first heard Thandiswa Mazwai perform live on Zoom while I was stuck inside during the COVID-19 pandemic and unable to travel. I witnessed two of her "live" performances—one at the Arts Alive Festival, streamed live, and the other celebrating the first anniversary of the Women and Gender Studies Center at Nelson Mandela University. Both followed after listening via Zoom to the rich thinking of the Johannesburg-centered but usually always traveling South African artist William Kentridge present the annual endowed lecture at the University of Pennsylvania's Arthur Ross Gallery. I will join these conversations in bringing this chapter to some closure by considering the radical shift in diasporic possibility brought about by the global COVID-19 pandemic—its denial of human movement and simultaneous encouragement of rapid virtual connectivity through the mobility of technology—how quickly the world moved to Zoom! The lack of containment of the virus in 2020–21 stands in stark contrast to the lockdowns and shutdowns experienced all over the world and our inability to move freely from place to place. COVID-19 brought record unemployment, public protests, and a renewed energy to the Black Lives Matter and Defund the Police movements, along with the often brutal suppression of dissent, especially in the United States. In South Africa, although there has been less death than in the United States, the monumental job losses and overwhelming hunger caused by immobility and extreme shutdown have meant that death would simply find another way in.

One of the effects of the COVID-19 pandemic has been to produce a moment reminiscent of the earlier era of South African exile and diaspora, where the capacity to travel outside boundaries of the nation state is suddenly and unexpectedly limited. People cannot rehearse together or travel internationally to record and earn US dollars. And yet, it has been impressive to see innovative responses to lockdown in South Africa on social media, perhaps because nobody can afford not to work and there is simply no social welfare safety net for South African artists—the government has failed miserably. This experience has given some musicians and artists time to reflect on what it means to be part of a larger African diaspora. And a key dimension of this capacity to reflect is a series of ongoing questions pertaining to reconfiguring a sense of a more African home, and of the place of Africa in the contemporary world, a place that many believe needs to be reevaluated.

In the COVID-19 moment, the world-renowned visual artist William Kentridge took us via Zoom into his artist's studio to consider the work of what he calls "the less good idea." It is a way of thinking, in my view, that gives South Africans an artistic means to explore new ways of valuing all things African and to create a more culturally coherent sense of South African home in the contemporary world (see Kentridge 2017). So often, Kentridge explains, the artist sets out with a very good idea. The work of art-making begins with this very good idea. The idea is strong, powerful, centered, and loud in its authority. But after a time, the certainty of the good idea begins to waiver; its logic begins to falter when it is put on stage. After spending months and months on the very good idea, the artist recognizes that the fragments that exist on the periphery, at the edges of vision, the traces of the idea, dangling in spaces of the unknown, of uncertainty, of contingency and difference, may eventually be the better sources for making art. This edge of vision, I suggest, is where the revaluing of things African takes shape. And, Kentridge argues, it is the [artist's] studio that is the safe place for such imagining and creation: playing with the less good idea, giving it its moment, then putting aside the good idea and giving space to the traces and the fragments. In Kentridge's studio, as in hip-hop, kwaito, Shangaan electric, and South African jazz, collage is the process for assembling the fragments into history, the space of experimentation for and by contemporary musicians.

Conclusion

So, South Africans wonder, what do we make of the center of good ideas in the Age of COVID-19, the Black Lives Matter movement, and the global focus on police brutality? What does diaspora mean now? Even if South Africa is the center of the pandemic in Africa, the spread of the virus in Africa so far does not seem to be nearly as severe as it has been in the United States. Africans are beginning to understand that America has never had Africa's deep history. Slavery denied African history, cultures, and languages to those who arrived in America, as did colonialism in Africa. Africans, and South Africans in particular, are beginning to recognize and process the violence of European partitioning, colonization, and silencing. And so it is in this moment that South African women singers are digging deeper, hovering in place, and seeking to come to terms with the destructiveness of colonial history. Resisting the urge to leave, they instead choose to celebrate those who have fought for freedom from that dominance, to come out from under the force of the pervasive good idea from the Global North, and to focus on seeking out the place of the less good ideas: fragments, traces, remnants, and small presences of a precolonial African past that could be imaginatively remade in a post-COVID-19 world.

Thandiswa Mazwai's voice reminds us that for women singers, the struggle to find one's place in a newly democratic, liberated context is ongoing because of the uneven nature of diasporic return. There is a complicated sense of "home" due to societal inattention to post-apartheid women's rights, ongoing violence against women, and the devastation of increasing poverty, all of which lead to contradictory feelings of unbelonging. The last decade has seen a gradual move toward greater gender equality and against gender-based violence, all in the shadow of an ever-present HIV/AIDS epidemic that has already killed and sickened so many. HIV/AIDS has required the labor of women in rural communities to care for the sick, the dying, and their children, who would otherwise be orphaned. And then there is the ongoing scourge of gang violence in the Cape. Living among the poor creates a feeling of unbelonging for a host of reasons, and history continues to seep into the everyday, with reminders of past struggles, victories, and the need to keep the struggle simultaneously in the present and the future. The old African diaspora and the new South African diaspora—diasporas as a state of ongoing internal unbelonging are all brought into new perspective by the immobility and forced homestay brought by the COVID-19 pandemic. These South African women singers all wonder through musical experimentation: Where will this moment take them in healing the ruptures and traumas of the past in the present?

Notes

1. For a documentary on the musical theatre piece produced and performed in New York City, see Noble 1988.
2. For more on the making of the *Princess Magogo* opera, see Opera Africa 2013.
3. For an interview with Sibongile Khumalo at Lincoln Center Jazz, see Muller and Khumalo 2018.

References

Benjamin, Sathima Bea. 2013. "Children of Soweto." www.youtube.com. https://www.youtube.com/watch?v=RRxST7XnOwU.
Expresso Show. 2013. "Interview and Performance with Melanie Scholtz and James Matthews 'Freedom's Child.'" www.youtube.com. https://www.youtube.com/watch?v=hoB_w8b6oDk.
Feldstein, Ruth. 2013. "Screening Anti-apartheid: Miriam Makeba, 'Come Back, Africa,' and the Transnational Circulation of Black Culture and Politics." *Feminist Studies* 39(1): 12–39.
Gilroy, Paul. 1993. *The Black Atlantic: Modernity and Double Consciousness.* Cambridge, MA: Harvard University Press.
Kentridge, William. 2017. "The Defence of the Less Good Idea." www.vimeo.com. https://vimeo.com/211476297.
Makeba, Miriam. 2015. "Miriam Makeba with Hugh Masekela—Soweto Blues (South Africa Freedom Song)." www.youtube.com. https://www.youtube.com/watch?v=dMSwlBGcSRs.
———, with James Hall. 1987. *Makeba: My Story.* New York: New American Library.

———, with Nomsa Mwamuka. 2004. *The Miriam Makeba Story*. Johannesburg: STE Publishers.

Muller, Carol Ann, and Sathima Bea Benjamin. 2011. *Musical Echoes: South African Women Thinking in Jazz*. Durham, NC: Duke University Press.

———, and Sibongile Khumalo. 2018. "South Africa's 'First Lady of Song' Sibongile Khumalo, Part One." www.youtube.com. https://www.youtube.com/watch?v=ynLrbN2pg2o.

National Arts Festival. 2009. "Standard Bank Young Artist Award 2010—Melanie Scholtz (Jazz)." www.youtube.com. https://www.youtube.com/watch?v=b1N9iXRNDYo.

Nelson Mandela University. 2020. "Celebrating CWGS One Year Anniversary with an Interview with Thandiswa Mazwai." www.youtube.com. https://www.youtube.com/watch?v=kNm5li0769s.

Noble, Nigel, dir. 1988. *Voices of Sarafina!* New York: New Yorker Films. https://www.youtube.com/watch?v=qoJ5bojx758.

Opera Africa. 2013. "The Making of an African Opera (Princess Magogo)." www.youtube.com. https://www.youtube.com/watch?v=zh3BJ4yx-Mg.

Roodt, Darrell James, dir. 1992. *Sarafina!* Burbank, CA: Buena Vista Pictures.

In addition to twenty years of conversations with Sathima Bea Benjamin, I have recorded interviews with Sibongile Khumalo (1995, 2016) and Melanie Scholtz (2019), though all quotes with Melanie Scholtz come from publicly accessible interviews and programs.

Multimedia Playlist

SATHIMA BEA BENJAMIN, "Children of Soweto" (written by Sathima Bea Benjamin) https://www.youtube.com/watch?v=Q9ZdVaEsbOQ

SIBONGILE KHUMALO, *Ancient Evenings* (full jazz album) https://www.youtube.com/watch?v=yQO1PUhw1go&list=OLAK5uy_maEWbB-5oExQJQwhj1WMk1shikDTlV76U

———, Sibongile Khumalo's conversation on the Opera *Princess Magogo* https://www.youtube.com/watch?v=riKYFGwNmRA

MIRIAM MAKEBA, "Soweto Blues" (written by Hugh Masekela) https://www.youtube.com/watch?v=YGbEQ210_J4

THANDISWA MAZWAI, "Iyeza" ("Medicine"—live version) https://www.youtube.com/watch?v=XDNwZ9UTPDo

———, "Zabalaza" ("Rebel") https://www.youtube.com/watch?v=kyY2r_iitas

MELANIE SCHOLTZ, "Freedom's Child" (poetry by James Matthews) with Soweto Kinch https://www.youtube.com/watch?v=cTbhWOKk9yY&list=OLAK5uy_nHXDqDhK3_8wjKb9vjaB-lLYInDJ_GVwU

PART IV

Singers and Songs as Interweaving Narratives

Introduction
Kwame Dawes

As a writer, nurtured on the anti-colonial and postcolonial texts of writers from Africa and the Caribbean emerging in the 1950s and '60s who were engaged in the complex challenge of constructing a literary aesthetic that sought to deconstruct the power of colonial traditions, and to, instead, derive their meaning and power from an activation of the aesthetics of sites of origin long denigrated and ignored by the colonial enterprise, I became a writer challenged by this core value, but also challenged by the demand of my moment of coming of age to find a poetics and an aesthetic that spoke to my lived experience. I found models in the aforementioned literature, and more urgently in the music that became a defining force in my world, the reggae music of the 1970s and 1980s. As this was taking shape in me intellectually and creatively, I was also growing as a scholar and an artist, and I knew fairly early on that the popular music of Jamaica would represent what *son* music was for Nichols Guillen, the blues for Amiri Baraka and Langston Hughes, rhythm and blues for Ntozake Shange, Irish folk culture and myth for Yeats, and so on. My two key books on the subject, *Bob Marley: Lyrical Genius*, a close study of Marley's lyrics, and *Natural Mysticism: Towards a New Reggae Aesthetic in Caribbean Writing*, a book of exploratory theory, are the products of this development in me. My work as a writer, an editor, a scholar, and a literary activist has been deeply influenced by my constant engagement with the rich store of insight and beauty in the music shaped in many of the cultures in which I have lived. I am as interested in these esoteric matters as I am in the sheer pleasure of enjoying music and its powerful impositions on my body and sensibilities.

It has struck me for years and in my own research around reggae music and culture, that one of the most fascinating and rewarding areas of study around global musical culture is the very capacity that we have to speak of such a thing. There is a long history, perhaps epitomized and repeated in western narratives about various cultures that are predicated around the idea of sound, meaning, and the function of music as a marker of understanding, civilization, and cultural value, especially when placed in direct contrast with the music of other cultures regardless of what the nature of that relationship might be.

In Shakespeare's *The Tempest*, we see enacted an understanding of language that opens the way for a certain cultural dynamic that dismisses a language as nonexistent and gibberish simply because it is not understood. Prospero does not claim to have taught Caliban *his* language, but that he has taught him how to speak, has taught him *language*. Prospero presumes that whatever Caliban spoke before he arrived was not language but mere gibberish, noise, a void of meaning. Caliban, to Shakespeare's credit, is able to make a distinction between what Prospero might have imagined, and what Caliban thinks of this transaction: "You taught me language, and my profit on 't/ Is I know how to curse. The red plague rid you/ For learning me your language!" (I.ii.). The obscenity of Prospero's assertion of hegemony and power is what has operated in various ways in which the colonializing or imperializing gesture has been about the denigrating of the sounds and the music of others as non-music.

In Jamaica's modern music history, the "noise" of the working class and religiously ostracized reggae artist is celebrated in metaphor and, in actuality, as a means to "disturb [the] neighbors" (as Bob Marley sings in "Bad Card") and shocking, as Lorna Goodison declares, "decent people's" sensibilities (1992, 61). Reggae is the recalibration of the idea of what constitutes music. This is an old dilemma and one that is complicated by technology. Indeed, when I teach my course on reggae music, I must begin with a brief history of the technology of music, or found recording, of the rapidly expanding ways in which we access music and how these means of access have complicated and shaped our cultures, our economies, and our ideas of aesthetics in deep and complex ways that eventually force us to have to reckon with the unreliability of notions of purity, of essentialism, and of originality.

For even while in the years before the twentieth century, efforts were made to try to find a kind of universal aesthetic of beauty and harmony by musicologists acting as anthropologists, the twentieth century has complicated this matter simply because technology has changed the way we apprehend music, how we access it, and how we engage it. And this transformation is rapid and continues unchecked. The quick, easy access to music from around the world via YouTube and Spotify and iTunes is startling when compared to what was available to us forty years ago. There is a generation of people who cannot easily de-couple music from the images generated in music videos. And the narratives of music videos have their own force and impact that can shape and reshape the way we apprehend the thing we imagine to be "pure" music.

Technology has brought with it the construction of a "mass" understanding of the individual—the advent of the global star. They have existed before, but not at such alarming and all-consuming regularity, and not with the level of incongruity between the substance of their fame and the fact of their fame. The "icon" is global because technology has invented global reach. And this phenomenon has effectively imposed its disruptive power on the idea of the "local," the conception of local value. When industry and capitalism establish a value system predicated on the monetizing of fame, they are assaulting the very idea of a value system predicated on the local, on the village, on the parochial. They are also creating a platform of power that effectively manipulates issues of gender, race, sexual identity, and nationalism in ways that are designed to sustain the commercial enterprise.

Human beings are remarkable in our capacity to bring invention and creativity to even the most dehumanizing of technologies, but we have to consider the ways in which technology is seriously transforming the very idea of indigeneity especially in music. The global conglomerate of the *Got Talent* and *American Idol* franchises is certainly worthy of study as a force that is affecting the idea of music and the way that music is consumed around the world. The chapters that follow offer fascinating ways of engaging this idea. Technology changes what we understand about music, whether it is the role of the film industry in India, vocal practices of female singers, or the Americanization of Arabic music in *Arabs Got Talent*. The reckoning with this fact of technology, and the function and role of how music is consumed in the world, as well as the ways in which it is weaponized, manipulated, and exported as a cultural product and as a product of imperial and colonial power is the historical context, often so much taken for granted that we never spell it out, of these bracing and sophisticated essays on quite varied music traditions.

Rich with information and offering fascinating insights into music traditions and experiences that are exciting and sophisticated, the chapters in this section function in an environment in which many readers' access to the videos, episodes, films, and so on that form the basis of their examination is quite remarkable, and has played a truly essential role in the readers' ability to bridge the differences of cultures, histories, and traditions that will confront many readers of these chapters. We can listen to the work, study the work, and meditate on the work through the possibilities of technology. Of course, I am cautious about the broad presumption around access, especially given the massive imbalance that exists globally around access to media, to the internet, and to other sources of information.

Natalie Sarrazin explores the history of playback singing in Indian film and its impact on the Indian film industry, offering an authoritative and well-researched discussion about the remarkable and influential career of Lata Mangeshkar (1929–2022). Grounded in an informed historical review of the phenomenon of playback singing performance in India, her chapter provides an engaging study of the peculiar manifestation of popular art in Indian society, examining issues of gender stereotypes, vocal practice, and the entire industry surrounding the female voice. Katherine Meizel, in turn, in her extremely insightful and well-informed examination of a singular moment in the global musical industry in which a white American singer Jennifer Grout (b. 1990) wins *Arabs Got Talent*, identifies a moment rich with all the questions surrounding globalization, musical authenticity, stardom, and the complex and fraught geopolitical relationship between the West and the Arab World, and effectively guides us through the nuances of musical theory and practice. Her chapter allows us to see the intersection between the personal and the political in the music industry, and all of this is shot through with matters of cultural appropriation and cultural hegemony.

References

Baraka, Amiri. 1999. *Blues People: Negro Music in White America*. New York: Perennial.

Dawes, Kwame. 1998. *Natural Mysticism: Towards a New Reggae Aesthetic in Caribbean Writing*. Leeds, UK: Peepal Tree Press.

———. 2007. *Bob Marley: Lyrical Genius*. New York: Bobcat Books.

Goodison, Lorna. 1992. *Selected Poems*. Ann Arbor: University of Michigan Press.

Shakespeare, William. 1958. *The Tempest*. Cambridge, MA: Harvard University Press.

Shange, Ntozake. 2010. *For Colored Girls Who Have Considered Suicide When the Rainbow Is Enuf*. New York: Scribner.

CHAPTER 10

The Vocal Narratives of Lata Mangeshkar

Gender, Politics, and Nation in India

NATALIE SARRAZIN

At a dinner party in the late 1990s, a colleague asked what field of research I studied. When I said, "Indian film music," he exclaimed, "Oh yes, I've seen some films, but why do the female singers all sound alike?" While this question might strike some as culturally uninformed, I could not deny its fundamental accuracy. The vocal similarity he referred to was due to the voluminous vocal contribution of one playback singer—Lata Mangeshkar (1929–2022). Not only were a huge number of film songs sung by Lata Mangeshkar during Hindi film's heyday—the 1950s–1980s—but almost all other singers during this time imitated her as well. A novice listener of Indian film music, therefore, could not help but hear a predominantly Lata soundprint.

Lata Mangeshkar's vocal aesthetic coupled with unique external factors catapulted her to the forefront of Indian film music, while her longevity, hegemony, and popularity subsequently captured the national limelight, making her a subject of considerable interest. Her life has been examined in documentaries, fanzines, websites, on radio, TV, in countless newspapers, and in numerous academic disciplines. Beyond the film music world, however, Lata's career offers a stimulating look at the integration of politics and music through a cinematic lens. Scholars from a wide range of fields have studied her impact.

Sociologist Sanjay Srivastava (2004, 2007) and economist Ashwini Deshpande (2004, 2015), for example, have contentiously debated Lata's popularity and impact on gender, politics, and the nation, particularly in relation to its connection to India's five-year plans. Film, media scholars, and ethnomusicologists such as Neepa Majumdar (2001), Pavitra Sundar (2008), and Gregory Booth (2008) contextualize her musical attributes in a larger sociopolitical perspective, while others such as Ashok Ranade (2006) and Peter Manuel (1993) focus primarily on the voice itself and its reverberations.

While India's film industry has certainly seen its share of female singers, the question of Lata's vocal prominence and long industry reign is front and center. How does her voice compare to those who came before her? How did her voice come to embody the ideals of a nation and shape certain standards of femininity to the exclusion of others? In this chapter, I will examine Lata's vocal imprint on the nation through a critical juncture in India's history as it navigated a confluence of postcolonialism, nationalism, and the creation of a new post-independence femininity, addressing her unique contribution, contextualized in sociopolitical and musical perspectives, and address how early film voices led to a Lata-dominated homogeneity. Ultimately, I argue, Lata's voice and stardom captured and embodied a complex system of signs outside of the film world, which exemplified a standard of female performativity and the goals of the nation itself.

Playback Singing in Indian Cinema

Indian cinema is the most prolific film industry in the world, producing over one thousand films per year, most containing songs. Indian cinema is unique in that its actors do not sing but lip-synch to songs pre-recorded by playback singers in a studio. Lata Mangeshkar's voice is one of India's most prolific playback singers. Her voice is instantly recognizable and iconic, having sung for actresses in hundreds of films and thousands of songs over her long career.[1] Her popularity is partly a result of being a productive playback singer in a high-volume industry,[2] and partly rooted in the fact that India's film music industry also functions as its popular music industry, dominating over 80 percent of the music market. This "double-duty" means that playback singers are pop stars as well and are often as or more popular than actors. Their voices not only sell soundtracks (which are sold separately as cassettes, CDs, or streaming) but the films themselves. Their value is undisputed, and a good playback singer can lend nuance to the role and characterization of an actor. Lata, for example, provided vocal interpretations that were highly admired by audiences, music directors, and actors over her extensive career.

An additional source of playback singer popularity concerns its disembodied nature, which provides singers with a longevity advantage in that they do not age in front of the camera. Audiences only hear Lata, but rarely see her perform. While most actors, particularly female leads, were replaced rather quickly by younger actors, playback singers often maintain their positions behind the scenes and work for decades. Lata and her playback-singing sister Asha Bhosle's (b. 1933) careers, for example, lasted almost seventy years, in part due to their off-camera work.

Lata: An Overview

Lata was born in 1929 in Indore, then a princely state in British India, during India's freedom struggle. From an early age, her life and identity revolved around theatre and music. Her Maharashtrian Brahmin father, Dinanath, was a classical singer and Marathi theatre actor (the spoken language of the state of Maharashtra) who changed the family name from Hardikar to Mangeshkar to better represent his family's Goan identity. Lata's given name was Hema, and she was renamed Lata after a character in one of her father's plays named Latika. Her first venture into performance was singing in her father's Marathi theatre productions. Lata had no formal schooling to speak of and may have attended school for only one day. Her father trained her as well as her siblings (Meena, Usha, Asha, and Hridaynath) in classical singing, and all are accomplished musicians.

Lata began her film career in 1942 at the age of thirteen, singing regional Marathi film songs. Lata's entry into the industry came after her father's death. As the oldest child, she felt responsible for supporting her family and moved to Mumbai where she spent the remainder of her career singing primarily for "Bollywood"—India's Hindi-speaking film industry. Lata sang for stars from Madhubala, Hema Malini, and Nargis in the 1940s up to Ashwariya Rai and Preity Zinta in the 1990s, and beyond.

Lata's sister Asha Bhosle, also a playback singer, rivals her in terms of luminary status and industry recognition. Both sisters have numerous recordings to their names, and although the exact number is unknown, Asha may have out-recorded her sister in terms of numbers of songs—in 2011, Asha earned the Guinness title of most recorded artist, citing eleven thousand solo, duet, and chorus-backed songs since 1947.

Lata became the most sought-after playback singer in Indian cinema from the 1950s–1980s and received dozens of film music awards for her work. In addition to her prolific film songs output, Lata recorded *ghazals* (short poems consisting of rhyming couplets), devotional *bhajan*-s and other light classical works, as well as songs in almost two dozen regional languages. A national-level award established in her name—The Lata Mangeshkar Award—rewards the highest caliber of music director or playback singer. In 2001, Lata Mangeshkar was awarded India's highest civilian honor, the Bharat Ratna, and on her ninetieth birthday in 2019, she received the "Daughter of the Nation" Award. She was known by a stream of illustrious titles, such as "Voice of the Nation," "Queen of Melody," "Voice of the Millennium," "Nightingale of India," and the most endearing moniker of all, *didi*, which means "sister."

An ambassador for the nation, Lata was highly regarded at home and abroad by actors, directors, politicians, and fans from all generations. She has been regularly accorded legend-status and is even discussed in terms befitting a deity—frequently compared to Saraswati, goddess of music, education, and the arts. Music directors from old contemporaries, such as Naushad Ali and Khayyam, to recent composers, like A. R. Rahman, recognize her contribution to Indian culture and praise her talent in singing as well as musical interpretation. "There is magic in this girl's voice," Khayyam said of a young Lata (Bichu n.d.), while music director Naushad Ali, a mentor and early supporter of Lata, believed she was the best thing to happen to playback singing. A. R. Rahman, in turn, waxed quite poetic about working with Lata for the soundtrack to *Dil Se* (*From the Heart*, 1997), citing her brilliant interpretation and song execution (Interview, February 12, 2006). Although she experienced a rather inauspicious start with early vocal criticisms, discussed below, once she achieved a certain level of notoriety, she was able to maintain a career mostly untouched by scandal or external forces.

Female Playback Voices: 1940s Pre-Independence

When Lata moved to Mumbai in 1945, she entered an industry well established in terms of vocal luminaries and standard musical practices. Her competition included the most dominant singers of the 1940s—Noorjehan, Suraiya, Rajkumari Dubey, Zohrabai Ambalewali, Amirbai Karnataki, and Shamshad Begum, the latter of whom was the most popular and highest paid female playback singer until 1955.

These playback singers were either classically trained in Hindustani or Carnatic (Hindustani is the music of North India, and Carnatic is from the South) traditions, or well-versed in folk music, and most were altos or mezzo-sopranos who sang in lower vocal ranges—from G_3 to E_5. Each playback singer had her own vocal soundprint, production style, and timbre. Rajkumari's voice was a warm, smooth, mellow mezzo-soprano, consistent when changing registers. Shamshad Begum, while not classically trained, was steeped in folk music traditions. Her voice is quite naturally produced and falls in an alto range, common for Indian folk music. Amirbai's voice is in a low contralto range, and her voice production is open throated with nasal resonance. Noorjehan's voice is deep, rich, powerful, open, relaxed, and well supported. She has a limited upper register but can bring her chest voice upward, keeping her sound open and not too narrow or focused. Actor-singer Suraiya has a much lighter voice—low, warm, a bit breathy, but entirely approachable and also in an alto range.[3]

When required, singers would alter their voices to match their on-screen characters. Women substituted for children's voices as there were no child singers. In *Taqdeer* (*Fate, Destiny*, 1943), for example, Shamshad manipulates her voice to imitate a young Nargis, adding vocal fry and removing any trace of vibrato. This early conflation of the female voice with children is significant and portends a shift in female vocal timbres that Srivastava describes as infantilization—relegating female voices as docile, pliable, and dominatable.

While Lata's signature voice would later become one of the hallmarks of Indian cinema, she was initially rejected as a teen by producer Sashadhar Mukherjee, who believed her voice to be "too thin and shrill." Lata, however, was industrious and ambitious, and took classical singing lessons, which she applied directly to her playback singing (Layton 2013, 158).

Initially, Lata's voice did not differ greatly from those of her contemporaries. Lata sang in the same style, pitch range, and tessitura of her cohorts. Lata's first Marathi film song was "Natali Chaitraachi Navalaai" ("The New Bride Has Come in Chaitra") from *Pahili Mangalagaur* (a religious celebration for new brides) (1942), sung when she was thirteen years old (Mangeshkar 2010). As was typical, the pitch range was low and limited, only one octave from B_3–B_4. In her first Hindi film song, "Paa Laagun Kar Jori Re" ("Touching the Feet as a Sign of Respect") from the 1946 film *Aapki Sewa Mein* (*At Your Service*), her voice is imitative of Noorjehan—low in pitch and range (B_3 to C_5). Lata's voice is smooth, somewhat but not excessively thin, and impressively flexible as she sings *gamak*-s (melismas) with expert flexibility despite her age.

For Lata's undeveloped voice, however, the low B_3 in these songs did not sit comfortably in her naturally soprano vocal range (from C_4 to C_6). Despite Lata's soprano voice and large range, she continued to sing mezzo-soprano/alto-ranged songs common in the era. Her song "Chidiya Bole Chu Chu Chu" ("The Bird Said Chu Chu Chu") from the 1946 film *Jeewan Yatra* (*Life Journey*), for example, is both narrow and low, extending from D_4–D_5. In "Dil Mera Toda" ("My Heart Broke") from the 1948 film *Majboor* (*Helpless*), the range is D_4 to E_5.

Soon after, Lata's individual style matured. Her very tight vibrato is the hallmark of her aesthetic but is deceptive in that it makes her voice seem much higher and lighter than it is.[4] By 1949, Lata's voice was well developed. Her control allowed her to deliberately imitate other singers such as Noorjehan, as in the duet "Darr Na Mohabbat Karle" ("Don't Be Afraid to Love") sung with Shamshad Begum from Naushad's *Andaz* (*Style*, 1949).

By industry standards and accounts of critics at the time, Lata's voice was not uniformly accepted as being traditionally "beautiful." Her voice was described as sweet, melodious, hauntingly expressive, ageless, pure, and flexible, with a few of the most common unflattering adjectives deeming it as thin, shrill, soft, too sweet, and high. Lata's thin sound, alternating between a tight vibrato and genderless straight tone, continued to invite non-musical monikers such as "girl-like" and "adolescent." As Srivastava (2004) argues, Lata's vocal beauty or sweetness is hardly the point as other factors intervened in her rise.

Lata's popularity only increased over time, as did her vocal dominance in the field. After being mentored by top music directors such as Naushad, she quickly became an industry favorite. By the late 1940s and early 1950s, her voice began to change the industry itself as music directors wrote songs to match her specific voice, which shifted the conventional pitch range of songs upward. For example, the song "Aayega Aanewala" ("The One Who Must Come Will Come") from the 1949 film *Mahal* (*Mansion*), which Lata sings for the actress Madhubala, is slightly higher (from E_4-E_5), marking the beginning of this upward pitch trend. Soon, music directors adopted soprano as the new standard for all Hindi film songs, and her sweet, pre-adolescent timbre became *de rigueur* in the industry. By the release of *Mother India* in 1957, for example, the pitch range in "Duniya Mein Hum Aaye Hain" ("We Have to Live as We Have Come in This World") was D_4-F_5, with G_4 as the tonal center. Whereas G_4 was roughly in the mid- to high-range of pre-independence-era songs, it is now one of the lowest notes. Congruent with the higher tonal center, the tessitura (range) of the songs moved upward as well. In the song "Ichak Dana Bichak Dana" ("One Little Seed, Two Little Seeds") from *Shri 420* (*Mr. 420*, 1955), not only is the pitch range higher—from G_4 to E_5—but the entire *antaara* (similar to a verse) rests in the upper pitch range of the song (C_5-E_5). This tessitura is quite high and is very difficult to sustain for any length of time without straining or fatigue.

Lata's popularity among music directors, actors, and audiences soon overcame early negative perceptions of her voice. Within a decade, audiences accepted her voice as an iconic entity imbued with meaning. According to the Marathi writer Gangadhar, "To me, and I believe, to every Indian, Lata Mangeshkar is not so much a person as a voice—a voice that soars high and casts a magic spell over the hearts of millions of Indians from the Himalayas to Kanyakumari . . . her voice has an ethereal quality, an undefinable something, with a unique appeal to Indians" (1967, 36). The perception that Lata's voice is separate from Lata the person is significant in that it symbolically allowed her voice to re-signify as nationhood, independence, and India.

Lata's Rise to Dominance

After ushering in a new sonic era, post-independence, within a few years, Lata and Asha replaced the heterogeneous, stylistically diverse vocal timbres of pre-independence singers with a more homogenous one. How could Indian audiences, steeped in a plethora of classical and folk traditions with varying styles and timbres, accept the dominance of two female voices? The answer is complex and combines the inner mechanizations of the Indian film industry on one hand with the nation-building imperative of the Nehru government on the other. Lata's rise, in other words, coincided with extraordinary external factors that facilitated her entry, rise, and prominence in the industry, as well as the ability to permanently transform it.

Playback Singing Is Normalized

In the 1930s, playback singing was not commonplace, nor was it accepted by Indian audiences. Many "singer-actors" sang their own songs, a practice championed by Indian film's first superstar, K. L. Saigal (Majumdar 2001, 166). According to film scholar Gregory Booth, the "singer-actor" began to fall out of favor with the death of K. L. Saigal in 1946 (2008, 44), leaving playback singers to thrive in their wake. Films began using playback singers, known as "ghost voices," in the 1940s, and singers were matched with actors' speaking voices (Majumdar 2001, 167). The practice, however, was criticized for being inauthentic, similar to reactions to the same practice in Hollywood films.

Playback singing became more common in the 1940s, gaining traction as the voice behind the actor added a layer of complexity and nuance. Majumdar (2001) notes that the audience penchant for a handful of voices relates to a "recognition" factor, where audiences could identify with the singer. In terms of marketing, singers and actors could be sold separately and repackaged with "hits." The result catapulted a small number of prominent female and male singers at the time into stardom, with singers such as Kishore Kumar, Mohammad Rafi, etc. dominating the music scene. Playback singers, entrenched in the industry's star system, were economically desirable as proven actors and singers minimized financial risk. Singers became stars in their own right, and were highly sought after by actors, directors, and producers who recognized the value of playback singers' voices. The actor Madhubala put a clause in her contracts requiring that only Lata sing for her, and according to Lata, actress Jaya Badhuri believed that heroines acquired additional stature when Lata sang for them (Jha 2016). A Canadian reporter commenting on Lata's status during her 1975 North American tour wrote that "if the actress is anyone important, her voice is supplied by Lata Mangeshkar" (quoted in Deora and Shah 2017, 45).

Post-Partition Impact

In 1947, India's independence and the subsequent partition of the country into East and West Pakistan (now Bangladesh and Pakistan, respectively) significantly changed playback singing on two fronts. First, it allowed a realignment of singers along nationalist lines, with some shifting to Pakistan and some remaining in India. Second, the resulting gap in India provided an opportunity to shape vocal timbres to appeal to Hindu sensibilities. The 1947 rift was bitter and bloody, and anti-Muslim sentiment in India was palpable. Postcolonialism was rife with anti-Muslim sentiment, and Lata's voice conveniently provided distance from the timbres of the previous era. As Srivastava notes, "When the 'Muslim problem,' and the search for a 'proper'— controllable—femininity (and hence a 'proper' masculinity) became part of the nationalist project of cultural redemption, certain kinds of voices came to be marked as an unacceptable aspect of 'proper' post-coloniality" (2004, 2024). In other words, Lata's high, light voice was read as "Hindu," whereas voices that were lower and darker in timbre were read as "Muslim."

After Partition, superstar playback singer and actress Noorjehan, who was Muslim, moved to Pakistan and continued her career in Pakistani cinema, a much less profitable and impactful industry at the time. The careers of other pre-independence singers began to wane as well, leaving a vocal void. According to Majumdar, Lata was actually quite shrewd, and took an active role in her own ascendance and taking advantage of the migration of singers to Pakistan after Partition (2001, 169). Absent Noorjehan and others, the deep, alto, contralto sound fell out of favor. Lata and Asha's light, high voices filled the gap, thus solidifying their dominance.

By the early 1950s, audiences not only accepted Lata and Asha's timbres as replacements for the deeper, richer timbres of the Muslim singers; they understood the new sound as expressly Hindu and expressly feminine in the new post-independence era.[5]

Lata as the Voice of the Heroine

Hindi films limit women in many ways, but especially by character type, breadth of agency, and access to singing. Traditionally, music is seen as a positive, humanizing force and a privileged expression. As such, the hero/heroine (the romantic couple) and their family, friends, etc. perform the majority of on-screen songs. The heroine and any mothers are depicted as traditional, devoted, pious, and representative of Indian culture. Amanda Weidman discusses the impact of female playback singing in two phases: in the 1940s, actresses were more likely than actors to have playback singers, laying the groundwork for stock female characters in the 1950s and allowing the disembodied singer's voice to stand for the nation rather than a particular female body (2021, 43). Weidman also notes that the "gendered prevalence" of female voice substitution not only covers any singing inability but also the immorality of actresses' on-screen characters (ibid., 37). By extension, the disembodied female playback voice allowed excursion into questionable moral territory on screen. Unlike male villains who don't sing, the "not-so-good" women of Hindi cinema, such as the vamp or cabaret dancer, are allowed to sing, despite being modern, "western," and of questionable morality. The characters of the vamp or cabaret dancer can be loosely traced to nineteenth-century female courtesans who performed for nobility and invited their gaze. Therefore, the highly sexualized "item numbers" are regarded as permissible as they now invite both the villain's and the audience's gaze.

Lata became synonymous with the heroine, singing almost exclusively for her, while her sister Asha sang for heroines and vamps alike. Critics deemed Asha's voice much more sensual and nuanced than Lata's—a teleological and somewhat manufactured description used to justify the types of roles for which Asha sang. In fact, their voices are quite similar in terms of timbre, range, vibrato, and the obligatory "sweetness" quality. Music directors regularly "voice cast" the sisters in these roles, sometimes hiring both for the same film. Critics, however, drew more distinction between their voices than actually existed, perhaps due to the limited pool of singers available for critiquing. One would think that their vocal similarities served to mitigate differences between the female roles. In other words, while the sisters' timbral similarity might have diminished the ideological divide between the female heroine and the vamp, it actually did no such thing. Asha's voice may have represented the licentiousness of the actress on-screen, but by voicing all facets of stock female characters between the two sisters, they honed their constructed differences to establish a monopoly that kept it all in the family.

This unique set of factors—the normalization of playback singing, the disruption of voices post-Partition, the limited number of playback singers, and the association of Lata's voice with the heroine—all contributed to her rise and acceptance. All of this occurred as India's flourishing middle class fueled an increased demand in film production for leisure-seeking pleasure. Lata's soprano became the preferred timbre, and the continuous use of her voice, along with a handful of other Golden Era singers, cemented her in the playback singing firmament. Nation-building, however, was just beginning.

A New Nation and a New Femininity

In the 1950s, post-independent India was in nation-building mode. Prime Minister Nehru created a series of five-year plans to reform the country both economically and socially. The Ministry of Information and Broadcasting was founded in 1949 to help the new nation reinvent itself after colonialism. State-sponsored institutions such as All India Radio came to the service of the nation. Although India's cinemas are private entities, the Indian film industry basically functioned as a state entity due to its reach and popularity (Virdi 2003, 9). Nation-building post-Partition was not free from religious contention. Information and Broadcasting Minister B. B. Keskar reclaimed India's traditional classical heritage for the "Hindu" nation in the hope of saving it from neglectful British and Muslim musicians who were seen as having corrupted the form (Lelyveld 1995, 117), thus continuing a bitter divide.

Films of the 1950s, by and large, were nationalistic in orientation and distinctly patriotic in tone.[6] Post-independence required images, sounds, and goals to which postcolonial Indians could aspire, and directors rushed to the challenge (Schulze 2002, 72). Rather than a single discourse, however, "nation" played out in a series of images revealing tropes of gender, sexuality, family, and community (Virdi 2003, xiii), while narratives and characters revolved around the nation as their moral universe (ibid., 12). The neo-realism of the postcolonial era, as Chakravarty notes, was incommensurate with the star system which the Bombay industry is rife with, and directors deglamorized stars to read them as "average man/woman" (1993, 98). Roles portrayed divisions of caste and class, while women, like the character Vidya in *Shri 420* (*Mr. 420*, 1955), were representative of a sign-system of the "average good woman" (ibid., 106). Lata supplied the voice for Vidya and most other iconic heroines of the 1950s, thus acquiring and representing these proper female qualities even in their everyday construction.

Gandhian ideals also impacted nation-building, such as establishing "home" as a spiritual space. Unlike the women's movements in the United

States and elsewhere, home became the focal point for women's issues in postcolonial India (Chatterjee 1993, 133). Home and family were the cultural and social heart of the new middle-class woman, while public vs. private life became gendered points of contention. Despite some Nehruvian[7] reforms for women, nation-building in India did little to dispel the paradigm of the traditional Brahmanic male.[8] Men were allowed license to operate in public spaces—bartering, working, negotiating, and politicizing—while women were invisible, relegated to private, household spheres of activity. The threat for women was that leaving these sanctuaries was akin to inviting risk if they became "conspicuously visible" in public spaces (Sunder Rajan 2001, 8). According to Srivastava, Lata's voice helped delineate public vs. private space in that the external excursions of the heroine into public (i.e., male-dominated space) is tempered by Lata's demure femininity, evoking a private/housebound, secondary status (Srivastava 2007, 88).

It is in this "inner" world of the home, as Chatterjee argues, that women acquire the "spiritual" (read "East") space of home and hearth, while men occupy the outer "material" world, which may be borrowed from the West in terms of science, technology, and materialism (1993, 129). As Virdi notes, inequalities between men and women became further exacerbated. "Male economic advantage in the public sphere continued in the private sphere, while discriminatory laws against women's rights in the family were enshrined in the new constitution" (Virdi 2003, 12). On-screen nationalism, however, depended on maintaining tradition, primarily through culture-bearers—that is, the nation's women. Women were represented as demure, devoted, self-sacrificing, long-suffering, and with little agency.

Radha, the long-suffering mother in the 1957 blockbuster *Mother India*, galvanized cultural ideals and established Lata as the ideal feminine voice of the nation. The film not only "evokes the myth of a powerful India" (Chakravarty 1993, 149), but also foundationally represents women as self-sacrificing upholders of tradition. Normalizing women's suffering and conflating it with nationhood helped delineate a national femininity, motherhood, and acceptable spheres of power and agency for women in service of the nation. Lata, as the voice of Radha, became the very sonic signifier of these ideals.

Lata's voice was endowed with symbolic figuration as the nation's culture-bearer of ideal femininity—an ideal embodied in her personal life as well. As a teenager, she often wore a white sari to recording sessions (Ali 2009). White, in India, is the color of the renouncer or widow. It is associated with purity, cleanliness, peace, knowledge, and the dress of Saraswati, Goddess of Knowledge and the Arts. Lata never married but was devoted to her audience (read nation), rather than to a self-serving career. Srivastava goes so far as to suggest that Lata's own sexuality as the virgin mother is part of her mystique as a national mother figure (2007, 89).

Lata's voice helped construct masculinity as well. Rather than being an irritant, Srivastava notes that Lata's pliable, young voice became a compelling part of a "heterosexual male fantasy of a Hindu adolescent girl—both controllable and ever-ready to please—that is an overwhelming aspect of the desire that congregates around Lata's voice" (2004, 2024). In addition, Srivastava suggests that the infantilization of the female, embedded in Lata's sound, marked the changing role of film heroines. This change helped discredit the de-masculinization that can occur in cities (ibid., 2024)—a sonic amelioration of the gendered impact of post-independence rapid urbanization.

The aspects of femininity prescribed to Lata are not rooted in the voice itself—there is nothing inherently more feminine about a thin voice vs. a thicker one—but emerged with on-screen roles and their cultural meanings. The self-sacrificing mother, devoted wife, and so on gave Lata her vocal power, positioning her as the "voice of a nation" that remains Brahmanical in its treatment of women. Her thin, light voice, interstitially located between childhood, adolescence, and womanhood, marked a useful feminine sound that would be continuously replicated in the Bombay studios to the exclusion of all others.

In terms of convincing audiences of her value, Srivastava brilliantly draws on the classical aesthetics analysis of Coomaraswamy, suggesting that Lata re-signified the traditionally dynamic relationship between performer and skilled audience. Lata *instructed* audiences with her particular interpretation of the feminine (2004, 2021). In other words, Lata rewrote the rules of aesthetics to prescribe her particular sound as the voice of an idealized femininity and the voice of the nation.

The term "Mangeshkar monopoly" was coined by *Stardust Magazine* to describe Lata and Asha's four-decade reign in the industry. While many in the business downplayed their control, relegating it to a mere ebb and flow of playback singer replacement, few would argue that their impact was anything but substantial. Lata, for example, won every Filmfare Award from 1955–66 until in 1969, she gave up the awards to allow room for new talent. Classical vocalist Arati Ankalikar notes that "from the morning wake-up *bhajan* [devotional songs], to ditties that entertain you during the day, to the lullaby that puts you to sleep, for six decades people heard nothing but Lata and Asha. How then can you expect listeners to accept other voices?" (Pawar 2011). Playback singer Shreya Ghoshal notes that whether they are singing or not, the two singers will continue to monopolize the industry (TNN 2006).

Shikha Jhingan's research on the "Age of Reproduction" (2013) further uncovers the breadth and influence of Lata's voice in particular. Her voice permeated all aspects of film song and was broadcast everywhere, including reproduction via radio, gramophone, and film. In the 1970s and '80s age of cassettes, her voice was imitated by "copy artists" who manipulated their voices to sound like hers. Given that the world of film music pervades almost all areas of Indian music, Lata's and Asha's dominance was a significant and pervasive musical obstacle. It wasn't until the 1990s that this began to change with new singers and more varied song ranges.

Disillusionment and Decline

By the 1990s, it became clear that Lata's dominance was waning. Her decline was precipitated by her advancing age as well as an increased appetite for authenticity and cinematic realism. After India's economic liberalization in 1991, the film industry responded to global markets by altering aesthetics to attract diasporic and other non-Indian markets. Corny cinematography, overly dramatic background scores, and over-worn tropes and techniques were gradually phased out. In addition, the disjuncture between studio playback singing and on-screen contexts became more obvious. Earlier songs in which Lata's vocal performance seemed to directly contrast the on-screen action were perceived as nostalgic and unrealistic. In this sense, the pre-recorded "falseness" of the studio-recorded voice created an authentic disease in audience perception that they were willing to forgo. For example, in the song "Duniya Mein Hum Aaye Hain" ("We Have to Live as We Have Come in This World"), the actress Nargis engages in excessive physical exertion as she plows the fields by herself in the scorching sun, projecting a strength and determination that is unmatched by Lata's demure and ethereal voice. In addition, it is almost impossible to tell the difference between her voice and the voices of her two children in the scene (for whom Lata's two sisters sang). Although this is very much Srivastava's (2004) point—that Lata's thin, pure, mother's voice does not threaten masculinity and evokes the inner world of home and hearth—the lack of realism, in retrospect, is jarring, particularly to audiences now conditioned to global realism.

Another incongruity surfaced in the 1990s toward the end of Lata's career. The suspension of disbelief required to listen to the aging Lata as she sang for young heroines was, in some cases, extreme. Seventy-something-year-old Lata singing for twenty-year-old heroines—despite her legendary status—is simply not believable. For example, in Ratnam's *Dil Se* (*From the Heart*, 1997),

Lata sings "Jiya Jale" ("My Heart Burns") with an aging vibrato that is less than ideal. One discussion of Lata's voice in the film writes, "While it is possible to believe that playback singer Roop Kumar Rathod's voice really belongs to Shah Rukh Khan, since the two men are of an approximate age, the idea that the distinctive Lata Mangeshkar sound could emanate from Preity Zinta is in fact ludicrous" (Layton 2013, 21). Her aging voice is a reminder that the once ethereal voice that was so frequently separated from the body through the playback singing process and grandiose metaphors is now grounded in mortality.

Although no longer as active, Lata continued to sing in the years before her death in 2022. In the 2010s, she recorded several film songs, released several albums, and launched her own production company. In 2019, she released the song "Saugandh Mujhe Is Mitti Ki" ("I Vow to the Soil of My Nation") in honor of India's army, continuing her support of nationhood through song. Lata also maintained an online footprint—she appears in memes, her Twitter account had almost fifteen million followers, and her Facebook page had eleven million with several dedicated fan clubs. Since she was not generating as much in terms of "new buzz," most of the content on these platforms is nostalgic in nature, celebrating past milestones, commenting on copycat singers, or offering birthday wishes. Lata, up through her early nineties, still remained a powerful icon, partly through Indian film's pervasive participatory culture. From the film song parlor game *antakshari*—where teams compete at remembering song lyrics—to the digital explosion in social media, online cyber communities of film fandom, and memes, Bollywood music and dance is a regular part of everyday lives, and Lata is part and parcel of that world.

Conclusion

Through her life and prolific career, Lata left an indelible, sonic mark on both the film and popular music industries in India. Her iconic imprint, associated with a particular set of signifiers forged through a confluence of events, cleaved pre-independence from post, establishing a new sonic femininity and national voice. As Ashwini Deshpande (2004) points out, the "woman" conjured by Lata Mangeshkar's singing voice is the product of certain developments that are peculiar to the processes of Indian modernity. That "shrill adolescent girl falsetto became the 'ideal' voice of a nation" and female sexuality, coinciding with India's post-independence search for women's role in the new national identity (Manuel 1993, 53).

Her personal life emulated her art, further imbuing her persona with mythical power. Her association with actresses and roles in the 1950s nation-building era and her own patriotic fervor connected her with specific on-screen female roles. Lata devoted herself to singing, to the exclusion of everything else. Her voice and personal life were marked by a distinct lack of sexuality. Lata's own life mimicked the ideal female of the heroine. Lata never married, was chaste, pious, devoted to her craft, and often wore a white sari when recording, presenting herself as a devotee or "renouncer"—almost widow-like in status.

Lata's true legacy, perhaps, is that her atypical voice became the accepted sound for a nation, dominating all voices around her. Lata's distinct vocal style is not found in any other style of North Indian music from folk genres to classical (Manuel 1993, 53), in a culture where "women's singing styles ... have been marked by a striking heterogeneity of tonal and other styles" (Srivastava 2007, 82). Her vocal style and tessitura inspired music directors to raise the pitch ranges of songs to fit her voice, which could lithely soar to a high G_5.

Of all the things Lata's voice may represent or prescribe in terms of nationhood and femininity, it struggles to truly represent the voice of the "every woman." And this was entirely the point. Lata's songs were not easily sung by the majority of women as she moved film music out of the grasp of everyday folk or even classical singing ranges. Lata's thin, adolescent sound was non-threatening to men both on-screen and off, but her heroine's voice set a bar for femininity that, despite occurring in Nehru's neo-realist nation, did not offer a realistic musical standard for India's women. It was a new voice representing a new era—just not one that was accessible by the everyday woman.

Regardless, the Mangeshkar monopoly endured as singers conformed to their vocal qualities in order to succeed. Even today, one still hears attributes of the "Mangeshkar style" flowing from Indian cinema's digital afterlife, replicated in millions of viewings on YouTube, inspiring millions more to mimic film songs and dances, participate in film music contests and flash-mobs, or post videos singing Lata's and Asha's evergreen hits on social media. Streaming platforms and over a dozen singing talent shows feature Lata's songs, breathing new life into the Indian film industry, and securing her legacy. Even as homage is paid, the eclipsing of her sound with new styles, lower ranges, and thicker timbres heralds the promise of a nation trying to renegotiate a female sexuality in a new, globalized India of the twenty-first century.

Notes

1. In 1974, Lata was in *The Guinness Book of World Records* as the most recorded artist in history with twenty-five thousand solo, duet, and chorus-backed songs in

twenty languages between 1948 and 1974. This claim was contested by singer Mohammad Rafi (1924–1980), a contemporary of Lata who recorded twenty-eight thousand songs. By 1984, Guinness listed Lata as recording thirty thousand songs between 1948 and 1984, but by 1991, her entry was deleted without explanation. Estimates put her recordings in the five-thousand range.

2. Playback singing is perceived unfavorably by many as an inauthentic practice that deceives the audience. Although the ubiquitous nature of playback singers in Indian cinema is widely accepted currently, this was not always the case (see below).

3. Many thanks to colleague Monica Ramich for her help with vocal descriptions.

4. For further examples, compare Shamshad Begum's full-throated sound in "Pi Ke Ghar Aj Pyari Dulaniya Chal" ("For Her Beloved's House, the Lovely Bride Leaves") in *Mother India* with Lata's thinner, more adolescent-sounding voice in "Duniya Mein Hum Aaye Hain" ("We Have to Live as We Have Come in This World") or in their duet "Teri Mehfil Mein" ("In Your Gathering") from the film *Mughal-e-Azam* (*The Emperor of the Mughals*, 1960).

5. Film scholar Gregory Booth notes the significant shift in the Bombay film industry post-Partition and counts Noorjehan's absence as crucial to the growth of Lata Mangeshkar's status as a singer (2008, 44).

6. Lata described herself as very patriotic and viewed the nation-building era in cinema as its best years. In an interview with Manvi Dhillon for NDTV in 2008, Lata discussed the early years of film and its penchant for the patriotic given the nation-building imperative. Her favorite song from this era was a patriotic one, "Aaye Mere Watan Ke Logon" ("Oh, People of My Homeland," 1963), about soldiers who died during the Sino-Indian War in 1962. Lata sang the song at a Republic Day event for Nehru himself, who cried after hearing her sing.

7. Of or relating to the policies of India's first Prime Minister, Jawaharlal Nehru (1889–1964), such as a commitment to secularism, a scientific temperament, and inclusive liberalism.

8. Related to Brahmanism, the Vedic religion that predates Hinduism. Brahmanism encouraged the authority of the Vedas put forth by the highest priestly caste of Brahmin males. By extension, it refers to the traditional perspective and power of the Brahmins, as well as its associated privileges, such as access to Vedic knowledge and the creation of a Brahmanic patriarchy.

References

Ali, Naushad. 2009. "Voice of a Nation." *Hindustan Times*, May 22. https://www.hindustantimes.com/delhi/voice-of-a-nation/story-uuRyu1lfkAmY7NED8Mt3MN.html.
Bharatan, Raju. 1995. *Lata Mangeshkar: A Biography*. New Delhi: UBS Publishers.
Bhimani, Harish. 1995. *In Search of Lata Mangeshkar*. New Delhi: Indus.
Bichu, Mandar V. n.d. "Khayyam Speaks on Lata." *Cinema Sangeet*. http://www.cinemasangeet.com/lata-mangeshkar/interviews/khayyam-speaks-on-lata.html.

Booth, Gregory. 2008. *Behind the Curtain: Making Music in Mumbai's Film Studios.* Oxford: Oxford University Press.

Chakravarty, Sumita S. 1993. *National Identity in Indian Popular Cinema, 1947–1987.* Austin: University of Texas Press.

Chatterjee, Partha. 1993. *The Nation and Its Fragments: Colonial and Postcolonial Histories.* Princeton, NJ: Princeton University Press.

Deora, Mohan, and Rachana Shah. 2017. *On Stage with Lata.* New Delhi: HarperCollins Publishers India.

Deshpande, Ashwini. 2004. "Lata Mangeshkar: The Singer and the Voice." *Economic and Political Weekly* 39(48): 5179–84.

———. 2015. "New Voices in Songs: Do Women in Hindi Films Have Greater Agency?" *Economic and Political Weekly* 50(37): 25–27.

Gangadhar, Gadgil. 1967. "Meet Lata Mangeshkar." *Illustrated Weekly of India,* April 30.

Jha, Subhash K. 2016. "'Ten Actresses I Loved to Sing For'—Lata Mangeshkar." www.bollywoodhungama.com. https://www.bollywoodhungama.com/news/features/10-actresses-i-loved-to-sing-forae%c2%a6-lata-mangeshkar/.

Jhingan, Shikha. 2011. "Re-Embodying the 'Classical': The Bombay Film Song in the 1950s." *BioScope: South Asian Screen Studies* 2(2): 157–79.

———. 2013. "Lata Mangeshkar's Voice in the Era of Cassette Reproduction." *BioScope: South Asian Screen Studies* 4(2): 97–114.

Kabir, Nasreen Munni. 2009. *Lata Mangeshkar in Her Own Voice: Conversations with Nasreen Munni Kabir.* New Delhi: Niyogi Books.

Layton, Myrna June. 2013. "Illusion and Reality: Playback Singers in Bollywood and Hollywood." PhD Dissertation, University of South Africa.

Lelyveld, David. 1995. "Upon the Subdominant: Administering Music on All-India Radio." In *Consuming Modernity: Public Culture in a South Asian World,* ed. Carol A. Breckenridge, 49–65. Minneapolis: University of Minnesota Press.

Majumdar, Neepa. 2001. "The Embodied Voice: Song Sequences and Stardom in Popular Hindi Cinema." In *Soundtrack Available: Essays on Film and Popular Music,* eds. Pamela Robertson Wojcik and Arthur Knight, 161–81. Durham, NC: Duke University Press.

Mangeshkar, Lata. 2010 [1942]. "Lata Mangeshkar's First Song." www.youtube.com. https://www.youtube.com/watch?v=0_5RfSE6ZRA&feature=emb_title.

Manuel, Peter. 1993. *Cassette Culture: Popular Music and Technology in Northern India.* Chicago: University of Chicago Press.

Pawar, Yogesh. 2011. "Women Playback Singers Get a Voice of Their Own." DNA, November 6. https://www.dnaindia.com/lifestyle/report-women-playback-singers-get-a-voice-of-their-own-1608143.

Ranade, Ashok. 2006. *Hindi Film Song: Music Beyond Boundaries.* New Delhi: Promilla Press.

Schultz, Anna C. 2013. *Singing a Hindu Nation: Marathi Devotional Performance and Nationalism.* New York: Oxford University Press.

Schulze, Brigitte. 2002. "The Cinematic 'Discovery of India': Mehboob's Re-Invention of the Nation in *Mother India*." *Social Scientist* 30(9/10): 72–87.

Srivastava, Sanjay. 2004. "Voice, Gender and Space in Time of Five-Year Plans: The Idea of Lata Mangeshkar." *Economic and Political Weekly* 39(20): 2019–28.

———. 2007. "The Idea of Lata Mangeshkar: Hindu Sexuality, the Girl-Child, and Heterosexual Desire in the Time of the Five Year Plans." In *Passionate Modernity: Sexuality, Class, and Consumption in India*, 79–115. New Delhi: Routledge.

Sundar, Pavitra. 2008. "Meri Awaaz Suno: Women, Vocality, and Nation in Hindi Cinema." *Meridians* 8(1): 144–79.

Sunder Rajan, Rajeswari. 2001. "Introduction." In *Signposts: Gender Issues in Post-Independence India*, ed. Rajeswari Sunder Rajan, 1–16. New Brunswick, NJ: Rutgers University Press.

TNN (Times News Network). 2006. "Mangeshkar Magic: Over the Hill?" *Times of India*, August 31. http://timesofindia.indiatimes.com/articleshow/1944999.cms?utm_source=contentofinterest&utm_medium=text&utm_campaign=cppst.

Virdi, Jyotika. 2003. *The Cinematic ImagiNation: Indian Popular Films as Social History*. New Brunswick, NJ: Rutgers University Press.

Weidman, Amanda. 2021. *Brought to Life by the Voice: Playback Singing and Cultural Politics in South India*. Berkeley: University of California Press.

Multimedia Playlist

Some of my favorite film soundtracks (some with Lata and some without!):
S. D. BURMAN, *Guide*, 1965
R. D. BURMAN, *Sholay* (*Embers*), 1975
JATIN-LALIT, *Dilwale Dulhania Le Jayenge* (*The Big-Hearted Will Take the Bride*), 1995
KHAYYAM, *Umrao Jaan*, 1981
GHULAM MOHAMMED AND NAUSHAD ALI, *Pakeezah* (*Pure*), 1972
SHANTANU MOITRA, *3 Idiots*, 2009
A. R. RAHMAN, *Dil Se* (*From the Heart*), 1997
———, *Rockstar*, 2011
SHANKAR-EHSAAN-LOY, *Bunty aur Babli* (*Bunty and Babli*), 2005
AMIT TRIVEDI, *Queen*, 2014
VARIOUS ARTISTS, *Gully Boy*, 2019

CHAPTER 11

Ya Toyour

One Song in Two Voices

KATHERINE MEIZEL

Toward the end of 2013, a series of headlines swept across the global internet, proclaiming "All-American Singer Jennifer Grout May Win *Arabs Got Talent*" (Jamjoom 2013), "One of the Finalists of 'Arabs Got Talent' Is a White Woman from Boston" (John 2013), "Move Over, Susan Boyle: Boston Irish Girl Jennifer Grout Is the Unexpected Star of 'Arabs Got Talent'" (Pizzi 2013), and from Italy, the somewhat colonially troubling "Jennifer Grout, l'Americana che ha Conquistato la Musica Araba" ["Jennifer Grout, the American Who Has Conquered Arab Music"] (Molinari 2013). *Arabs Got Talent* is part of a global reality TV competition franchise developed by Simon Cowell's SYCOtv, first aired in the UK and then in dozens of versions worldwide, each tailored to its regional or national audience. The variant airing on MBC-1 to Arabic-speaking populations in the Middle East and North Africa premiered in 2011. The franchise features all kinds of performance, not only musical, and its musical performances range across music genres and styles, and languages. Within the widespread *Got Talent* franchise, despite the locality of each version, performers may hail from anywhere, and even make the rounds—for example, Austrian acrobat troupe Zucaroh appeared on both *France's Got Talent* (*La France A Un Incroyable Talent*) and on *America's Got Talent*.

In that international context, and in the internally international context of the *Arabs Got Talent* audience, the 2013 headlines pitch Ms. Grout (b. 1990) as not only American, but "*all*-American"—a representative of the essence of US identity, although she was living in Morocco at the time of her audition and had attended college in Canada. She is Bostonian, the headlines declared, from a vital seat of American history, and white, of Irish heritage—although she has publicly identified her heritage as "English, Scottish, and Native American" (Crouse 2013). Hers was an unexpected voice, like that of Susan Boyle, the seemingly awkward singer whose talent famously surprised *Britain's Got Talent* audiences in 2009. In the Arabic-language version of British media mogul Simon Cowell's *Got Talent* format, the language and vocality she performed were received as disjunct. Western media reports made much of her non-fluency in Arabic, often claiming that she spoke "not a word," although she had a year of classical Arabic in school.

When she first sang for the jury of *Arabs Got Talent*, she walked onstage with her oud (a pear-shaped, short-neck, lute-type stringed instrument) and, after some theatrical cross-linguistic fumbling by the judges, obeyed their pantomimed order to begin. On a cosmopolitan variety competition that has seen impersonations of Michael Jackson and fluteboxing with a plastic recorder, Ms. Grout chose to perform a song from the repertoire of the ultra-iconic classic *tarab* singer Umm Kulthum, "Baeed Anak" ("Away From You," composed by the nearly equally iconic Baligh Hamdi). *Tarab* is understood by practitioners and Arabic-speaking listeners as referring to a repertory of older, "classic" songs (in the sense of being known and beloved by a large population) that are focused on establishing a mutual feeling of emotional transportation and ecstasy between performer and audience. There is a body of famous *tarab* songs that originated in multiple Arabic-speaking cultures, recorded by singers from multiple Arab countries and regions, which then became well known across them. When Ms. Grout sang Umm Kulthum instead of an American song, the stunned jury was shown responding first with amused smiles and then concentrated attention. The Lebanese singer and *Arabs Got Talent* judge Najwa Karam exclaimed, "You don't speak a word of Arabic, yet you sing better than some Arab singers . . . We have for so long imitated the West, and this is the first time that a person who has no link whatsoever to the Arab world, an American girl who does not speak Arabic, sings Arabic songs" (Crouse 2013). It was a moment that magnified many of the concerns about reception some ethnomusicologists encounter when their ensembles, typically made up of students coming from outside of the relevant music culture, have the opportunity to perform for or with culture-bearers.

It wasn't only her linguistic flexibility that intrigued her audience, but also her ability to adopt a way of singing in which she wasn't expected to perform—a *vocality* that evoked beloved singers of *tarab*, the classic genre of Arab music that centers conceptually on "the merger between music and emotional transformation" (Racy 2003, 5). I have noted elsewhere (Meizel

2020) that singing in any culturally shaped way may be considered a social practice of being-in-the-world (Heidegger 1962), of acting in the world. In 1966, avant-garde composer and singer Cathy Berberian linked this function with the idea of vocality, as she encouraged classical singers to develop a collectively "New Vocality" by exploring many ways of singing—using a wider range of vocal qualities and capabilities—as "'ways of being' for the voice" (Berberian 2014 [1966], 47). Singers frequently find multiple ways of being and acting in the world through voice, and they apply the inherent intersubjectivity and interstitiality of voice to navigate the borderlands and border-crossings of twenty-first-century identities (see Meizel 2020). These crossings are not unidirectional; they do not require the complete leaving behind of any singular aspect of identity, or of any voice. Rather, they result in a singer's collection and combination of layered cultural practices, absorbed into new modes of self-knowledge and self-performance.

In my research, I have explored intersections of culture and consciousness, the material and the metaphorical in the vocal navigation of identity. I think about voice as physiological and agentive, and as both personal and cultural. As I study vocalities with the view that they are vocal ways of being, I aim to position sounds, practices, techniques, and meanings in the context of the truths singers experience, and in the complicated epistemologies of voice that mirror and shape both self and culture in discrete or overlapping ways. When singers perform across the borders mapped between styles, genres, spaces, cultures, and temporalities, they are performing not only *in multiple vocalities*, but more importantly they are *performing multivocality* in the negotiation of self (cf. Meizel 2020).

Voice, and multivocality in particular, can serve as strategies of de-bordering, re-bordering, border-dwelling, and border-crossing (Meizel 2020, 14). This chapter centers on how one song serves two singers in their navigation of cultural and geographical borders. It is a song written to intentionally showcase a flexibility of vocality, a flexibility of music culture in an increasingly globalized world, having originated at a geopolitically volatile moment, during a war that entangled the Arab world in the machinations of European governments once again. It neatly demonstrated the historical colonial impact on North African and Levantine musics, and the ways in which an Egyptian composer and Syrian-Egyptian singer might employ such a song in the crossing of borders. And seventy years later, it similarly became an instrument for two singers traversing borders in very different circumstances.

"Taghrid al-Balabil" (a.k.a. "Ya Toyour")

On *Arabs Got Talent*, Ms. Grout's cultural-vocal flexibility pushed her through to the last rounds of the competition, singing Muhammad al-Qasabji's famous "Taghrid al-Balabil" ("The Warbling of the Nightingales," with lyrics by Yusuf Badrus). More popularly known as "Ya Toyour" ("Oh, Birds"), due to its opening words, the song adopts a popular literary motif of both East and West: a narrator exhorts a bird (or group of birds)—frequently a nightingale—to deliver a message to a lover describing the narrator's pining pain, or, in some cases, to a person who has committed sexual violence against the narrator. For example, in ancient Greek mythology, Philomela survives an assault by her sister's husband, and subsequently becomes a nightingale, her singing the only way she can tell her story. Seventeenth-century Italian composer Giovanni Felice Sances's *ciaccona* (a type of baroque musical composition with a repeating bass line) "Accenti Queruli" twists the motif of the lamenting birds, as a man asks birds to deliver word of his unhappiness to the girl whose "honor" he has violated and to remind her that if she doesn't tell anyone, she can still pretend to be a virgin. Inscribed with a range of similar meanings (both sacred and secular) across cultures, and found throughout centuries of poetry and song in East Asian literatures, ancient Greek myth and literature (Williams 1997), medieval and subsequent European literature, Arabic poetry, Turkish poetry (see Halman and Warner 2005), Persian poetry (famously epitomized by Hafiz's motif of the rose and the nightingale—see Krasnowolska 2006), and Urdu poetry in South Asia (Kugle 2007) as well, the nightingale becomes an especially appropriate sign of border-crossing in "Ya Toyour."

In "Ya Toyour," the narrator asks the birds to sing their discontent and sorrow to a beloved who does not notice the narrator's love or pain. Descriptive lines highlight natural phenomena such as tree branches, breezes, flowers, and a brook in sensory language, so that mundane imagery and experience appear heightened by the love the narrator feels. But that love is tragically not returned, or at least it seems so to the narrator:

> Oh birds, sing of my love and chant/recite my passion and hopes,
> To the one next to me who sees what's happening to me.
>
> I complain to him but he smiles and increases my fondness [for him].
> Oh birds, describe to him my state of sleeplessness and my tears.[1]

"Ya Toyour" puts singers through both Arabic-style *tarab* and Italian-style bel canto paces, shifting between lyrical *maqam* (the system of melodic modes used in traditional Arabic music) sadness and a bright *Lucia di Lammermoor*-esque imitation of birds. It also intersperses *maqam* vocal virtuosity and challenging light-operatic coloratura in quick alternation between one phrase and another, while the orchestra follows largely in *tarab* style with occasional bursts of clearly tonal arpeggios and major chords. When Al-Qasabji wrote the song in 1941, he first tried to give it to Umm Kulthum, in whose career he had played an important part as composer and oud player—but, according to Samim al-Sharif, as quoted by Sherifa Zuhur, "[Umm Kulthum's] golden throat hadn't reckoned with the science of Western music, solfegio [*sic*]" (Sharif 1981, 227, quoted in Zuhur 2000, 101). So, al-Qasabji offered the song instead to a rival of Umm Kulthum: Asmahan. Asmahan (born Amal al-Atrash) came from a branch of the politically noteworthy, Syrian Druze al-Atrash clan, which had relocated to Egypt. Asmahan's brother Farid al-Atrash became the renowned "King of the Oud."

Asmahan, whom Fatima Mernissi (1994) positioned as an adventurous border-crosser herself in breaking from tradition, had a film career that coincided with those of two younger contemporaries in Hollywood—Deanna Durbin and her successor Kathryn Grayson. In an interview, the Syrian singer Lubana Al-Quntar told me that al-Qasabji had decided to compose "Ya Toyour" when he heard Johann Strauss's 1882 piece "Frühlingsstimmen (Voices of Spring) Waltz," an also-nightingale-centered showcase for soprano inundated with trills, ornaments, and staccato ornithological imitation; possibly, al-Qasabji based his own operatic passages on these. Although I have been unable to locate a reference in any scholarship in the languages I read (English, Spanish, French, Italian, German), I wonder if it may be important that Kathryn Grayson performed "Frühlingsstimmen" in her debut film, *Andy Hardy's Private Secretary*, in 1941—the very year that al-Qasabji wrote "Ya Toyour." In her work on Asmahan, Sherifa Zuhur has suggested that the coloratura passages in "Ya Toyour," which she calls "the 'Queen of the Night' section of the song," showed that the singer "could musically equal the Deanna Durbins or the Jenny Linds of any country" (Zuhur 2000, 101). She was film-worthy and her voice could appeal to an extensive audience; she brought a classic quality to pop culture, and was a cultural icon.

Al-Qasabji and Asmahan, especially with the success of "Ya Toyour," are both considered artists who skillfully integrated aspects of European elite genres into Arab music. Ali Jihad Racy describes a dominant Cairene musical aesthetic of the twentieth century as a "neutral canvas" with Arab musical sounds hosting patches of color, including musical forms on a continuum from fully "neutral"—precomposed songs with *tarab* characteristics—to a linear structure with successive segments in contrasting styles. Music from

Western classical influence and film music are significant sources of color in Racy's canvas, as in "Ya Toyour," a song that clearly exhibits stylistic contrast. For Racy, contrasting sound colors can also be located using the concept of *lawn* (literally "color" in Arabic), an important idea in the context of Arab music discourse. In *Making Music in the Arab World: The Culture and Artistry of* Tarab (2003), Racy defines *lawn* as a musical style or "flavor," but also adds that it can refer to "a stylistically distinct segment within an eclectic piece of music" (227). The neutral-canvas model, Racy explains, is often referred to as *lawn tarab*, while the "patches of color," or sounds from a Western palette, provide *lawn gharbi* (literally "Western color"). And the interpolation of bel canto in Asmahan's performance of "Ya Toyour" might even be termed *lawn upira*, or "opera color" (Racy 1982, 395–96).

Compositions using such a model highlight tradition, innovation, and an artist's individual quality, or *lawn khāss* ("special color," *lawn* meaning "color," *khāss* meaning "particular"), which may involve vocal timbre and/or ornamentation (Racy 1982, 400); Racy offers Asmahan as an example. Ilyas Sahhab described her as "proficient in the area of *tarab*," as well as "highly innovative," with the ability to "inlay the fundamentals of European singing into Arab singing" (Sahhab 1980, 64, quoted in Racy 1982, 393). Sherifa Zuhur (2000), in turn, warns readers not to focus on Asmahan's operatic abilities, arguing that Asmahan is too skilled in *lawn tarab* to simply be thought of as a singer with a Westernized sound. Additionally, it is key that al-Qasabji and Asmahan did not intend to cross over into Western markets, but only to experiment with the sort of eclectic modern Arab style that had excited musicians present at the Congrès du Caire in 1932.[2]

In Asmahan's recording of "Ya Toyour," she oscillates between two *lawn*-s, two vocalities. During the *tarab* sections, she employs a medium-to-heavy register commonly heard in contemporary Arab film songs, and during the most Straussian moments of the song, she sings with a consistently vibratoed, lighter register—as in her final cadenza, which features a birdlike call-and-response between her soprano and a violin (in a role comparable to that of the flute in "Frühlingsstimmen"). When her voice follows diatonic scales and triadic arpeggios in distinctively Western ornamental motives, she stays in her lighter register, whether singing higher or lower pitches. In the *tarab* segments of the music, she tends to sing the virtuosic passages of modal exposition (up to D_5) in her heavier register. Asmahan's performance goes as high as a staccato A_5, although the highest parts mostly settle around G_5.

One difference between the vocalities may reside in the idea of vocality as a kind of vowel-ness, considering Italian vowels favored in Western classical diction, such as the singular open vowel for /a/, and Egyptian Arabic vowels including a range of /a/-related vowels between a front-positioned /æ/ and a back-positioned version (Cowan 1970, 96). But there are moments in "Ya Toyour" where East and West overlap musically, for example Asmahan's final cadenza that shifts the singer's operatic staccato into *maqam* modulation, or the pervasive use of descending and ascending portamenti (sliding pitches); the latter being characteristic, albeit in different ways, of both Arab and Western styles.

An American in Beirut

Ms. Grout's reception on *Arabs Got Talent* was largely celebratory, though some critics at the time didn't believe she was American or that she spoke Arabic (Shanahan and Goldstein 2013), and she recounts some later disapproval from Arab musicians in the United States (Interview, June 2, 2016). "I can see where they are coming from," she acknowledges, "because I received all of this praise. I wouldn't have received this much praise had I been an Arab girl singing at the same level, or playing oud at the same level. So the whole marketing thing is [that] I'm American and I'm singing in Arabic" (Interview, June 2, 2016). This last statement is an especially important insight; if we are free to collect aspects of our identity in a global cultural supermarket, we cannot guarantee that we won't end up on the shelf ourselves.

Ms. Grout told me that she was halfway through her university studies when she heard the Lebanese superstar Fairuz on YouTube and "fell in love with her voice" (Interview, June 2, 2016). She thought she might try singing Arab music someday, but decided to start with lessons on the oud, studying *maqamat* and adjusting her ear to the unfamiliar three-quarter-step intervals. A few months in, she tried the singing. She found a teacher on the online music site Zaman al-Wasl, and he began working with her, on Skype, as her coach. She took language courses in classical Arabic, found herself fascinated with *tarab*, the classic genre rooted in Arabic poetic traditions, and listened to the ultra-iconic *tarab* singer, Umm Kulthum. In her youth in Egypt, Umm Kulthum famously studied Qur'an at village *kuttab*-s (primary religious schools) and absorbed the fundamentals of recitation there (Danielson 1997, 22). As with other singers of her time, her later reputation in secular music partly hinged on how strongly her expressive performance style was informed by her knowledge of *tajwid*, the rules of Qur'anic recitation. In her biography of Umm Kulthum, Virginia Danielson describes Umm Kulthum's singing as a combination of these qualities with "what the cognoscenti of Cairo taught as historically Arab aesthetics" (Danielson 1997, 92). She demonstrated vocal strength with a range beyond two octaves, an admired ability to sing long phrases, and the meaningful changes in tone color that Egyptian listeners associated with religiously learned musicians—a hoarseness or break (*bahha*), a nasality called *ghunna* or *khanaafa*, and the judicious use of falsetto, vibrato, and trill.

From Ms. Grout's point of view as a Western classical vocal major, one of the key distinctions between operatic and *tarab* vocalities lies in where the resonance is perceived by the singer—for operatic singing, in the head and face (known as the "mask"); in Arab singing, the chest and nasal area. Fairuz, she says, employs head resonance more than many other Arab singers, and she muses that perhaps hearing Fairuz's voice and its culturally diverse qualities was a reason why she found the music accessible in the first place. Working on two vocalities at once created some tension. Simultaneously studying voice at McGill University, she encountered bafflement from her instructors, and the practical differences between her two repertories made them seem incompatible—"the equivalent of training to be a ballerina and a heavyweight boxer at the same time" (Interview, June 2, 2016), an analogy that suggests two disparate ways of shaping the muscles, of using the body. She began to see her senior recital primarily as the end-goal that would finally free her to focus on Arab singing full-time. (Her former voice teacher has since expressed support of her work, as her success has grown.)

As she listened to celebrated singers, picking up the pronunciation by ear was nearly automatic, as she had studied diction and previously sung in Italian, German, French, Spanish, and Russian. But to better attain the appropriate vocal sound for *tarab*, with a view toward the parameters set by Umm Kulthum, Ms. Grout's online instructor insisted that she listen to recordings of Qur'anic recitation by the renowned Muhammad Siddiq al-Minshawi and Muhammad Tantawi. Although she had not begun practicing Islam at the time, and did not understand the texts, she listened carefully and constantly, not only picking up enunciation, phrasing, and timbral quality, but also developing her aural "intuition" (her term) for the *maqam*—modal—practices that structure both religious recitation and singing in Arab music. Although both employ *maqam*, the two are separated, Ms. Grout notes, due to the "*samāʿ* polemic" (Nelson 1985; Marcus 2006) that debates the permissibility of music in Islam, and as a result positions sacred recitation as non-musical. Virginia Danielson, asked to comment for *The Guardian* on Ms. Grout's initial *Arabs Got Talent* performance, heard her style as successful, although she gently critiqued her musical knowledge:

> Her resonance—that slightly nasal sound—is particularly compelling and very expressive in this style of singing. Her voice is strong, very pretty

and she commands the style of the repertory very well. If I were going to criticise, I'd say the rhythmic structure of the piece escapes her a bit, but otherwise she sang very well, I thought. (quoted in Kingsley 2013)

Ms. Grout acknowledges that she is still learning, still listening: "For me, I'm still in an imitation phase; I'm still imitating what I hear. I'm not yet at a level where I can interpret a piece in my own, purely Jennifer artistic way" (Interview, June 2, 2016). Many of the singers I've interviewed have brought up imitation as a vital part of cultivating vocality. It's worth noting, too, that Umm Kulthum wrote about imitating her father in her childhood (Danielson 1997, 22), and that many Arab singers after her have attributed their own vocal abilities to early imitations of Umm Kulthum (Danielson 1997, 66). Ms. Grout attributes her facility with *tarab* vocality to a lifelong imitative ability and describes playing with accents during her childhood to make her family laugh (Interview, June 2, 2016). CNN reported in 2013 that some *Arabs Got Talent* viewers doubted she was actually American, due to a unique style of speaking English that offers no obvious regional phonetics. Her response at the time questions the validity of a fixed relationship between location and speech, indicating a belief in cultural flexibility and the mutability of identity in a globalized society:

> I like my accent. I like the fact that it's unique, and I think it's narrow-minded to believe that just because you're from a certain place, you have to speak a certain way. Because people learn and people change and people travel, and things about them change all the time. Why does that not include accents? (quoted in Jamjoom 2013)

And if not accents, why not singing?

Her ease with imitation was put to the test following her time on *Arabs Got Talent*. That show airs on MBC4, the Middle East Broadcasting Center channel that re-launched in 2005 with new programming designated specifically for the "modern Arab woman" ("Reaching the Modern Arabic Woman" 2005). Its scheduling features several Western formats, including dramas, talk shows (including *The Oprah Winfrey Show*), and, besides *Arabs Got Talent*, other reality competitions. Ms. Grout was invited to participate in one of these, titled *Shaklak Mish Gharib* (*Your Face Sounds Familiar*, part of a global franchise developed by Dutch and Spanish media companies), which requires celebrity contestants to impersonate popular singers—both Western and Arab—of the twentieth and twenty-first centuries. The show assigned her diverse personas, asking her to deliver imitations of stars including Asmahan, Madonna, Shadia (famous in the 1950s and '60s), the more recent sensation Ahlam, and Alicia Keys. Each undertaking was rushed and difficult, Ms. Grout says; she had one week to learn the style and music of singers with whom, in many cases, she was completely unfamiliar. A vocal coach was tasked with helping her to sound like the target voice, and an acting coach assisted with presentation—sometimes, as with her impersonation of Shadia, even reproducing a famous film scene. As she prepared, she was admonished to give up any aspirations of beautiful singing in the service of precise imitation, and the acting coach told her, "Actors don't act; they just *are*. Don't act, *be* . . . You have to *be* Shadia" (Interview, June 2, 2015).

Because other singers had told me that multivocality could cause some personal confusion about vocal identity, I asked Ms. Grout whether she had identified one way of singing that was "really [her]." She said, without hesitation:

> I'm one hundred percent *tarab*. For me, Arabic music is just so full of soul, and it's, like, effortlessly so. And I—maybe this is a personal thing, there might be some objectivity to it, but I feel like in [Western] classical music, I had to work so much harder to get worked up to get a feeling, but with Arabic music, I just *listen* to it and I'm immediately transported to that special place that artists get when they're immersed in what they're doing . . . I don't know, maybe I was reincarnated or something, and I used to be an Arabic singer! Maybe if I had grown up in the Umm Kulthum period I would have been obsessed with classical Western music. I have always had the need to veer out from the norm; I've always had this sense that when everyone around me is doing something, I want to be doing something different. (Interview, June 2, 2016)

Jennifer Grout's performance of "Ya Toyour" on *Arabs Got Talent*, a blue-lit, fog-suffused staging with dancers in diaphanous bird-winged gowns, was an abbreviated one at three minutes—likely due to the show's time constraints—and did not include the spectacular final cadenza. However, even the shortened version allowed Ms. Grout to demonstrate her *lawn*-traversing skills and served as a perhaps ideal choice of repertoire—a kind of reverse- or even circular-Asmahan feat in which the American opera singer, who had previously surprised her audience with her knowledge of *tarab*, now surprised viewers again with her operatic ability. She was awarded third place in the competition.

Refuge

Just as the dual *lawn*-s of "Ya Toyour" helped Ms. Grout to cross a border from Western opera into the world of Arab music, they worked in an analogous way in the opposite direction for Syrian singer Lubana Al-Quntar. The song is featured frequently in Ms. Al-Quntar's programs, including that of a performance I heard in 2016 at the Toledo, Ohio, event *Mideast x Midwest: A Dialogue of Music, Food, and Fun at America's Crossroads*. Publicity billed her as Syria's first opera singer. Before the revolution, before she became a refugee in the United States, Ms. Al-Quntar had taught both Western classical/operatic singing and *tarab* at the Conservatoire in Damascus, Syria. She had grown up with Arab music in a family notably directly linked to Asmahan's—her grandmother was a cousin of Asmahan and Farid al-Atrash's mother. Ms. Al-Quntar told me that her family and others observed in her from an early age a vocal likeness to Asmahan. She loved the repertoire she heard from Asmahan and Umm Kulthum, but always wanted to do something "different" in singing. When Damascus's conservatory opened its opera department, she leaped at the opportunity—although at the time she didn't know a lot about opera or Western classical music, she was sure that she wanted to learn about the processes of singing: "I was fascinated about the idea of *learning* how to sing. It doesn't matter what style it is, but I wanted to know more about the voice and the breathing and all this" (Interview, December 4, 2016). She studied at the Damascus Conservatory for four years from 1993, then at the Royal College of Music in London for two years, and then attended Holland's Maastricht Academy of Music. When she started to learn operatic singing, her teacher asked her not to sing Arab music or in any style other than what she was studying. She entirely abandoned singing Arab music for seven years, but after that time, she felt that her technique and the awareness she had acquired of her physical instrument's mechanics would allow her to improve her *tarab* vocality too.

Her dual vocal history served her well when she returned to Syria, this time appointed to head the opera department at the Damascus Conservatory. Although she taught Western classical singing there, she also founded an "Arabic singing technique department" (Interview, December 4, 2016). In that area, she applied Western classical training techniques to Arab music, asking her *tarab* students to practice the same kinds of exercises her opera students did, including triadic arpeggios—but with discrete modes of resonance in each style. The way breathing and vowels are conceptualized in bel canto, she believes, work well in *tarab*. For her, the primary difference lies in the embodied, corporeal location in which the singer feels the strongest vibration:

> In opera, I teach the same method in terms of breathing, of the vowels; there are specific rules you can follow at the same time with opera and with Arabic [music]. But in terms of the *place* of singing, like where the sound has to vibrate, it's different. In Arabic, you are completely singing from your throat, exactly from the throat and from the chest. The vowels have to be with the mouth and the articulation the same as opera, but in opera you are using the head voice, and you use your body just to support your higher notes, and your resonance, and the vowels. In Arabic [music] you do much the same, but you open your throat . . . Instead of making the head voice resonance, I tell my students to open the throat and the chest, so the chest is the place of the vowels [for] resonance. So, it's the same method. (Interview, December 4, 2016)

Ms. Al-Quntar's training in *tarab* had not been so different from Jennifer Grout's, in that it consisted primarily of studying the recordings of renowned singers such as Asmahan and Umm Kulthum. Although not herself Muslim, Ms. Al-Quntar says that she analyzed and absorbed elements of Umm Kulthum's foundations in the study of Qur'anic recitation. She considered these practices again when she began teaching *tarab* at the conservatory. In particular, she notes that the study of Qur'anic recitation has historically had a useful impact on *tarab* singers' breathing, the long phrases of Qur'anic recitation allowing them to manage the similar demands of *tarab*. The breathing techniques required across Qur'anic recitation and the music of *tarab* and bel canto, she believes, are one and the same. "You cannot divide one sentence, you cannot breathe in each word" (Interview, December 4, 2016).

Ms. Al-Quntar has sung "Ya Toyour" many times, including two very different performances: One was included in the official recording released for the 2000 Queen Elisabeth Competition in Brussels, where she placed fifth in singing. The other was recorded at the Festival de la Medina in Tunisia more than a decade later (Al-Quntar 2013). Typically, when she performs the song, she shifts between two *lawn*-s like Asmahan; however, in her Brussels performance, where she was participating in a Western classical singing competition, she sang it truncated (but including the final cadenza), a cappella, and at a pitch higher than it is written, centered on B-flat instead of G. This change in pitch helped her to emphasize the high tessitura highlighted in the Western classical vocality, and she avoided any heavy-registered *tarab* vocalizations at all, finishing on a suitably operatic B-flat$_5$. Conversely, and more like Asmahan's rendition, the performance recorded in Tunisia showcases her ease with both *tarab* and bel canto singing, low and high pitch ranges, heavy and light registration, and ornamental practices specific to each style. Ms. Al-Quntar finds special meaning in this way of performing the song: "Singing the *tarab* is very dear to me, because this is what we sing, and what we embrace, and this is our culture. And then to go to the opera part, I feel like the song was made for me . . . I like the style, I like the idea so much, the East and the West in music" (Interview, December 4, 2016).

I asked her whether she feels that one way of singing is more "her" than the other. "Actually," she answered, "I ask myself this question a lot, and [other] people ask me this question, and always I cannot choose. So, apparently both are me . . . I feel both actually, I really feel both equally" (Interview, December 4, 2016). Two vocalities reside in one singer, wherever she resides, and "Ya Toyour" encapsulates them both.

In her study of displaced Syrian musicians in Turkey, Dunya Habash writes that "music and music-making can create avenues for agency, resilience, and resistance in diaspora and displacement by allowing migrants to have a political voice in their new societies" (Habash 2020, 1372). Citing the ethnomusicologists Alan Lomax and Martin Stokes, Habash also draws on ideas about musical practice as an embodiment of social identity, describing a Syrian choir in Istanbul that demonstrates music's home-making and identity-sustaining power for displaced singers (ibid., 1373). Her work thus presses up against two ideas with special significance in voice research: first, the metaphorization of the sonic voice as "political voice" and personal agency; second, the embodiment of social identity through music, a concept amplified in the context of the supremely embodied instrument—voice. Though the lives of the musicians she interviews ostensibly reinforce the understanding of music as a vehicle of agency and embodied identity, Habash also finds a tension between cultural identity and the more immediately urgent needs of socioeconomic survival (ibid., 1383), so musicians adapt to the performance practices of their new home rather than maintain the musical memory of the home they left. In the context of Lubana Al-Quntar's experience, her already dual cultural capabilities perhaps mitigated some of this professional tension as she moved into her North American career. The embodiment of two cultural practices, even within the space of a single song like "Ya Toyour," allows Ms. Al-Quntar to create with and within her voice a sense of home and identity that spans across borders. Her voice is a *borderscape*, in itself, a place where the sounds of multiple homes compete, conflict, and ultimately establish a fluid new personal map of identity. Prem Kumar Rajaram and Carl Grundy-Warr have written of the concept of borderscape (based on Arjun Appadurai's -scapes concept), that any borderscape is identifiable by the kinds of specific conflicts that arise within it about belonging and non-belonging (2007, xxviii), and that it is "a zone of multiple actors and multiple bodies each calling on different histories and solidarities . . . experiences, economies, and politics that are concealed" (ibid., xxix). In my framework of multivocality, voice is such a zone, inhabited sonically by multiple, invisible—but not inaudible—social interactions, histories, and politics. Thus, Ms. Al-Quntar's voice both creates and navigates border spaces and can be heard as a sonic borderscape.

Conclusions

The two *lawn*-s demanded by "Ya Toyour" allowed Ms. Grout and Ms. Al-Quntar to cross borders in opposite directions—Ms. Grout toward a career in Arab world music and entertainment, and Ms. Al-Quntar toward Europe and North America, even if eventually that move was forced. The song helped Ms. Al-Quntar cross not only vocal borders but also geographic ones, as well as to establish a global career, and subsequently to endure in exile.

* * *

To find an agentive voice, a singer may chart their route through multiple vocalities. Even though pervasive essentialist discourse about voice is an important feature of many singing traditions—positioning each person as the possessor of a singular sonic character, a single way of singing—singers may in many ways abandon one vocality for another or embody multiple vocalities. They may use changes in vocality as sonic modes through which to negotiate the boundaries and intersections of geographical, musical, and cultural spaces, and to sound their own intersubjective individualities in new places. Their singing choices may be directed by culture-specific discourses of self and/or relationships to broader cultural identities. In some ways, the freedom to choose and change vocality is a privilege provided by the accessible, messy twentieth- and twenty-first-century global sonic marketplace. Multivocality can be used as a strategy in cultural interaction, and as a form of branding that can make a singer an ideal neoliberal subject, marketable across audiences. And reality-TV singing competitions like those within the *Got Talent* franchise provide a tempting path to becoming rich and famous, however illusory that path might be. Writing on the concept of voice as metaphor for agency in neoliberal capitalism, Nick Couldry warns against seeming offers of voice that in reality merely support the market system and not true agency, delivering only the "opportunity to compete as a commodity" (Couldry 2010, 13). This has played out on twenty-first-century singing competitions over and over, ostensibly giving all young artists equal, democratic opportunities to be heard, but in the end just shaping them into products (Meizel 2011; cf. Stahl 2013). In the case of Ms. Al-Quntar, who sang "Ya Toyour" at the Belgian competition, a similar if somewhat less commercialized process took place, her choice of song hinting at her marketability in the world of opera, where women singers, especially sopranos, must stand out from one another to be hired. Additionally, the experiences of both Ms. Grout and Ms. Al-Quntar highlight how vocalities that are largely perceived as culturally fairly homogenous—Western classical singing, for example (see also Meizel 2020), or *tarab* singing—can be inscribed with extremely heterogeneous meanings for the complex people who use them. And, as this chapter has illustrated, those multiple vocalities and multiple meanings may all exist within the performance of one song.

Notes

1. Translated by Lillie Gordon.
2. Al-Qasabji himself had a fraught relationship with the Congrès. He apparently felt that the invited European scholars, and he names Curt Sachs, were being paid to insult cultivated Arab music (positioning it as less important than Arab "folk" musics), and he was concerned that many important musicians had not been invited (Vigreux 1992, cited in Danielson 1994, 135).

References

Al-Quntar, Lubana. 2013. "Lubana al Quntar—Ya Touyour (Asmahan)." www.youtube.com. https://www.youtube.com/watch?v=EPyMyrLgNiM.
Appadurai, Arjun. 1990. "Disjuncture and Difference in the Global Cultural Economy." *Theory, Culture & Society* 7: 295–310.
Berberian, Cathy. 2014 [1966]. "The New Vocality in Contemporary Music." Translated by Francesca Placanica. In *Cathy Berberian: Pioneer of Contemporary Vocality*, eds. Francesca Placanica, Pamela Karantonis, Pieter Verstraete, and Anne Sivuoja Kauppala, 47–50. Surrey, UK: Ashgate.
Couldry, Nick. 2010. *Why Voice Matters: Culture and Politics after Neoliberalism*. Thousand Oaks, CA: Sage.
Cowan, William. 1970. "The Vowels of Egyptian Arabic." *Word* 26(1): 94–100.
Crouse, Lindsay. 2013. "Surprising New Face in Arabic Music." *New York Times*, December 3. http://www.nytimes.com/2013/12/04/arts/music/jennifer-grout-sings-umm-kulthum-hits-on-arabs-got-talent.html?_r=0.
Danielson, Virginia. 1994. "Reviewed Work: *Musique Arabe: Le Congrès du Caire de 1932*, by Philippe Vigreux." *Yearbook for Traditional Music* 2(6): 132–36.
———. 1997. *"The Voice of Egypt": Umm Kulthūm, Arabic Song, and Egyptian Society in the Twentieth Century*. Chicago: University of Chicago Press.

Habash, Dunya. 2020. "'Do Like You Did in Aleppo': Negotiating Space and Place Among Syrian Musicians in Istanbul." *Journal of Refugee Studies* 34(2): 1370–85.

Halman, Talat S., and Jayne L. Warner, eds. 2005. *Nightingales and Pleasure Gardens: Turkish Love Poems*. Syracuse, NY: Syracuse University Press.

Heidegger, Martin. 1962. *Being and Time*. New York: Harper & Row.

Jamjoom, Mohammed. 2013. "All-American Singer with Very 'Arab' Voice May Win 'Arabs Got Talent.'" www.cnn.com, December 5. https://www.cnn.com/2013/12/05/world/meast/mideast-arabs-got-talent.

John, Arit. 2013. "One of the Finalists of 'Arabs Got Talent' Is a White Woman from Boston." *The Atlantic*, November 25. https://www.theatlantic.com/international/archive/2013/11/one-finalists-arabs-got-talent-white-woman-boston/355506/.

Kingsley, Patrick. 2013. "All-American Singer Wows Arabs Got Talent with Umm Kulthum Cover." *The Guardian*, November 25. https://www.theguardian.com/tv-and-radio/2013/nov/25/american-jennifer-grout-arabs-got-talent-umm-kulthum.

Krasnowolska, Anna. 2006. "The Epic Roots of Lyrical Imagery in Classical Persian Poetry." In *Ghazal as World Literature II: From a Literary Genre to a Great Tradition: The Ottoman Gazel in Context*, eds. Angelika Neuwirth, Michael Hess, Judith Pfeiffer, and Börte Sagaster, 109–20. Würzburg: Ergon Verlag Würzburg in Kommission.

Kugle, Scott. 2007. "*Qawwālī* Between Written Poem and Sung Lyric, or . . . How a *Ghazal* Lives." *The Muslim World* 97(4): 572–610.

Marcus, Scott. 2006. *Music in Egypt*. New York: Oxford University Press.

Meizel, Katherine. 2011. *Idolized: Music, Media, and Identity in American Idol*. Bloomington: Indiana University Press.

———. 2020. *Multivocality: Singing on the Borders of Identity*. Oxford and New York: Oxford University Press.

Mernissi, Fatima. 1994. *Dreams of Trespass: Tales of a Harem Girlhood*. New York: Addison Wesley.

Molinari, Maurizio. 2013. "Jennifer Grout, l'Americana che ha Conquistato la Musica Araba." *La Stampa*, May 12. http://www.lastampa.it/2013/12/05/spettacoli/jennifer-grout-lamericana-che-ha-conquistato-la-musica-arabatQB50ZMP2hJ3s6ktliZffM/pagina.html.

Nelson, Kristina. 1985. "The Samāʿ Polemic." In *The Art of Reciting Qurʾan*, 32–51. Austin: University of Texas Press.

Pizzi, Michael. 2013. "Move Over, Susan Boyle: Boston Irish Girl Jennifer Grout Is the Unexpected Star of 'Arabs Got Talent.'" *The Daily Beast*, December 5. http://www.thedailybeast.com/articles/2013/12/05/boston-irish-girl-jennifer-grout-is-the-unexpected-star-of-arabs-got-talent.html.

Racy, Ali Jihad. 1982. "Musical Aesthetics in Present-Day Cairo." *Ethnomusicology* 26(3): 391–406.

———. 2003. *Making Music in the Arab World: The Culture and Artistry of* Tarab. Cambridge, UK: Cambridge University Press.

Rajaram, Prem Kumar, and Carl Grundy-Warr, eds. 2007. *Borderscapes: Hidden Geographies and Politics at Territory's Edge*. Borderlines 29. Minneapolis: University of Minnesota Press.

"Reaching the Modern Arabic Woman—MBC4 Goes On-Air with a Totally New Look." 2005. *Albawaba*, November 23. http://www.albawaba.com/news/reaching-modern-arabic-woman-mbc4-goes-air-totally-new-look.

Sahhab, Ilyas. 1980. *Difaʿan ʿan al-Ughniyah al-ʿArabiyya*. Beirut: al-Muʾassasah al-ʿArabiyya li-al-Dirasat wa-al-Nashr.

Shanahan, Mark, and Meredith Goldstein. 2013. "Jennifer Grout Places Third in 'Arabs Got Talent.'" *Boston Globe*, December 7. https://www.bostonglobe.com/lifestyle/names/2013/12/07/namesgrout/0e6yIc92J4QqnO2IswWSwO/story.html.

Sharif, Samim. 1981. "Al-Qasabji wa Asmahan wa al-Aswat al-Jamila fi al-Marhala al Simimaʾiyya." In *Al-Ughniyya al-ʿArabiyya*, 221–22. Damascus: Wizarat al-Thaqafa wa al-Irshad.

Stahl, Matt. 2013. *Unfree Masters: Recording Artists and the Politics of Work*. Durham, NC: Duke University Press.

Vigreux, Philippe, ed. 1992. *Musique Arabe: Le Congrès du Caire de 1932*. Cairo: CEDEJ.

Williams, Jeni. 1997. *Interpreting Nightingales: Gender, Class and Histories*. Sheffield, UK: Sheffield Academic Press.

Zuhur, Sherifa. 2000. *Asmahan's Secrets: Woman, War, and Song*. Austin: Center for Middle Eastern Studies, University of Texas at Austin.

Multimedia Playlist

LUBANA AL-QUNTAR, "Ya Toyour," *Queen Elisabeth Competition: Singing*, 2000

———, "Ya Touyour," Festival de la Medina de Tunis, 2013: https://www.youtube.com/watch?v=EPyMyrLgNiM

ASMAHAN, "Ya Toyour" (also spelled "Ya Touyour"), *La Sublime, Vol. 2*, 1994

———, "Ya Toyour," *Farid El Atrache & Asmahan*, 2000

JENNIFER GROUT, "Ya Toyour," *Arabs Got Talent*, 2013: https://www.youtube.com/watch?v=IQ4QFqTeFw8

SOUZAN HADDAD, "Ya Toyour," with the Syrian National Symphonic Orchestra, 2011: https://www.youtube.com/watch?v=Ij-V1f0Ybes

NESMA MAGHOUB, "Ya Toyour," 2013: https://www.youtube.com/watch?v=nAIXpjoj2h4

FARRAH YOUSEF, "Ya Toyour," 2016: https://www.youtube.com/watch?v=QItSQdOZv90

Afterword

The Power of Song

ELIJAH WALD

What is the power of song?

Reading the pieces in this book, it seems to me that it is above all the power of identification. We hear songs and singers as speaking directly to and for us; when we love a singer's work, we feel we know them and often that they know us in deep and meaningful ways. When we see someone else singing, dancing, or even just nodding along to the same song, we feel a sense of connection no other form of art can provide, a bond that goes far beyond music. We may share enthusiasms for paintings, books, or movies, but there is no equivalent in those media for "our song" or the way a brief snatch of melody or a familiar vocal or instrumental timbre can evoke a wave of memories and associations. The songs we share symbolize shared culture, not only implicitly but explicitly—nations have anthems, and all sorts of organizations use songs to signal and cement their group identity.

The power of song to provide that sense of unity and shared experience, often over great distances and divides, is wonderful and precious. But power is a tricky thing.

My father was born in 1906 to parents who had emigrated from Central Europe, and he grew up as the only Jewish kid on a tough Irish block in Brooklyn. He was not happy about that and escaped first by reading, then by joining another boy in a song and dance act that performed for local social clubs. He knew all the pop songs of the 1920s, and I grew up with that music: "When Francis Dances with Me," "Three O'Clock in the Morning," and all sorts of songs that marked ethnicity and ethnic differences: "Mammy," "Mother Machree," "The Sheik of Araby," and its Jewish immigrant parody, "The Sheik of Avenue B."

That was a high point of immigration to the United States, and sheet music publishers, vaudevillians, and record companies were marketing songs that connected people to the communities and languages they had left and helped them to shape new communities and identities—as well as shaping their views of the people around them.

My father was the first member of his family to go to college, emigrating from Brooklyn to Manhattan, where he found a new world, an intellectual European high culture of classical music, fine art, and theater. He got a doctorate in biology, married a young woman from Philadelphia's main line, and after his graduation they went to Germany, where he did a year of postdoctoral work in Heidelberg. He enjoyed speaking German, which his parents had sometimes spoken at home, and was entranced by the old-world charm of the town: the narrow streets lined with cobblestones, the old stone houses, and the medieval castle on the hill. Their apartment was on a small square, and early every morning, through his bedroom window, he could hear groups of young men singing as they walked through the streets. He remembered how lovely that sounded, the young voices echoing off the ancient stones.

That was 1933, and those young men were the Nazi Brownshirts, singing the "Horst Wessel Lied." My father knew who they were; he was Jewish and a moderate leftist, and he hated and feared them and understood that the point of their morning marches was to show who was now running Germany. But he was also a romantic young American embarking on a new life and escaping the streets of Brooklyn, and he always remembered how beautifully they sang.

I suppose that story could be framed as an example of the power of music to transcend politics; that my father could appreciate the beauty of the singing, despite what the singers represented. He always spoke of those mornings with nostalgia and never lost that sense of connection to an old, romantic Germany—which was, of course, why the Nazis sang and sponsored concerts of the great German composers and a national revival of *volksmusik*. The power of song.

I spent several years playing music around Europe in the 1970s and 1980s. The German folk scene was very active at that time, but although the British, Irish, French, Italian, Scandinavian, and Eastern European folk scenes were full of groups reviving their various traditions, the young Germans were all singing songs from the United States, Ireland, and Latin America, or new songs in the styles of Bob Dylan and Joan Baez—but never German folksongs. That music was still associated with the Nazis, and ninety years after my father's postgraduate year, the "Horst Wessel Lied" is still illegal there, still regarded as too dangerous to be sung. I have to wonder whether the song's old associations are really so powerful that Germans must be protected from it, or if the prohibition has by now become another source of its power.

I started playing music at age seven, hit the road as a performer at eighteen, and earned my living for the next dozen years as a singer and guitarist. I had grown up in Cambridge, Massachusetts, in the years of the US folk revival, surrounded by the songs of Pete Seeger, Woody Guthrie, Lead Belly, and Josh White. My mother's parents, Jewish Communist refugees from Nazi Vienna, bought records of those artists in the 1940s, and I fell in love simultaneously with the music and the idea of being a rambling proletarian hobo guitar player. My timing was perfect: in the 1960s, that music became the sound of youth and civil rights and the antiwar movement, and by the 1970s it had been embraced by young people around the world, along with the Beatles and Rolling Stones, and Motown, and Willie Nelson. As an American guitarist and singer, I was welcomed wherever I traveled, not only in Europe but in Asia, Africa, and Central America. The power of song.

I refer to myself as an "American" guitarist consciously: that was what people called me, almost everywhere, and the word "America" had a magical quality, beyond the prosaic "United States." It referenced a mythological place people everywhere knew from movies, television, recordings, advertisements, and news stories, an idealized (even when demonized) evocation of wealth and power, and a dream of access to that wealth and power. Although I was hitchhiking and playing for tips on sidewalks and café terraces, I symbolized an ideal of freedom that went along with being American, unlike the local people who hitchhiked and begged on the street because they had no choice.

That is a simplification, of course. People reacted to me and my music in all sorts of ways, including, much of the time, ignoring me. But it was true enough to take me around the world, always able to earn enough to live fairly decently, and always feeling the protective power of being a white man with a US passport. All of that mattered, even when I played Spanish or Swahili songs: I was on national television in Zaire, not simply because I played the music of Edouard Masengo and Jean-Bosco Mwenda, who were my teachers there, but because I was a white American playing that music. I was able to write a book on Mexican narcocorridos, the ballads of the cross-border drug traffic, because, although I arrived on their doorsteps on foot with a guitar slung over my shoulder, the composers and musicians welcomed me as an emissary from a world of money and power. And they were right; I went home and wrote a book that was published by a major publisher and my advance would have bought a nice house in most Mexican towns—though not the opulent mansions of the top corrido composers, bought with royalties from songs heard all over Mexico, Central America, and the United States and treasured by millions of immigrants, and their children and grandchildren, as the sound of home, or homeland, or heritage—something, in any case, older and more meaningful than a tenuous identity as immigrant outsiders. The power of song.

This is a huge subject, and I am fascinated by the different ways the writers in this volume, and the artists they are writing about, have approached and understood it. I have devoted these few pages to exploring some aspects of my own relationship to music and power as a reminder that we all start with our own experiences and viewpoints, our own power and relationships to power, some chosen, some not. Music is always heard in larger contexts, and the power of song is never just the power of a song itself, or of the singer—there are always infinite powers and relationships shaping its context, its intended and unintended meanings, and our various understandings and relationships to all of that.

I also want to remind readers that, much as we may love music, its power is not only a metaphor. It can unite and inspire people in wonderful ways, and also in horrific ways—and if the deep associations and fervent love it inspires are uniquely precious and seductive, that is a reason to celebrate and also to be wary of its power.

Contributors

CHRISTINA D. ABREU is Associate Professor of History and Director of the Center for Latino and Latin American Studies at Northern Illinois University. Her research focuses on the role of race, nationalism, and migration in the Cuban and Spanish Caribbean diasporic communities of the United States with a particular emphasis on popular culture. She is the author of *Rhythms of Race: Cuban Musicians and the Making of Latino New York City and Miami, 1940–1960* (University of North Carolina Press, 2015) and is currently working on a second book, *Patria over Profits: The Story of Afro-Cuban Boxing Champion Teófilo Stevenson*, under contract with the University of Illinois Press, looking at race and sport in Cuba and US-Cuba relations in the 1970s and 1980s using the story of Teófilo Stevenson, an Afro-Cuban heavyweight boxer who won three gold medals in the 1972, 1976, and 1980 Olympic Games.

MICHAEL K. BOURDAGHS is Robert S. Ingersoll Professor in East Asian Languages and Civilizations and the College at the University of Chicago. He previously taught at UCLA and received his PhD in Asian Literature from Cornell University. A specialist in modern Japanese literature and culture, he is the author of *The Dawn That Never Comes: Shimazaki Tōson and Japanese Nationalism* (Columbia University Press, 2003), *Sayonara Amerika, Sayonara Nippon: A Geopolitical Prehistory of J-Pop* (Columbia University Press, 2012; Japanese translation, 2012), and *A Fictional Commons: Natsume Sōseki and the Properties of Modern Literature* (Duke University Press, 2021). He is also a prolific translator, most recently of Kojin Karatani's *The Structure of World History: From Modes of Production to Modes of Exchange* (Duke University Press, 2014). He is the recipient of a 2019 Guggenheim Fellowship and numerous other fellowships and awards.

KWAME DAWES is the author of numerous books of poetry and other books of fiction, criticism, and essays. His most recent collection, *UnHistory*, was co-written with John Kinsella (Peepal Tree Press, UK, 2022). Dawes is a George W. Holmes University Professor of English and Glenna Luschei Editor of *Prairie Schooner*. He teaches in the Pacific MFA Program and is the Series Editor of the African Poetry Book Series, Director of the African Poetry Book Fund, and Artistic Director of the Calabash International Literary Festival. He is a Chancellor for the Academy of American Poets and Editor of American Life in Poetry. Kwame Dawes is the winner of the prestigious Windham-Campbell Award for Poetry and was a finalist for the 2022 Neustadt International Prize for Literature. His book *Bob Marley: Lyrical Genius* (Bobcat Books, 2007) remains the most authoritative study of the lyrics of Bob Marley.

LEVI S. GIBBS is Associate Professor of Asian Societies, Cultures, and Languages at Dartmouth College. His research focuses on the social roles of singers and songs in contemporary China and the cultural politics of regional identity. He is the author of *Song King: Connecting People, Places, and Past in Contemporary China* (University of Hawai'i Press, 2018) and the editor of *Faces of Tradition in Chinese Performing Arts* (Indiana University Press, 2020). His work has appeared in *China Quarterly*, *Modern China*, *Asian Ethnology*, *Prism: Theory and Modern Chinese Literature*, *CHINOPERL: Journal of Chinese Oral and Performing Literature*, and *Journal of Folklore Research*.

NANCY GUY is Professor of Music at the University of California, San Diego. Her interests include the musics of Taiwan and China, varieties of opera (including European and Chinese forms), music and state politics, and the ecocritical study of music. She is the author of *Peking Opera and Politics in Taiwan* (University of Illinois Press, 2005), which won the ASCAP Béla Bartók Award for Excellence in Ethnomusicology and was named an "Outstanding Academic Title for 2006" by *Choice*, and *The Magic of Beverly Sills* (University of Illinois Press, 2015), as well as the editor of *Resounding Taiwan: Musical Reverberations Across a Vibrant Island* (Routledge, 2022).

RUTH HELLIER is a Professor and scholar-creative artist at the University of California, Santa Barbara (UCSB), USA. Dr. Hellier is particularly interested in issues of memory, embodiment, experimentation, political economy, and creativity. She focuses on experimental performance-making, the politics~poetics of national and touristic performance in Mexico and Europe, embodied vocality and singing, environmental and community arts, and engages with performance studies, ethnomusicology and music studies, critical dance and theatre studies, history and feminist studies. Her principal publications include: *Embodying Mexico: Tourism, Nationalism, and Performance* (Oxford University Press, 2011); *Women Singers in Global Contexts: Music, Biography, Identity* (University of Illinois Press, 2013); and *Performing Palimpsest Bodies: Postmemory Theatre Experiments in Mexico* (Intellect and University of Chicago Press, 2019). She was editor of the multidisciplinary journal *Mexican Studies/Estudios Mexicanos* for five years. Trained as a musician at the Guildhall School of Music and Drama (1973–80), and followed by a BA Music, Drama, Dance (Birmingham University, 1983, including opera training with Janet Edmunds at Birmingham Conservatoire); PGCE Drama in Education (UCE, 1991), and PhD (UCE, 2001), Dr. Hellier had successful careers as an actor/performer (1983–91) and Head of Music (1992–95) before commencing her professorial career in 2000. In relation to voice and singing, Dr. Hellier has a wide range of professional experience, including as a singer, choir director (adults and children), and musical theatre vocal coach (Birmingham Theatre School).

JOHN LIE is Distinguished Professor of Sociology at the University of California, Berkeley. His recent publications include *K-Pop: Popular Music, Cultural Amnesia, and Economic Innovation in South Korea* (University of California Press, 2015), *The Dream of East Asia: The Rise of China, Nationalism, Popular Memory, and Regional Dynamics in Northeast Asia* (Association for Asian Studies, 2018), and *Japan, the Sustainable Society: The Artisanal Ethos, Ordinary Virtues, and Everyday Life in the Age of Limits* (University of California Press, 2021).

TREVA B. LINDSEY is Professor of Women's, Gender, and Sexuality Studies at The Ohio State University and the co-founder of Black Feminist Night School at Zora's House. Her research and teaching interests include African American women's history, Black popular and expressive culture, Black feminism(s), hip-hop studies, and sexual politics. She is the author of *America, Goddam: Violence, Black Women, and the Struggle for Justice* (University of California Press, 2022), which explores the combined force of anti-Blackness, misogyny, patriarchy, and capitalism in the lives of Black women and girls in the United States today, and was described as "required reading for all Americans" in a starred Kirkus review. Her first book, *Colored No More: Reinventing Black Womanhood in Washington, DC* (University of Illinois Press, 2017), was a *Choice* 2017 "Outstanding Academic Title." She has published in numerous peer-reviewed journals. She was a 2020–2021 Mellon/ACLS Scholars and Society Fellow and the inaugural Equity for Women and Girls of Color Fellow at Harvard University (2016–2017). She has been the recipient of several awards and fellowships. She also writes for and contributes to outlets such as *Time, NBC News, Al Jazeera, BET, Complex, Vox, Huffington Post, Billboard, Teen Vogue, Grazia UK, TheGrio, The Washington Post, Women's Media Center*, and *Cosmopolitan*.

ERIC LOTT teaches American Studies at the Graduate Center of the City University of New York. Lott has published widely and lectured at dozens of universities and other institutions on the politics of US cultural and performance history, and his work has appeared in a range of periodicals including *The Village Voice, The Nation, The Chronicle of Higher Education, PMLA, Representations, Transition, Social Text, American Literary History*, and *American Quarterly*. He is the author of *Love and Theft: Blackface Minstrelsy and the American Working Class* (Oxford University Press, 1993; 20th Anniversary ed., 2013), from which Bob Dylan took the title for his 2001 album *"Love and Theft"*; *The Disappearing Liberal Intellectual* (Basic Books, 2006); and *Black Mirror: The Cultural Contradictions of American Racism* (Harvard University Press, 2017), a study of race, culture, and fantasy across the long twentieth century. Lott has appeared on *The Daily Show with Trevor Noah, CBS Sunday Morning, Turner Classic Movies, C-SPAN Book TV, Al Jazeera TV*, and various radio shows and podcasts.

KATHERINE MEIZEL is Professor of Ethnomusicology at Bowling Green State University. Her book *Idolized: Music, Media, and Identity in American Idol* (Indiana University Press) was published in 2011, and *Multivocality: Singing on the Borders of Identity* (Oxford University Press) in January 2020. Her work has appeared on Slate.com, NPR.org, NewRepublic.com, and TheConversation.com, and she also recently coedited the *Oxford Handbook of Voice Studies* (2019).

CAROL A. MULLER is Professor of Music at the University of Pennsylvania. She has published widely on South African Music at home and abroad; on women and religious practices (four books plus articles). She is currently writing a book on the *Music of Contemporary Africa* for Routledge; working on a project, *Faith of Our Fathers*, with Tshepo Masango on the unlikely friendship of two Presbyterian ministers under apartheid; is at the start of a large South African jazz podcasting project; and is working on a Master's in Public Health to address issues of childhood trauma and the arts. She is a faculty fellow in one of Penn's College Houses and deeply engaged in online and community partnership pedagogy. Muller is a seasoned gumboot dancer.

NATALIE SARRAZIN is Professor of Music at SUNY Brockport. She holds a PhD in Ethnomusicology from the University of Maryland, College Park, and a Master's degree in Music Education from Peabody Conservatory at Johns Hopkins University. Dr. Sarrazin's area of teaching and scholarship includes ethnomusicology, Indian popular music, Hindi film music, and Indian music education. Dr. Sarrazin's recent publications include *Focus: Popular Music in Contemporary India* (2019), published as part of Routledge's Focus on World Music series, and *Music in Contemporary Indian Film: Memory, Voice, Identity* (co-author J. Beaster-Jones, Routledge, 2016). She is also the editor of a South Asia popular book series forthcoming for Bloomsbury's 33 1/3 Global.

ANTHONY SEEGER is Distinguished Professor of Ethnomusicology, Emeritus, at the University of California, Los Angeles, and Director and Curator Emeritus of Smithsonian Folkways Recordings. He holds a BA from Harvard University and a PhD in Anthropology from the University of Chicago. He is the author of three books on the Suyá/Kĩsêdjê Indians in Brazil, coeditor of three books, and author of over 120 articles and book chapters on ethnomusicology, anthropology, audiovisual archives, applied ethnomusicology, intellectual property, and American vernacular music. He served as President of the Society for Ethnomusicology and President and later Secretary General of the International Council for Traditional Music. He is a nephew of Pete Seeger.

CAROL SILVERMAN is Professor Emerita of Cultural Anthropology and Folklore at the University of Oregon. She has done research with Roma for over thirty years in the Balkans, Western Europe, and the United States. Her work explores the intersection of politics, music, human rights, gender, and policy with a focus on issues of representation. She is also a professional vocalist and teacher of Balkan music, curator for Balkan music for the international RomArchive, and works with the NGO Voice of Roma. Her book *Romani Routes: Cultural Politics and Balkan Music in Diaspora* (Oxford University Press, 2012, winner of the Merriam Prize from the Society for Ethnomusicology) explores how Romani music is both an exotic commodity in the world music market and a trope of multiculturalism in cosmopolitan contexts. Her 2021 book *Ivo Papazov's Balkanology* (Bloomsbury) analyzes the history and politics of Bulgarian wedding music.

ANDREW SIMON is a historian of media, popular culture, and the Middle East. He was a fellow at the Center for Arabic Study Abroad in Cairo during the 2011 Egyptian Revolution and is serving as a Senior Lecturer at Dartmouth College. Andrew's interdisciplinary research has received generous support from the Social Science Research Council and the American Research Center in Egypt and has been the subject of numerous presentations in and outside of the Arab world. His first book, *Media of the Masses: Cassette Culture in Modern Egypt* (Stanford University Press, 2022), explores how audiotapes empowered an unprecedented number of people to create culture, circulate information, and challenge ruling regimes long before the internet entered our daily lives. Andrew is currently examining what Shaykh Imam might teach us about misinformation, national narratives, and the making of the modern Middle East. You can follow Andrew on Twitter @simongandrew.

JEFF TODD TITON is Professor of Music, Emeritus, at Brown University, where for twenty-seven years he directed the PhD program in Ethnomusicology and led an old-time string band. He is the author or editor of numerous recordings, films, and articles, as well as nine books, including *Early Downhome Blues: A Musical and Cultural Analysis* (University of North Carolina Press, 1994, 2nd ed.), *Powerhouse for God: Speech, Chant, and Song in an Appalachian Baptist Church* (University of Tennessee Press, 2018, 2nd ed.), *The Oxford Handbook of Applied Ethnomusicology* (Oxford University Press, 2015), and most recently *Toward a Sound Ecology: New and Selected Essays* (Indiana University Press, 2020). In 2015, his field recordings were selected for preservation in the National Recording Registry, and in 2020, he received the American Folklore Society's lifetime scholarly achievement award.

ELIJAH WALD is a musician, writer, and historian who has published on a broad range of music and related cultural subjects. He started playing guitar after seeing his first Pete Seeger concert at age seven and spent many years traveling and performing in North and Central America, Europe, Asia, and Africa. In the early 1980s, he began writing for the *Boston Globe*, first covering gospel and other "roots" styles, then becoming the regular "world music" reporter. Wald has an interdisciplinary PhD in Ethnomusicology and Sociolinguistics, has taught at UCLA, Boston College, and Temple University, and travels widely as a speaker on the history and culture of popular music. He is particularly known for exploring musical styles within broader sociocultural contexts, as well as for original research on early blues, Mexican ranchera, and the folk revival. Wald has published well over a thousand articles in the *Globe*, the *Los Angeles Times*, and various magazines and journals, and his dozen books include *Global Minstrels: Voices of World Music* (Routledge, 2007); *Narcocorrido: A Journey into the Music of Drugs, Guns, and Guerrillas* (Rayo, 2002), a survey of the modern Mexican ballads of drug smuggling, migration, and political corruption; *Dylan Goes Electric! Newport, Seeger, Dylan, and the Night that Split the Sixties* (Dey St., 2015); *How the Beatles Destroyed Rock 'n' Roll: An Alternative History of American Popular Music* (Oxford University Press, 2009); *Escaping the Delta: Robert Johnson and the*

Invention of the Blues (Amistad, 2004); and Dave Van Ronk's memoir of the New York folk revival, *The Mayor of MacDougal Street* (Da Capo Press, 2013, the inspiration for the Coen Brothers' movie *Inside Llewyn Davis*). His awards include a 2002 Grammy for Best Album Notes, an ASCAP-Deems Taylor award, and special mention for the American Musicological Society's Otto Kinkeldey award. Currently, Wald is finishing a book on Jelly Roll Morton and early blues; planning a project about nationalism, migration, and borders; and performing occasional concerts. There is plenty of additional information at his website: http://www.elijahwald.com.

Index

Abbate, Carolyn, 129
'Abd al-Wahhab, Muhammad, 50
Abiyoyo and Other Story Songs for Children (P. Seeger), 40, 43
Abreu, Christina D., 13, 14, 80, 81, 98–114
Abu-Lughod, Lila, 143
activism. *See* political/social activism
Adichie, Chimamanda Ngozi, 137
Adorno, Theodor W., 66–67
Afro-Cuban music/professional singers, 98–111; cha cha cha, 99; Latin jazz, 81, 98, 100, 105–6, 107; Latin soul, 98–99; male musician partners and, 101–4, 105, 108, 109; mambo, 99, 105; migration to the U.S., 100–104; playlist, 114; relationships among contemporary singers, 98, 101–10; rumba, 99; salsa, 81, 98–100, 104–8, 110. *See also* Celia/Celia Cruz; Graciela/Graciela Pérez Grillo; La Lupe/Lupe Victoria Yolí
Ahmad, Zakariyya, 50
Ahmed, Sara, 143
AIDS epidemic, 175, 181, 187, 193
"Airport"/"Kūkō" (Teng, 1974), 168–69
al-Hakim, Ayman, 49–51
al-Hariri, Darwish, 50
Ali, Muhammad, 56
Ali, Naushad, 204, 206, 211
Allaire, Christian, 5
All India Radio, 210
Almanac Singers, 34, 35
al-Qasabji, Muhammad, 222–25

Al-Quntar, Lubana, 17, 229–33; awards and honors, 230; operatic training, 229–31; personal background, 229; playlist, 235; *tarab* training, 229–31; vocality/multivocality and, 229–32
American Musicological Society, 127
"America the Beautiful," 5
Ames, Katrine, 117
Ampiah, Kweku, 165
Anderson, Benedict, 69
Ankalikar, Arati, 212
Aparicio, Frances R., 99, 108
Appadurai, Arjun, 231–32
Arabic music/singers of, 11; challenges to the Egyptian government, 11–13; *maqam* system, 222–23, 225, 226; oud playing, 50, 52, 59, 220, 223, 225; playlist, 235; *tarab* singing, 17, 220–32. *See also* Al-Quntar, Lubana; Asmahan; Grout, Jennifer; Imam, Shaykh; Umm Kulthum; "Ya Toyour" ("Oh, Birds")
Arab left, 48, 55–57
Arabs Got Talent (Beirut television program), 7–8; *Got Talent* franchise and, 197, 219–20; Jennifer Grout and, 17, 198, 219–20, 222, 225–27, 228, 232–33
Arab Spring, 7, 47, 48, 57–59
Araki Hitohisa, 170
Ardoin, John, 124
Arita Yoshifu, 175
Armbrust, Walter, 59
Asch, Moses, 40

Asian music/professional singers. *See* Japanese music/singers of; K-pop/K-pop fandom; Teng, Teresa
Asmahan (1918–1944), 223–25, 228–30, 232–33
Athanasopoulos, George, 164
"Atonement"/"Tsugunai" (Teng, 1984), 170–72
Audiotopia (Kun), 8
authenticity: cultural narratives/politics in, 12, 26–27 (*see also* political/social activism); iconicity and (*see* iconicity); Indian film playback singing and, 213–14, 216n2; K-pop groups and, 27, 67, 69–71, 76; nature of, 11, 26, 69; technology and, 18 (*see also* media/technology of music)
autobiographical interludes, 9–10; Kwame Dawes, 10, 195–99; Ruth Hellier, 10, 135–38; Eric Lott, 10, 79–82; Jeff Todd Titon, 10, 25–27; Elijah Wald, 18, 237–40
Azizi, Arash, 4–5

Bachechi, Kimberly, 13
Badrus, Yusuf, 222–25
Bandung Conference of Asian and African Nations (1955), 165–67, 170, 174
Baraka, Amiri, 195
Barendregt, Bart, 8, 14, 15
Barthes, Roland, 1
Bauman, Richard, 9
Bauzá, Mario, 98, 101–2
Begum, Shamshad, 204–6
Belafonte, Harry, 180, 182, 184–85
bel canto singing style, 17, 38, 124, 128, 222–23, 224, 229–30
Benjamin, Sathima Bea (1936–2013), 16, 178, 182–87; awards and honors, 183; diasporic moments in life of, 180, 182–83, 184–87; male musician partners and, 182–83, 184–85, 187; motherhood and, 186, 187; playlist, 194; political activism, 180–87; repertoire, 183, 185–86
Benjamin, Walter, 69
Benson, Devyn Spence, 100
Berberian, Cathy, 221
Berlin, Irving, 6
Bernheimer, Martin, 118
Betancourt, Bianca, 5
Beyoncé Giselle Knowles Carter (b. 1981), 14, 80–81, 83–95; albums/visual albums and singles, 81, 83–84, 87–88, 89–95; awards and honors, 89, 92; as Coachella headliner (2018), 93–95; "crossover appeal," 88–95; Destiny's Child and, 81, 83–84, 86–87, 88, 89, 93; iconicity/superstardom and, 84–85, 88–89, 95; playlist, 97; political stance, 88; racialized misogyny and, 85; *Saturday Night Live* sketch (2016) and, 12, 85–86; social media and, 93; songwriting of, 85, 86, 92–93, 95; US Black South/Global South and, 14, 80, 84–85, 90–95; vocal/performance style of, 86–95
Bhosle, Asha (b. 1933), 203, 207–10, 212–13, 215
Bichu, Mandar V., 204
Biden, Joseph, 4–7
Big Hit Entertainment, 65
Bing, Rudolph, 117–18
Black Atlantic, The (Gilroy), 180
Black Is King (Beyoncé, 2020), 81, 83–84, 89, 91, 94–95
Black Lives Matter movement, 66, 74, 191, 192
Black music/professional singers: Afropop, 94; Black diasporas and, 179, 180–93; blackface minstrels and, 79–80; blues, 10, 25–26, 90, 91, 92, 195; country music, 90, 91, 92; hip-hop, 87, 90, 91; Jamaican music and, 195–99; jazz, 98, 182–83, 187, 188; K-pop as appropriation of, 27, 65, 66; "neo-soul," 86, 87; rap music, 86, 91; reggae, 10, 94, 172, 195–97; rhythm and blues, 84, 86, 87, 89, 92, 195; rock and roll, 91, 92; "sonic color line" of Black American music (Stoever) and, 151–52; soul, 87, 88, 89, 98–99; superstardom and, 84–85; zydeco, 90, 91, 92. *See also* Afro-Cuban music/professional singers; Beyoncé Giselle Knowles Carter; Black South African music/professional singers
Blackness, 80–81, 83, 85–95
Blackpink, 70, 76
Black South African music/professional singers, 178–93; Black middle class and, 189, 190; gender-based violence and, 179, 181, 184–85, 186, 189, 192–93; "new" African diasporas and, 179, 180–93; playlist, 194. *See also* Benjamin, Sathima Bea; Khumalo, Sibongile; King Tha/Thandiswa Mazwai; Makeba, Miriam; Scholtz, Melanie
Blair, Elizabeth, 5

Boggs, Vernon W., 99
Booth, Gregory, 202, 207
Booth, Marilyn, 51
border crossing/multivocality, 15–16, 136, 156, 229–31. *See also* Al-Quntar, Lubana; Beyoncé Giselle Knowles Carter; Black South African music/professional singers; Grout, Jennifer; King Tha/Thandiswa Mazwai; Redžepova, Esma; Teng, Teresa
Bourdaghs, Michael K., 16, 137, 161–77, 173
Boyle, Susan, 219, 220
Boylorn, Robin M., 90
Bradley, Regina N., 91
Brahmanism, 211, 212, 216n8
Brand, Dollar/Abdullah Ibrahim, 182–83, 184, 187
Brass, Perry, 131n9
Briggs, Charles L., 9
Brooks, Daphne, 84, 88
Brooks, Garth, 4
Brown, Lyn Mikel, 136
Browne, Kesewaa, 65
BTS/BTS ARMY, 63–66, 69, 70–71, 72, 74–75, 76

Caballé, Montserrat, 117–18, 125
Callas, Maria, 124, 125
Campbell, Martha, 121
Campos, Carlos do, 172
Caramanica, John, 85
Carmichael, Stokeley/Kwame Toure, 182, 184
Carson, Johnny, 120
Castro, Alicia, 100
Castro, Fidel, 100
Cavett, Dick, 120
Celia/Celia Cruz (1925–2003), 14, 80, 81; awards and honors, 110; comparisons with other singers, 107, 109, 110; male musician partners and, 101, 103, 108, 109; playlist, 114; relationships with contemporary singers, 98, 102, 105–9, 110; as salsa "queen"/"queen of Latin music," 98, 100, 103, 105–7, 110; and La Sonora Matancera, 100, 107; straight-laced performing style, 107–9
Cepeda, María Elena, 99
Chakravarty, Sumita S., 210, 211
Chambers, Veronica, 85
Chatterjee, Partha, 210–11
Cheng, Chen-Ching, 164, 167–68

Cheng, William, 4, 13–14
"Children of Soweto" (Benjamin, 2013), 185–86
Ching, Leo T. S., 166
Choe Sang-Hun, 27, 77
Choi, JungBon, 63
Chow, Rey, 163
ciaccona, 222
La Cieca (James Jordan), 124–26
Cinquemani, Sal, 89
City Pop, 171, 172
Clinton, Hillary, 5
Coachella (2018), 93–95
colonialism: in East Asia, 162; Indian film music in the pre-independence 1940s, 204–7; power of colonial traditions, 195–96
Columbia Records, 39, 40
Conzo, Joe, 100
Coomaraswamy, Ananda K., 212
"cosmopolitan" musicians, 178–79
costumes/dress: of Celia Cruz, 107; of Jennifer Lopez, 5; of Lata Mangeshkar, 211, 215; Esma Redžepova and the gendered respectable body, 144–51, 154–55, 156; social conversations concerning, 5; symbolism of white clothing, 5, 211, 215
Couldry, Nick, 232
counternarratives, 11, 13, 27, 48, 52
COVID-19 pandemic, 6, 12, 63, 189–92
Cowan, William, 224–25
Cowell, Simon, 219–20
Critic of Music, 86
Crouse, Lindsay, 219–20
Cruz, Celia. *See* Celia/Celia Cruz
Cuban music/professional singers. *See* Afro-Cuban music/professional singers

Dangerously in Love (Beyoncé, 2003), 87–88, 89
Danielson, Virginia, 8, 11, 60, 225, 226–27, 233n2
Darling Corey (P. Seeger, 1950), 37
Darwish, Adel, 56
Davis, Angela, 90
Davis, Peter G., 123–24, 126–27, 129
Dawes, Kwame, 10, 17, 195–99
Deng Lijun. *See* Teng, Teresa
Denning, Michael, 6
Deora, Mohan, 208
Deshpande, Ashwini, 201–2, 214
d'Estaing, Valéry Giscard, 26, 48, 52–55

Index 251

"d'Estaing" (Imam, 1975), 26, 48, 52–55, 58, 61
diasporas/diasporic musicians: Afro-Cubans in the U.S. and, 100–104; Black diasporas and, 179, 180–93; nature of diasporas, 179. *See also* Black South African music/professional singers; Redžepova, Esma
Dil Se (From the Heart, 1997 film), 204, 213–14
Doherty, Thomas, 35
Dove, Ian, 98, 104
DuBois, Thomas A., 8
Dunaway, David King, 12, 31, 34, 35, 41
Dunn, Leslie, 144–45
Dus, Tawfiq, 51–52
Dwight, John Sullivan, 127
Dylan, Bob, 7, 30, 46, 238
Dyson, Michael Eric, 13

Easter, Makeda, 84–85
Edell, Dana, 136
Edwards, Leigh H., 3, 13
Ehrlich, Dimitri, 86
Eide, Elisabeth, 144
Eidsheim, Nina Sun, 13
Ekapa label, 183
Eliot, T. S., 79–80, 81
Ellington, Duke, 183, 184
enka (Japanese music genre), 162, 168–69, 171–74
entertainment industry, 14, 35, 99, 101
environmental activism, 26, 30, 35
European Roma Rights Centre, 154
Expresso Show, 189
Eyerman, Ron, 8

Facebook, 58, 65, 68, 214
Fairuz, 225, 226
Fania Records, 101–2, 103, 105, 106, 108–9
Feldman, Martha, 127
Fernández, Raul A., 99, 101, 105, 106
film: *Come Back, Africa* (1959), 181–82; *Dil Se (From the Heart,* 1997), 204, 213–14; *Mother India* (1957), 211; music videos/visual albums, 81–85, 89, 153, 197; *The Power of Song* (2007), 30; *Sarafina!*, 185; *El Shaykh vs. Imam* (YouTube documentary), 58–59. *See also* Indian film music/professional singers
Fiol-Matta, Licia, 99

Fiske, John, 3
Fitzgerald, Ella, 107
Fleck, Bela, 37
Fleetwood, Nicole R., 2–3
Fleming, Renée, 124, 125
Flores, Juan, 99
Floyd, George, 66
Folkways Records/Smithsonian Folkways Recordings, 30–31, 37, 40
Fonseca, Felicia, 6
"Forbidden" ("Al-Mamnuʿat") (Imam), 56
Fox, Pamela, 13
FRA (European Union Agency for Fundamental Rights), 157n3
Franklin, Aretha, 107
Freedom's Child (Scholtz and Matthews), 188–89
"Frühlingsstimmen (Voices of Spring) Waltz" (J. Strauss), 223, 224

Gangadhar, Gadgil, 206–7
García, David F., 100
García, María Cristina, 100
Garman, Bryan K., 31–32, 42–43
Gay y Blasco, Paloma, 141
Ghoshal, Shreya, 212
Gibbs, Levi S., 1–2, 3, 7, 8
Gilbert, Ronnie, 35
Gilroy, Paul, 91, 180
Giscard d'Estaing, Valéry, 26, 48, 52–55
Global North, 16, 178–79, 180, 190, 192
Global South, 14, 16, 80, 90–95
"God Bless America" (I. Berlin), 6
Gold, Michael, 5
Goldstein, Meredith, 225
González-Wippler, Migene, 98, 103, 104, 108, 109
Goodison, Lorna, 196
"Goodnight, Irene" (Lead Belly/The Weavers), 35
Gordon, David B., 163
Gordon, Max, 184
Gorman, Amanda, 4
Gossett, Philip, 128, 129
Gourse, Leslie, 98, 104, 109
Graciela/Graciela Pérez Grillo (1915–2010), 14, 80; awards and honors, 110; as Latin jazz "queen", 98, 100, 105–6, 110; male musician partners and, 100, 101–2; performative sexuality/hypersexuality and, 102–3; playlist, 114; relationships with

252 Index

contemporary singers, 101–2, 105–6, 110; "Sí, Sí, No, No" as signature piece, 102–3, 106, 107
Grant, Stan, 6
Gray, Lila Ellen, 1, 3, 8
Grayson, Katherine, 223
Greene, Andy, 6
Griffin, Merv, 120
Grossberg, Lawrence, 8
Grout, Jennifer (b. 1990): on *Arabs Got Talent* (Beirut television program) and, 17, 198, 219–20, 222, 225–27, 228, 232–33; awards and honors, 228; linguistic flexibility, 220–21, 227–28; personal background, 219–20, 225–27; playlist, 235; repertoire, 222, 225–28, 232–33; on *Shaklak Mish Gharib* (*Your Face Sounds Familiar*), 227–28; social media and, 225, 226; vocality/multivocality and, 219–21, 222, 226–28, 232
Grundy-Warr, Carl, 231–32
"Guevara Is Dead" (Imam), 57
Guillermoprieto, Alma, 103, 107
Guthrie, Arlo, 41
Guthrie, Woody, 31–34; "This Land Is Your Land," 4–7
Guy, Nancy, 13, 14–15, 80, 81, 115–33

Habash, Dunya, 231
Hadden, Joey, 5
Hafiz, ʿAbd al-Halim, 51–52
Hall, Stuart, 180
Hall-Witt, Jennifer, 127
Hallyu (Korean Wave), 65
Halman, Talat S., 222
Hamdan, Zeid, 58
Hamdi, Baligh, 220
Hamilton, Jack, 91–92
Ha Miu Yin Serina, 174
Hancock, Ian, 144
Harootunian, H. D., 166
Harris, Kamala, 5
Hays, Lee, 35–36, 43
Heidegger, Martin, 220–21
Hellerman, Fred, 35
Hellier, Ruth, 1, 4, 10, 13, 15–16, 135–38, 144, 145
Hemmasi, Farzaneh, 8
Henderson, W. J., 127
Herrera, Ixya, 135
Herzfeld, Michael, 69

Hill, Joe, 2, 43
Hirano Kumiko, 162, 170, 171, 173
Hirschkind, Charles, 52
HIV/AIDS epidemic, 175, 181, 187, 193
"Ho Chi Minh" (Imam), 57
Hoffman, Henry, 121
Hofman, Ana, 144
Holmes, Jessica, 13
Homecoming (Beyoncé, 2019), 89, 91, 93, 97
Hong, Euny, 65
hooks, bell, 83
"hootenannies," 36
Horkheimer, Max, 66–67
Hosono Haruomi, 172
How to Play the Five-String Banjo (P. Seeger), 37
Hubbard, Madeleine, 6
Hubbs, Nadine, 118, 126
Hughes, Charles, 91–92

Ibrahim, Abdullah/Dollar Brand, 182–83, 184, 187
iconicity: of Beyoncé, 84–85, 88–89, 95; as global, with music technology, 197; of Shaykh Imam, 11–13, 26–27, 47–50, 59, 60; of K-pop groups, 11–13, 26, 27, 63–64, 66–69, 71–75, 77; of Lata Mangeshkar, 202, 204, 206, 209–10; politics of, 12; of Pete Seeger, 11–12, 26, 27, 29–31; of Teresa Teng, 162, 164–68; of Umm Kulthum, 59–60
identity: construction of new, 8; "power of identification" and, 18, 237–40
idolatry: idol-fan relationship and, 73–75, 76–77; of K-pop groups, 11, 13, 26, 27, 63–64, 66–69, 71–77; nature of idols, 71–73; of popular music stars, 67, 72
"If I Had a Hammer"/"Hammer Song" (P. Seeger), 29, 39, 41, 43
IFPI, 65
Igarashi, Yoshikuni, 166
Imam, Shaykh (1918–1995), 14, 47–62; cassette technology and, 7, 11–13, 26–27, 47–48, 51–53, 55, 56–59; death (1995), 48, 49, 59; Egyptian government challenges by, 7, 11–13, 26–27, 47–48, 52, 53–59; Ahmad Fuʿad Nigm's poetry and, 47–51, 56; "ordinary" iconicity of, 11–13, 26–27, 47–50, 59, 60; as oudist, 50, 52, 59; personal background, 48–51; playlist, 62; resurgence during Arab Spring,

Index 253

Imam, Shaykh (1918–1995), (*continued*)
7, 47, 48, 57–59; social media and, 7, 13, 48, 52–53, 57–59; songwriting of, 12–13, 26, 47–51, 52–53, 55–61; state-controlled radio and, 26–27, 47–48, 50, 51–53
Inani, Salah, 59
Indian film music/professional singers, 197–98, 201–16; Shamshad Begum, 204–6; Asha Bhosle, 203, 207–10, 212–13, 215; economic liberalization (1991) and, 213–14; film music industry as popular music industry and, 202, 207–8, 212–13, 214; gendered roles of women and, 209–13, 215; Amirbai Karnataki, 204, 205; Noorjehan, 204–6, 208; playback singing/lip-synching in Indian cinema, 198, 202–3, 207–14; playlist, 218; in the post-independence period (1947-), 207–14; in the pre-independence 1940s, 204–7. *See also* Mangeshkar, Lata
Indigenous people, social conversations concerning, 6–7
Inomata Kōshō, 168–69
In Search of Opera (Abbate), 129
Instagram, 64, 65
intersectionality: nature of, 13; of personal and political questions and concerns, 88; of professional singer identities, 3–7
Itō Tsuyoshi, 170
iTunes, 197
"Iyeza"/"Medicine" (Mazwai/King Tha), 190

Jackson, Marie, 65
Jacobs, Paul DuBois, 40
Jamjoom, Mohammed, 219, 227
Japanese music/singers of: *enka* genre, 162, 168–69, 171–74; Misora Hibari, 171–73; *yonanuke* pentatonic scale, 168–69. *See also* Teng, Teresa
Japan Polydor Records, 167–69
Jay-Z, 87, 91
Jha, Subhash K., 208
Jhingan, Shikha, 213
Jimenez, Mary, 34
John, Arit, 219
Jones, Andrew F., 164, 167, 172
Jones, Joseph, 107
Jones, Nancy, 144–45
Jordan, James (La Cieca), 124–26
JYP Entertainment, 67

Karnataki, Amirbai, 204, 205
Katin, Slave Nikolovski, 140, 142, 146, 153–55
Kaufman, Will, 5
Kennedy, Louise, 7
Kentridge, William, 191–92
Kesler, Sam Yellowhorse, 6, 7
Khumalo, Sibongile (1957–2021), 16, 178; awards and honors, 187, 188; male musical partners and, 187–88; as opera/jazz singer, 181, 187–88; personal background, 187–88; playlist, 194; repertoire, 188
Kim, Gooyong, 68
Kim, Sul-Young, 63
Kim, Yông-dae, 63
Kim Jong-Un, 27
Kingsley, Patrick, 226–27
Kingston Trio, 39
King Tha/Thandiswa Mazwai (b. 1976), 16, 178, 185; in Bongo Maffin (group), 190; as multi-genre performer, 181, 190–91; personal background, 190; playlist, 194; political activism and, 190, 192–93; repertoire, 190
Kirby, Fred, 98, 109
Koestenbaum, Wayne, 124
Kō Mamoru, 172
Kooijman, Jap, 86, 89
Kosovsky, Bob, 123
K-pop/K-pop fandom, 63–77; agencies supporting, 65, 67–69; appeal to members of ethnic and other minority groups, 75; appropriation of Black music and, 27, 65, 66; ascent and impact of, 64–69; authenticity and, 27, 67, 69–71, 76; awards and honors, 65; Blackpink, 70, 76; BTS/BTS ARMY, 63–66, 69, 70–71, 72, 74–75, 76; critics of, 75–77; digital revolution and, 66, 68, 73; English as language of, 64; as export-oriented product, 67–68; iconicity/idolatry of K-pop genre and, 11–13, 26, 27, 63–64, 66–69, 71–75, 77; individuality and, 67, 69–71; playlist, 78; political influence of, 27, 63, 65–66, 74; social media and, 12, 27, 64, 65–66, 68–69, 73; Super Junior, 71
Krasnowolska, Anna, 222
Kriegsman, Alan M., 128
Kristeva, Julia, 143

Ku, Lin-hsiu, 161
Kugle, Scott, 222
Kun, Josh, 3, 6, 8

Lady Gaga, 4, 5
Latinx music/professional singers: cha cha cha, 99; Ixya Herrera, 135; Latin jazz, 81, 98, 100, 105–6, 107, 110; Latinx population growth in the U.S. and, 99–100; Jennifer Lopez, 4–7; mambo, 99, 105; rumba, 99; salsa, 81, 98–100, 104–8, 110; social conversations concerning identity, 4–7. *See also* Afro-Cuban music/professional singers
lawn tarab, 224, 228–30, 232
Layton, Myrna June, 205, 214
Lead Belly (Huddie Ledbetter), 35, 37
Leaves of Grass (Whitman), 32
"Leaving It Up to the Flow of Time" (Teng, 1986), 170, 172
Lee, Hark Joon, 68
Lee, Ken, 141
Lee, Su-hyun, 77
Lehmann, Lilli, 124
Leida, Linda, 106–7
Leight, Elias, 84
Lelyveld, David, 210
Lemonade (Beyoncé, 2016), 81, 89–93
Leventhal, Harold, 40–41
Levine, Lawrence W., 127
Levine, Robert, 125
Leymarie, Isabelle, 99
Lie, John, 11–13, 26, 27, 63–78, 64, 65
Lin, Pei-yin, 164
Lindsey, Treva B., 12, 14, 80–81, 83–97, 86, 88–89
Lions of the North (Teitelbaum), 8
Lipshutz, Jason, 86
Lipsitz, George, 8
listening: as a political act, 13; positionality of, 136–37
Lloyd, Marie, 79–80, 81
Lohman, Laura, 11, 60
Lomax, Alan, 32–34, 38, 231
Lomax, John, 32, 38
Lopez, Jennifer, 4–7
López, René, 101, 105
Lopez, Trini, 39
Lordi, Emily J., 13
Lott, Eric, 10, 13, 14, 79–82
Love and Theft (Lott), 79

La Lupe/Lupe Victoria Yolí (1936–1992), 14, 80, 81; Afro-Cuban religious practices and, 108; awards and honors, 98–99, 110; Black motherhood and, 103–4; comparisons with other singers, 109, 110; as Latin salsa/soul "queen," 98–99, 100, 110; male musician partners and, 98–99, 101, 103–4, 105, 109; performance style, 108–10; playlist, 114; "Que Te Pedí," 104; relationships with contemporary singers, 106–7, 108–9, 110
Lutz, Catherine, 143
Lyan, Irina, 75

Machito, 100–102, 104
Madhubala, 203, 206, 208
Maeda Yoshitake, 174
Magowan, Fiona, 144, 145
Mahon, Maureen, 85, 92
Majumdar, Neepa, 202, 207, 208
Makeba, Miriam (1932–2008), 16, 178; awards and honors, 181–82; in *Come Back, Africa* (1959 film), 181–82; diasporic moments in life of, 180, 181–82, 184–87, 189; male musician partners and, 180–82, 184–86; motherhood and, 186; playlist, 194; political activism of, 180–82, 184–87; repertoire, 181–82, 185–86
Making Music in the Arab World (Racy), 223–24
Malvinni, David, 143
Manabe, Noriko, 168
Manawishi, Ahmed, 58–59
Mandela, Nelson, 180–81, 182, 184, 185, 187, 191
Mangeshkar, Lata (1929–2022), 201–16; awards and honors, 203–4, 212; contemporary singers and, 204–7, 208, 213–14; decline of career, 213–14; iconicity of, 202, 204, 206, 209–10; in the Indian post-independence period (1947–), 207–14; in the Indian pre-independence 1940s, 204–7; Mangeshkar monopoly and, 209–10, 212–13, 215; personal background, 203, 211–12, 214–15; as playback singer in "Bollywood"/Hindi-speaking film industry, 17, 198, 201–16; playlist, 218; popularity and longevity in Indian film, 201–3, 206–13; repertoire, 204, 206, 213–15; social media and, 214, 215;

Mangeshkar, Lata (1929–2022), (*continued*)
  vocal style, 201–3, 205–14; voice invoking post-independence femininity, 202, 208, 210–12
Manuel, Peter, 202, 214, 215
Marcus, Scott, 226
Markovic, Alexander, 143
Marley, Bob, 10, 195–96
Massenburg, Kedar, 86
Masucci, Jerry, 101, 103, 109
Matthews, James, 188–89
"Maybe Tonight, Maybe Tomorrow" (Teng, 1974), 168
Mazwai, Thandiswa. *See* King Tha/Thandiswa Mazwai
McCarthy era, 6, 12
media/technology of music: access and, 198; authenticity and, 18; cassettes, 7, 11–13, 26–27, 47–48, 51–53, 55–59, 164, 170, 202, 213; compact discs (CDs), 29, 30, 37, 68, 124–26, 175, 202; DVDs, 37, 68; film (*see* film; Indian film music/professional singers); and global reach vs. local value, 197–98; holograms, 60; impact of, 12, 197–98; music videos/visual albums, 81–85, 89, 153, 197; power relations and, 196–97; radio (*see* radio); television (*see* television programs); virtual technology, 18, 59–60, 73, 189–92, 225 (*see also* social media). *See also* social media
Meizel, Katherine, 4, 7, 15, 17, 156, 198, 219–35, 220–21, 232–33
Mercado, Ralph, 103
Merino, Juan Fernando, 105
Mernissi, Fatima, 223
Michelmore, Peter, 117
Miki Takashi, 170
Milenkovska, Vesna, 155
Miller, Karl Hagstrom, 13
Misaka Hiroshi, 171
Misora Hibari (1937–1989), 171–73
Miyagi, Taizo, 167
Molinari, Maurizio, 219
Moore, Deedee, 98, 104, 109
Moore, Robin D., 108
Moreno-Velazquez, Juan A., 103
Morris, Wesley, 85
Mother India (1957 film), 211
Mubarak, Husni, 47, 56, 57, 60
Mukherjee, Sashadhar, 205
Muller, Carol A., 12, 16, 137, 178–94
multiculturalism, pan-Yugoslav, 16, 146, 147

multivocality. *See* border crossing/multivocality
Musical Echoes (Muller and Benjamin), 180
music industry, 27, 69, 85, 86, 103, 104, 106, 108, 169, 198, 202
Mwamuka, Nomsa, 178

Nakajima Miyuki, 171
Nakamura Tōyō, 168, 171, 173
Nargis, 203, 205, 213
National Arts Festival, 178
nationalism, 12, 18, 154–55, 197, 202, 208, 210–11
Neal, Mark Anthony, 87
Negrón-Muntaner, Frances, 107–8
Nelson, Kristina, 226
Nelson Mandela University, 178
"New Music" genre, 171–72
Newport Folk Festival, 34, 36
"New Vocality" (Berberian), 221
Nguyen, Viet Phuong, 76
Night, Pedro, 108
Nigm, Ahmad Fuʾad (1929–2013), 47–51, 56
Nixon, Richard, 6
"Nixon Baba" (Imam), 58
Noorjehan, 204–6, 208
Nora, Pierre, 7
Norma (1973 compact disc release), 124–26
NPR (National Public Radio), 139, 152, 156, 188

Obama, Barack, 6, 41
Obomsawin, Mali, 6–7
Ocasio-Cortez, Alexandria, 5
Oguma, Eiji, 166
Okabayashi Nobuyasu, 172
Okoth-Obbo, Vanessa, 86
"One Grain of Sand" (P. Seeger), 40
opera. *See* Al-Quntar, Lubana; bel canto singing style; Grout, Jennifer; Khumalo, Sibongile; Scholtz, Melanie; Sills, Beverly
"orientalism" (Said), 141, 157n4, 173
Ortiz, Isabelle, 101
Otmazgin, Nissim, 75
oud performers, 50, 52, 59, 220, 223, 225

Pacheco, Johnny, 101, 103, 105
Pacini Hernández, Deborah, 99
Palmer, Robert, 107
Panofsky, Erwin, 71

Pareles, Jon, 98, 107
Pawar, Yogesh, 212
Pérez Grillo, Graciela. *See* Graciela/Graciela Pérez Grillo
performative presences: connection with audience and, 14, 80; nature of, 14, 79–81. *See also* Afro-Cuban music/professional singers; Beyoncé Giselle Knowles Carter; Sills, Beverly
Peter, Paul, and Mary, 39
Petric, Faith, 50
Petrova, Dimitrina, 140
Piaf, Edith, 107, 109
Pizzi, Michael, 219
Platon, Adelle, 87
Poey, Delia, 99, 107
political/social activism: Sathima Bea Benjamin's opposition to apartheid, 180–87; Béyonce as a "voice of black female discontent" (Brooks), 88; Black Lives Matter movement, 66, 74, 191, 192; carousel mirror metaphor for professional singers, 3–4; gender-based violence and, 179, 181, 184–85, 186, 189, 192–93; of Woody Guthrie, 4–7; Shaykh Imam and challenges to the Egyptian government, 7, 11–13, 26–27, 47–48, 52, 53–59; K-pop activities, 27, 63, 65–66, 74; Miriam Makeba's opposition to apartheid, 180–82, 184–87; Lata Mangeshkar's embodiment of Indian post-independence standards of femininity, 202, 208, 210–12; in multiple identities of professional singers, 3–7; Esma Redžepova's gender norm resistance, 142, 144–51; Pete Seeger as the voice of popular protest, 7, 12, 26, 29–31, 34–36; Beverly Sills's popularity with the masses, 117–18, 121, 123–30; Teresa Teng's support for democratic movements in China, 164–65
popular culture, 8, 14–15, 64, 66–67, 72, 86, 99–100, 110, 118, 162, 174
popular music stars: idolatry of, 67, 72; Jennifer Lopez, 4–7. *See also* Beyoncé Giselle Knowles Carter; K-pop/K-pop fandom; Teng, Teresa
Porter, Andrew, 130
Power of Song, The (2007 film), 30
power relations: in the auditory profiling process (Stoever), 151–52; in colonialism, 195–96 (*see also* colonialism); "giving voice" through song and, 8–9; Global North vs. Global South and, 16; global reach vs. local values and, 197; power of identification and, 237; power of song and, 4–7, 31–32, 35–36, 42–43, 237–40; technology of music and, 196–97; voice as metaphor for agency in, 4–7, 65–66, 101, 156, 211, 231, 232–33, 237–40. *See also* political/social activism
Powers, Ann, 1
Preston, Katherine K., 131n8
professional singers/singers: Afro-Cuban (*see* Afro-Cuban music/professional singers); of Arabic music (*see* Arabic music/singers of); Black (*see* Black music/professional singers; Black South African music/professional singers); carousel mirrors metaphor and, 3–4, 10; costumes of (*see* costumes/dress); Egyptian (*see* Imam, Shaykh; Umm Kulthum); of folk music (*see* Seeger, Peter "Pete"); as icons/public figures, 2–3, 4 (*see also* iconicity); Indian (*see* Indian film music/professional singers); of Japanese music (*see* Japanese music/singers of); Latinx (*see* Afro-Cuban music/professional singers; Latinx music/professional singers); Macedonian (*see* Redžepova, Esma); multiple identities of, 3–7; narratives of overcoming and, 13–14; opera and (*see* Al-Quntar, Lubana; Grout, Jennifer; Khumalo, Sibongile; Scholtz, Melanie; Sills, Beverly); as polysemic, 3–4; risk of essentializing, 10; Romani (*see* Redžepova, Esma); social conversations and, 4–9, 13–14 (*see also* political/social activism); South African (*see* Black South African music/professional singers); South Korean (*see* K-pop/K-pop fandom); Syrian (*see* Al-Quntar, Lubana; Asmahan); Taiwanese (*see* Teng, Teresa); voice as metaphor for agency and, 4–7, 65–66, 101, 156, 211, 231, 232–33, 237–40
Puente, Tito, 98–101, 103, 104
Purvis, Jennifer, 88

Qabil, Muhammad, 48–49

Race of Singers, A (Garman), 31–32, 42–43
Race of Sound, The (Eidsheim), 13
Racy, Ali Jihad, 220, 223–24

radio: All India Radio, 210; National Public Radio (NPR) in promoting professional singers, 139, 152, 156, 188; Pete Seeger's ban from, 30, 40; state-controlled radio in Egypt and, 26–27, 47–48, 50, 51–53
Radulescu, Dominica, 144
Rahman, A. R., 204
Rajaram, Prem Kumar, 231–32
Ranade, Ashok, 202
Reagan, Ronald, 6
Redžepova, Esma (1944–2016), 16, 137, 139–57; awards and honors, 139, 142, 146, 147, 153, 155; as bridge from Romani to non-Romani world, 145–53, 155–56; emotion/affect in vocal style, 142–44, 151–53; "fostered" children, 140, 149–50, 155; gendered respectable body in dance/costume, 144–51, 156; humanitarian stance, 140, 149–50, 153, 155, 156; legacy of, 139, 155–56; move to Belgrade (1960), 146; multiple performative identities of, 16, 137, 156; non-Romani mentor/husband, 139–42, 145–56; personal background, 142, 146, 154; playlist, 159–60; political stance, 154–55, 156; repertoire, 147–53; Romani "otherness" and, 140–43, 144, 154; social class and, 142, 150
Reiser, Bob, 8
representations: carousel mirror metaphor for professional singers, 3–4; components of, 2, 135–36; constructing new identities, 8 (*see also* K-pop/K-pop fandom; Redžepova, Esma); media choice and, 12 (*see also* Indian film music/professional singers); multiplicities of (*see* border crossing/multivocality); nature of, 2; positionality of listening and, 136–37; questioning, 10; risk of essentializing, 10; via song, 8–9
The Richmond Organization (TRO), 40–41
Rifa, Muhammad, 50
Rifati, Šani, 154
Rinzler, Ralph, 32–34
Risen, Clay, 124
Robinson, Dylan, 136
Rockwell, John, 98
Rodríguez-Seeger, Tao, 41, 42
Rogosin, Lionel, 181–82, 184
Rojek, Chris, 16
Romani music/professional singers. *See* Redžepova, Esma

Roodt, Darrell James, 185
Rosaldo, Michelle, 143
Rota, Nino, 172
Russo, Frank A., 2

Saal, Hubert, 115
Sadat, Anwar, 53–55, 56
Sahhab, Ilyas, 224
Said, Edward W., 141, 157n4
Saigal, K. L., 207
Sainte-Marie, Buffy, 7
Sakamoto Fuyumi, 172
Salazar, Max, 99, 101, 103, 108, 109
Saleh Maryam, 58
Sanneh, Kelefa, 84
Santamaría, Mongo, 101, 103
Santana, Matthew Leslie, 4
Sarafina! (theater piece/film), 185
Sarrazin, Natalie, 8, 12, 17, 198, 201–18
Saturday Night Live, 12, 85–86
Schippers, Thomas, 129
Scholtz, Melanie (b. 1979), 16, 178; awards and honors, 187; *Freedom's Child* project, 188–89; male musical partner, 188–89; as opera/jazz singer, 181, 187; personal background, 188–89; playlist, 194
Schulze, Brigitte, 210
Seeger, Anthony, 2, 8, 12, 14, 26, 29–46, 43
Seeger, Kate, 8, 43
Seeger, Mike, 35, 38
Seeger, Peggy, 35, 38, 39
Seeger, Peter "Pete" (1919–2014), 2, 8, 29–44; awards and honors, 30; children's books and songs, 39–40, 43; family and home of, 30, 33, 35–36, 38, 40–41, 44n1; financial resources of, 37, 39–41, 44n3; grandson, Tao Rodríguez-Seeger, 41, 42; group singing and, 29, 34, 35, 42; health issues, 41–42; iconicity of, 11–12, 26, 27, 29–31; instruments of, 37–38, 42; McCarthy-era censorship and, 12, 30, 34, 35–36, 39–41, 44n2; personal background, 32–37; playlist, 46; record labels and, 37, 39, 40–41, 44n3; as "singer of folksongs," 26; songwriting of, 29, 30, 31, 39–40, 41, 43; "This Land Is Your Land" (W. Guthrie) and, 5–6; vocal style of, 38–39, 41–42; as the voice of popular protest, 7, 12, 26, 29–31, 34–36
Seeger, Ruth Crawford, 33, 38, 43
Seeger, Toshi Aline Ohta, 31, 34, 36, 40–41
Shah, Rachana, 208

258   Index

Shakespeare, William, 196
Shalabi, Hilmi Ahmad, 51
Shanahan, Mark, 225
Shange, Ntozake, 195
Sharif, Samim, 223
Shaw, Sophie, 5
"Sí, Sí, No, No," 102–3, 106, 107
Siff, Ira, 123
Sills, Beverly (1929–2007), 14–15, 80, 81, 115–31; administrative roles of, 120, 122, 123; critics of, 117–18, 121, 122–30; death and *Farewell Guestbook*, 120–22, 130–31n5; mainstream media appearances, 118–20, 121, 122, 123, 127, 130; as member of the New York City Opera, 115–18; Metropolitan Opera debut (1975), 117–18, 129; *Norma* compact disc release (1973), 124–26; personal background and style, 117–26, 127–30; playlist, 133; repertoire, 115–17, 119, 124–26, 128, 129; retirement from singing (1980), 117, 120, 130; sacralization of culture problem and, 126–30; social class and, 81, 117–18, 121, 123–30; social media and, 125–26, 130n4; vocal/performance style, 115–18
Silverman, Carol, 16, 137, 139–60, 140, 141, 145
Simon, Andrew, 7, 11–14, 26–27, 47–62, 52
Sinatra, Frank, 183
singers. *See* professional singers/singers
Skype, 225
slavery/enslaved people: in the Americas (1616–1865), 94, 179–81, 183; in Romania, 140
SM Entertainment Agency, 67, 68
Smith, Charles Edward, 2, 43
Smithsonian Folkways Recordings (formerly Folkways Records), 30–31, 37, 40
social activism. *See* political/social activism
social class: Black South African music/professional singers and, 189, 190; Marie Lloyd and, 79–80; Esma Redžepova and, 142, 150; sacralization of culture problem and, 126–30; Beverly Sills and, 81, 117–18, 121, 123–30; upward mobility of professional singers and, 13–14, 16, 126
social media: Beyoncé and, 93; Jennifer Grout and, 225, 226; Shaykh Imam and, 7, 13, 48, 52–53, 57–59; K-pop/K-pop fandom and, 12, 27, 64, 65–66, 68–69, 73; Lata Mangeshkar and, 214, 215;

power of, 197; Beverly Sills and, 125–26, 130n4
Song Jung-a, 65
songs: bel canto singing style, 17, 38, 124, 128, 222–23, 224, 229–30; as changing multiplicities (Adichie), 137; defined, 43; *enka*, 162, 168–69, 171–74; lyrics and, 2, 6–7, 16–17; melody and, 2; new technologies in "apprehending music" (Dawes), 17 (*see also* media/technology of music); power of song and, 4–7, 31–32, 35–36, 42–43, 178–79, 237–40; as public expressions, 2–3; repetition and, 2; representation via, 8–9 (*see also* representations); singer's persona and, 2, 17; social conversations and, 4–9; *tarab* singing, 17, 220–32; voice and, 2
"sonic color line" (Stoever), 151–53
La Sonora Matancera, 100, 107
SoundCloud, 13, 58
South African music/professional singers. *See* Black South African music/professional singers
southern-ness, 14, 42–43, 80–81, 83–86, 89–95, 180
South Korean music/professional singers. *See* K-pop/K-pop fandom
"Soweto Blues" (Makeba, 2015), 185
Spitzer, Nick, 6
Spivak, Gayatri Chakravorty, 144
Spotify, 13, 58, 68, 197
Springsteen, Bruce, 6, 32, 41
Sprinkel, Katy, 63
Srivastava, Sanjay, 201–2, 206, 208, 211–13, 215
Stahl, Matt, 232–33
Stallings, L. H., 90–91
Sternheimer, Karen, 13
Stoever, Jennifer Lynn, 13, 151–53
Stokes, Martin, 69, 231
Strauss, Johann, 223, 224
Sulayman, Shaykh Mahmud, 49–50
Sundar, Pavitra, 202
Sunder Rajan, Rajeswari, 211
Super Junior, 71

"Taghrid al-Balabil" ("The Warbling of the Nightingales," al-Qasabji). *See* "Ya Toyour" ("Oh, Birds")
Tansman, Alan M., 8
tarab singing, 17, 220–32
Taurus Records, 170, 171

Index 259

Taylor, Lori B., 2, 43
technology of music. *See* media/technology of music
Teitelbaum, Benjamin R., 8
television programs: *Arabs Got Talent* (Beirut television program), 7–8, 17, 198, 219–20, 222, 225–27, 228, 232–33; *Beverly Hillbillies*, 81, 126; Béyonce sketch on *Saturday Night Live* (2016), 12, 85–86; *Shaklak Mish Gharib* (*Your Face Sounds Familiar*), 227–28; Beverly Sills and, 118–20, 121, 122, 123
Teng, Teresa (1953–1995), 16, 161–75; awards and honors, 168, 170; as cultural intermediary, 174–75; iconicity/superstar status, 162, 164–68; in Japan, 137, 165–75; movement across the Cold War Sinosphere, 162–68, 169, 170, 172; multiple names of, 161–62; passport incident (1979), 161–63, 167, 170; personal background, 161–63, 164, 166, 167–68; playlist, 177; repertoire, 164, 166–73; vocal/performance style, 158, 161, 163–64, 168–74
Teodosievski, Stevo, 139–42, 145–56
"This Land Is Your Land" (W. Guthrie), 4–7
Thompson, William Forde, 2
Tico Records, 109
TikTok, 65, 68
Titon, Jeff Todd, 10–12, 16, 25–27, 69
TNN (Times News Network), 212
Toure, Kwame/Stokeley Carmichael, 182, 184
transnational musicians: nature of, 179. *See also* Afro-Cuban music/professional singers; Black South African music/professional singers; Redžepova, Esma; Teng, Teresa
Troyano, Ela, 103, 108, 109
Trump, Donald, 4–5, 7, 27, 63, 66
Trumpener, Katie, 141
Tsutsumi Kyōhei, 168
"Turn, Turn, Turn" (P. Seeger), 39, 41, 43
Twitter, 64, 68, 214

Umm Kulthum, 11; iconicity of, 59–60; personal background, 225–26; repertoire, 223; virtual technology and, 60; vocal style of, 220, 226, 227, 228, 230
United States: antiwar movement, 7, 30, 34–35, 239; Black Lives Matter movement, 66, 74, 191, 192; Black South African professional singers and, 180–82, 183, 186, 188; civil rights movement (1954–1968), 8, 22, 30, 34, 180, 186, 239; Cuban exiles and, 99–104; immigrant experiences and, 99–104, 180–86, 237–38; Latinx population growth, 99–104; power of identification and, 239–40; slavery/enslaved people and, 94, 179–81, 183, 192

Valdés, Fabio, 107
Valentin-Escobar, Wilson A., 99
Vamping the Stage (Weintraub and Barendregt), 8
Van de Port, Mattijs, 143
Vandross, Luther, 87
Varela, Jesse, 101, 102
Vargas, Deborah R., 13
Vaughan, Sarah, 107
Vazquez, Alexandra T., 99, 103, 105
Vigreux, Philippe, 233n2
Village Vanguard (New York City), 36, 182, 184
Virdi, Jyotika, 210, 211

Wajima Yusuke, 169
Wald, Elijah, 4, 8, 18, 30, 237–40
Walther, Joseph B., 130–31n5
Warner, Jayne L., 222
Watanabe Productions, 168
Watanabe Yasushi, 173
"Water Is Wide, The" (P. Seeger), 29
Waxer, Lise, 99
The Weavers, 34, 35
Weidman, Amanda, 8, 209
Weintraub, Andrew N., 8, 14, 15
Weisbard, Eric, 80
Where Have All the Flowers Gone (P. Seeger songbook), 31, 39, 41
"Where Have All the Flowers Gone?" (P. Seeger), 39, 41, 43
Whitman, Walt, 31–34, 39, 42–43
"Who Are They?" (Imam), 56, 57
Williams, Jeni, 222
Wills, Garry, 129
Wilson, John S., 98, 109
womanhood, 14, 80, 83, 89, 90, 99, 212
Women Singers in Global Contexts (Hellier), 15, 136
world musicians: nature of, 179. *See also* Benjamin, Sathima Bea; Makeba, Miriam; Redžepova, Esma

Wortham, Jenna, 85
Wrazen, Louise, 144, 145

Yamagami Michio, 168
Yamaguchi Yoshiko, 172–73
Yano, Christine R., 169
"Ya Toyour" ("Oh, Birds"), 222–25; Lubana Al-Quntar and, 17, 230–32; Asmahan and, 223–25, 228–30, 232–33; Jennifer Grout and, 226–27, 228, 232–33; playlist, 235
Years of Art, Prison, and Tears (al-Hakim), 49–51

YG Entertainment, 67
Yolí, Lupe Victoria. *See* La Lupe/Lupe Victoria Yolí
YouTube, 13, 57–59, 64, 68, 93, 197, 215, 225

"Zabalaza"/"Rebel" (Mazwai/King Tha), 190
Zhuang, Yan, 76
Zhuang Nu, 167
Zimmerman, Paul D., 98, 104, 108, 110
Zinta, Preity, 203, 214
Zoom performances, 18, 190–92
Zuhur, Sherifa, 223, 224

The University of Illinois Press
is a founding member of the
Association of University Presses.
———————————————

University of Illinois Press
1325 South Oak Street
Champaign, IL 61820-6903
www.press.uillinois.edu